Atlantic Lives

Atlantic Lives

A Comparative Approach to Early America

TIMOTHY J. SHANNON

Gettysburg College

PEARSON
Longman

New York   San Francisco   Boston
London   Toronto   Sydney   Tokyo   Singapore   Madrid
Mexico City   Munich   Paris   Cape Town   Hong Kong   Montreal

Vice President and Publisher: Priscilla McGeehon
Acquisitions Editor: Ashley Dodge
Executive Marketing Manager: Sue Westmoreland
Production Manager: Joseph Vella
Project Coordination, Text Design, Photo Research, and Electronic Page Makeup: Shepherd Inc.
Design Manager/Cover Designer: John Callahan
Cover Illustration: Burgis, William (18th century) © New York Public Library/Art Resource,
    NY. Southeast view of the great town of Boston in New England in America (probably
    1731–1736). Colored engraving (issued probably after 1764). Engraver: John Carwitham.
    I. N. Phelps Stokes Collection, Miriam and Ira D. Wallach Division of Art, Prints, and
    Photographs. Location: Wallach Division, New York Public Library, New York, NY, U.S.A.
Manufacturing Buyer: Roy L. Pickering, Jr.
Printer and Binder: Courier Corporation
Cover Printer: The Lehigh Press

Library of Congress Cataloging-in-Publication Data

Shannon, Timothy J. (Timothy John), 1964–
    Atlantic lives : a comparative approach to early America / Timothy J. Shannon.
      p. cm.
    Includes bibliographical references.
    ISBN 0-321-07710-5
    1. America—History—To 1810. 2. America—History—To 1810—Sources.
    3. Indians—Biography. 4. Africans—America—Biography.
    5. Europeans—America—Biography. 6. America—Relations—Europe.
    7. Europe—Relations—America. 8. America—Relations—Africa.
    9. Africa—Relations—America. I. Title.
E18.82.S53 2003
970.02—dc22   2003062345

Visit us at http://www.ablongman.com

ISBN 0-321-07710-5

1 2 3 4 5 6 7 8 9 10—CRS—06 05 04 03

To my parents, John and Elizabeth Shannon, and

Mary,

Jim,

Mike,

Meg,

and

Dave.

Contents

Preface

This book has grown out of a course I started teaching in 1997 at Gettysburg College. At that time, the History Department had decided to revamp its introductory courses. In particular, the World History survey was at once too familiar and too daunting to students and instructors. It required covering an enormous amount of material at a breakneck speed, without providing the depth necessary to introduce students to the study of history at the college level. Those of us who had taught the World History course decided we would slice up the pie, each of us developing a new course that would deal with history on an intercontinental scale, but in a time frame small enough to allow in-depth concentration on specific themes and ideas. As a historian of Early America, I decided to focus on the interaction between Europe, Africa, and the Americas, from the Age of Columbus through the Age of Revolutions. It was an idea that would have appealed to Goldilocks: If World History was too big for what I hoped to accomplish and the standard U.S. History survey too small, then the Atlantic World seemed just right.

As soon as I began teaching the course, I became aware that the subject lacked a good, comprehensive textbook. There were many books on particular aspects of the course—the Atlantic Slave Trade, the Columbian Exchange, Atlantic Migrations—that my students and I found useful and thought-provoking, but I could find no single, overarching narrative that could guide the students through the semester. As I thought about how I would design such a text, it also occurred to me that I would like to have my students reading more of the primary sources of Atlantic History, so that they might meet and listen to many of the individuals who lived this history firsthand. As I taught the course in ensuing years, I collected references for such primary sources: slave and captivity narratives, travel journals and diaries, political tracts and promotional pamphlets, letters, and autobiographies. Ultimately, I decided to combine my ideas for a narrative text and primary source collection into one project, the result of which you are reading now.

This book presents a history of the Atlantic World from about 1450 to 1830. After the Introduction, the chapters follow a rough chronological order, but are conceived and organized thematically. The objective of this design is to provide both the skeleton of a narrative overview of the Atlantic World and an introduction to the major topics in the field. Each chapter presents reading selections from two or three primary sources related to its topic. I have chosen to devote the bulk of the book's content to these sources because they provide comparative, first-person perspectives on the issues at hand. Whenever possible, I have incorporated the narratives of people who traveled between the Americas, Africa, and Europe. Their voices give immediacy to the subject matter in a way that a textbook narrative cannot. Too often, the teaching of history loses its human content as students and instructors focus on -*isms* (feudalism, mercantilism, capitalism, industrialism, and so on) instead of individuals. This book has its share of -*isms*, but I hope that readers will find in these selections the voices and personalities of those individuals whose lives shaped and were shaped by the history of the Atlantic World.

Acknowledgments

A Faculty Development and Research Grant from Gettysburg College helped support the research for this project. I would like to thank Lauren Rocco, Amber Moulton, and Jen Chesney for their work as research assistants. Also, my thanks to Susan Roach and Linda Isenberger for their help in locating materials, and to Barbara Sommer for sharing her expertise in Latin American history and to Charlie Zabrowski for his help in Latin translations. My students have helped me identify many of the reading selections included here and to refine my own ideas about the content and meaning of Atlantic History. The kind folks at the Ragged Edge Coffee House (the real reason to visit Gettysburg) supplied my caffeine and a nice place to work when I could get away from the office. This book has been much improved by the thoughtful commentary of the following reviewers: John Thornton, Millersville University; Edward H. Tebbenhoff, Luther College; Robert A. Becker, Louisiana State University; Melissa Walker, Converse College; Brenda Thompson Schoolfield, Bob Jones University; David Armitage, Columbia University; Anna Bates, Aquinas College; Armand S. La Potin, State University of New York College at Oneonta; Jessica Kross, University of South Carolina; B. R. Burg, Arizona State University; Hal M. Friedman, Henry Ford Community College; H. Warren Gardner, University of Texas of the Permian Basin; Peter Moore, University of Georgia; Constance M. McGovern, Frostburg State University; James H. Williams, Middle Tennessee State University; Michael P. Gabriel, Kutztown University; and Wade Shaffer, West Texas A&M University who reviewed it for Longman, and I also appreciate the advice and assistance of Ashley Dodge and Jacob Drill during the editing and production stages.

Colleen thought this project was a good idea from the start, and it would not have been completed without her encouragement. Caroline and Daniel supplied welcome diversion from beginning to end, and Elizabeth joined them just in time to make the Acknowledgments (good work, kid!). I thank them all for their patience whenever I pleaded for five more minutes. The dedication reflects my gratitude to my parents and siblings, for the love and support that they have always provided in my endeavors.

TIMOTHY J. SHANNON

Atlantic Lives

Introduction: What Is Atlantic History?

By anyone's accounting, David George led a remarkable life. He was born of African parents in Essex County, Virginia, in the mid-eighteenth century and spent his early years working as a plantation slave. As a young man, he ran away and found work in South Carolina and then Georgia. When his freedom seemed in jeopardy, he escaped into the Georgia backcountry, only to be captured by Creek Indians, who reenslaved him. He worked for several months for a Creek chief who spoke some English and arranged to sell George back to his original master, 800 miles away in Virginia. George fled again before that transaction could be completed but ended up working as a slave for a master on the Savannah River. Here he was introduced to Christianity by another slave, and after his conversion, became a Baptist minister.

When the British invaded Georgia during the American Revolution, George again sought his freedom. Now married and the father of two children, he abandoned his patriot master and sought refuge for himself and his family among the British. George survived the siege of Savannah and a case of smallpox, and at the end of the war, he accepted a British offer for free passage to Nova Scotia, along with other white and black loyalist refugees. In Nova Scotia, he became a leader of the black community, despite the persecution he faced from whites for preaching before interracial audiences.

His travels were not over yet. After enduring several years of hard times in Nova Scotia, George decided to move again, this time to Africa. In 1792, he joined about a thousand other black loyalists in founding the colony of Sierra Leone. As conceived by British anti-slavery advocates, Sierra Leone would be populated by former slaves from British colonies, who would bring Christianity and European civilization to Africa and help end the slave trade there. George continued to work as a minister in Sierra Leone, often mediating when resentments flared between his fellow settlers and British agents. He died there in 1810.

What are we to make of David George? During his life he moved between freedom and slavery not once, but several times. He participated in two colonizing ventures on opposite sides of the Atlantic: Nova Scotia and Sierra Leone. At various times he lived among Indians, American slaves and slaveholders, British soldiers, and West Africans. He pursued liberty during the American Revolution, but not in a fashion typically associated with that conflict; he became a loyalist rather than a patriot and preserved his freedom by leaving the United States instead of remaining there. His travels took him hundreds, and then thousands, of miles from his place of birth. Over all that time and distance, how did he come to identify himself? Was he an African who lived in America, or an American who lived in Africa? In a brief autobiographical narrative he composed in the 1790s, George expressed consciousness of his race, noting his parents' African origins and his introduction to Christianity by a "man of my own color," but his most insistent self-identification was as a Christian. After his conversion, he sought the company of other Baptists, black and white, and he worked closely with whites to organize the black loyalist emigration to Sierra Leone.

David George's life defied the conventions by which historians typically tell the story of early America. He was not an immigrant who became American by adopting the New World as his homeland. Neither was he a slave who gained freedom by taking up arms in the patriot cause during the War of Independence. He was a slave who converted to Christianity and learned to read and write the English language, but who also abandoned America to live in the country of his ancestors. George's story is too expansive and too contradictory to be told only in the context of the thirteen colonies that became the United States. It demands a much larger geographic arena for its action and a framework for its themes and events that can connect and explain his experiences in the American South, Nova Scotia, and Sierra Leone.

Atlantic History provides that framework. Focusing on the period between 1450 and 1830—from the earliest European encounters with sub-Saharan Africa to the demise of the Atlantic Slave Trade—Atlantic History examines the ramifications of long-distance contact, exchange, and conflict between human populations in Europe, Africa, and the Americas. While the term *Atlantic History* has only recently gained widespread currency in academic conferences, graduate programs, and college catalogues, historians have been pursuing it in various ways for quite some time. The first scholars to define it as a field of inquiry were interested in the transatlantic revolutionary movement of the late eighteenth century. They explored ideological links between the French Revolution and the North and South American colonial wars of independence. Some of the most prolific practitioners of Atlantic History have been scholars who recognized the need to move beyond traditional geographic boundaries when writing about the Atlantic Slave Trade, which forcibly dispersed Africans throughout the Americas and the Caribbean. Attempting to survey the demographic, economic, and cultural impact of this migration on both sides of the Atlantic required evaluating data from the Old World as well as the New and from a variety of regions within the Western Hemisphere. Uncovering the economics that governed the Atlantic Slave Trade often meant dealing with commodities rather than nations; studying the rise of an international plantation complex that produced sugar, tobacco, coffee, and other cash crops for world markets.

Likewise, those historians who have investigated the biological and ecological consequences of contact between the Old World and the New have often found national borders irrelevant to their purposes. Microbes, plants, and animals moved into new environments oblivious to man-made boundaries, and their introduction to an ecosystem could wreak havoc regardless of the political or religious differences that divided human societies. When historians have tried to measure the impact of such biological exchange on human populations, they have often done so on an international or intercontinental scale. Human migrations are another topic fit for analysis on a transatlantic scale. What historical forces created the displaced peoples who moved between the Old World and the New? How did the experience of forced migration differ from that of voluntary migration? What were the varieties of bound or indentured labor that could bring a person across the Atlantic? What effect did such migrations have on the indigenous populations who encountered them?

Some of these questions have already been addressed in the familiar narratives of European colonization of the Americas. Each European colonial power produced its own national heroes for this story, from Spain's conquistadors to England's Pilgrims to France's missionaries. These nationalist narratives, however, fall short in several respects. All emphasize the exceptional quality of their subjects' experiences, be it their superior bravery, piety, or humanity. In doing so, they also downplay the consistencies and similarities between these stories that would allow for comparative analysis across national or ethnic borders. Nationalist narratives tend to leave many groups involved in colonization out of the story; they hide or obscure the roles played by stateless people in building the connections between the Old World and the New. For example, many of the sailors whose labor made transatlantic shipping possible were people of mixed ethnicity or no fixed nationality, who lived their lives in flux between two or more places that they might have called home. Pirates, slaves, and fur traders lived and worked among hybrid populations that combined African, European, and Native American identities. Such communities did not fit easily into national categories, and they often ignored whatever claims distant powers made to dominion over them, yet their importance in shaping the Atlantic World is undeniable.

What distinguishes Atlantic History from previous narratives is its transnational quality. Rather than splitting the story of the colonization of the Americas into discreet national units that would have made sense to only a fraction of the people involved, it asks questions that are best answered by taking a comparative perspective on the evidence. How did the Native American response to European missionaries differ in various regions of the Americas, and what circumstances explain those differences? Why did some New World slave societies create large biracial populations that occupied a middling social status between freedom and slavery while others did not? Did the colonial wars of independence originate from common grievances against European empires? If so, why were the results of those wars so different? Contemplating these questions reduces the emphasis on exceptionalism that has shaped nationalist narratives of Early America and helps us recapture the connections and overlaps that contemporaries would have recognized between these topics.

Let us return to the story of David George. His life illustrates several of the topics that make up the backbone of Atlantic History: slavery, the plantation economy, migrations, revolutions. More significantly, he illustrates this notion of transnationality, of the movement of peoples and their identities across geographic, cultural, and political borders. George's life was marked by his ability to reinvent himself. He ran away from slavery no fewer than three times to assume the life of a free man. He became a part of the loyalist exodus to Nova Scotia by choosing to align himself with the British cause in the War of Independence. He thought of himself as a Christian and as an African, and that identity led him to emigrate to Sierra Leone. His life reflected a willing, even restless, movement between social and political categories that at first seemed hard and fast. The history of the Atlantic World is the story of David George writ large, of intercontinental exchanges and conflicts between human societies set in motion by the collision of Europe, Africa, and the Americas.

In a way, it is not surprising that historians have latched onto the concept of Atlantic History in recent years. There is much about the Atlantic World that seemed to anticipate the issues and problems of our own. Just as the Atlantic World was made possible by technologies and migrations that broke down previous barriers to human contact and exchange, so too our modern world has been reshaped by an explosion of global relationships. The earth's population is more integrated than ever before. Intercontinental travel occurs with an ease and regularity that few would have expected even fifty years ago. International corporations make products, from cars to clothes to films, which are aimed as much at international audiences as local ones. The Internet and World Wide Web have a global reach and impact, but so do AIDS, greenhouse emissions, and overpopulation. Just as the generations that followed Columbus had to deal with a world that was suddenly much larger than they had previously thought, so too must we deal with a world that is shrinking before our eyes, bringing formerly isolated peoples into contact and conflict with each other, turning local and regional problems into international ones. We should not expect the study of Atlantic History to provide solutions to our current crises, but it can help us understand how human societies in the past have created and dealt with problems of similar global dimensions.

Suggested Readings

David George's autobiography can be found in John Rippon, *The Baptist Annual Register, including Sketches of the State of Religion Among Different Denominations of Good Men at Home and Abroad* (London, 1793–1802), 473–484. For more on the black loyalists and the Sierra Leone colony, see Ellen G. Wilson, *The Loyal Blacks* (New York: G. P. Putnam's Sons, 1976).

For essays that trace and define the emergence of Atlantic History as a scholarly field, see David Armitage, "Three Concepts of Atlantic History," in David Armitage and Michael J. Braddick, editors, *The British Atlantic World, 1500–1800* (New York: Palgrave, 2002), 11–29; Nicholas Canny, "Writing Atlantic History; or, Reconfiguring the History of Colonial British America," *Journal of American History* 86 (1999): 1093–1114; and Bernard Bailyn, "The Idea of Atlantic History," *Itinerario* 20 (1996): 19–43. Other works that are useful for how they conceptualize a transnational history of the Atlantic are: J. H. Elliott, *Do the Americas Have a Common History?* (Providence, R.I.: John Carter Brown Library, 1998); D. W. Meinig, *The Shaping of America: A Geographic Perspective on 500 Years of History, Volume I: Atlantic America, 1492–1800* (New Haven, Conn.: Yale University Press, 1986); and Philip D. Curtin, *The Rise and Fall of the Plantation Complex: Essays in Atlantic History* (Cambridge, England: Cambridge University Press, 1990). For more specialized studies that make use of an Atlantic framework, see Alfred W. Crosby, Jr., *The Columbian Exchange: Biological and Cultural Consequences of 1492* (Westport, Conn.: Greenwood Press, 1972); Ralph Davis, *The Rise of the Atlantic Economies* (Ithaca, N.Y.: Cornell University Press, 1973); and Peter Linebaugh and Marcus Rediker, *The Many-Headed Hydra: Sailors, Slaves, Commoners, and the Hidden History of the Revolutionary Atlantic* (Boston: Beacon Press, 2000).

Tupinamba Indian Family

The illustrations included in Jean de Léry's narrative (see Selection 2) were some of the earliest visual images of Indians published in Europe. What does this image tell its viewers about the Indians' family life, material culture, diet, and dress? What reactions do you think it would have elicited from a sixteenth-century European?

Source: Courtesy of the John Carter Brown Library at Brown University

Into the Atlantic Crucible

Introduction

The year of Christopher Columbus's first voyage to the Americas, 1492, might seem like a logical point at which to date the origin of the Atlantic World. Columbus's voyage was certainly a momentous event in world history, but the foundations of the Atlantic World are to be found in trends and circumstances that were altering Europe's relations with the outside world long before the famed navigator set sail.

Columbus had learned his trade plying the ports of the Mediterranean Sea, the highway of exchange between North Africa, the Near East, and southern Europe in the fifteenth century. He was a native of Genoa, which along with the other Italian city-states of Venice and Florence, dominated Europe's access to the consumer goods of this Mediterranean marketplace: silks, porcelain, and spices from Asia; cloth and sugar from India; gold, ivory, and slaves from Africa. Italian merchants secured these items through Muslim middlemen, who controlled the caravan routes to sub-Saharan Africa and China.

The impetus for Columbus and other explorers to navigate the Atlantic Ocean (see Figure 1.1) came from the gradual unraveling of this Mediterranean system after 1350. The spread of the bubonic plague devastated populations along its major trade routes, and the decline of Mongol power in China closed the access to the Far East that Europeans had enjoyed since the early thirteenth century. In 1453, the conquest of Constantinople by the Turkish Ottoman Empire dealt a severe blow to European interests in the eastern Mediterranean. When Columbus sailed west across the Atlantic almost forty years later, he was expecting to arrive in China, thus opening a new route to Asia that would bypass entirely the Muslim peoples in North Africa and the Near East. He was not alone in this quest. Since the fourteenth century, Portuguese and Spanish ships had been nudging their way into the uncharted waters of the Atlantic, hoping to open direct trade with the kingdoms of sub-Saharan Africa and ultimately to find a sea route to India, the Spice Islands, and China. When Columbus made his fateful voyage, the idea of sailing to the Far East was very old; what was new was his willingness to abandon a southern route along the African coast for a bold foray west across the Atlantic.

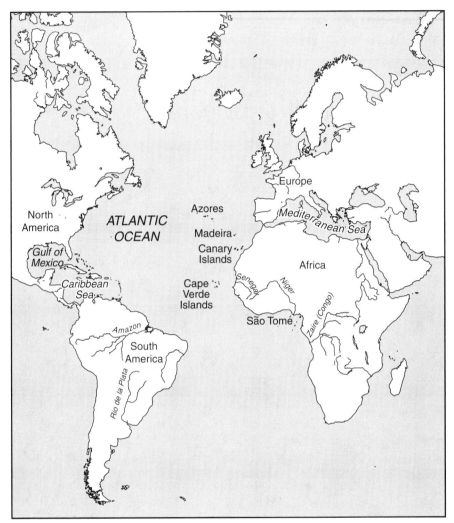

Figure 1.1 The Atlantic World
The Atlantic Ocean, bordered by Europe, Africa, North America, South America.

So, in a sense, the origins of the Atlantic World lay in a century-long effort by Europeans to go east, not west, in pursuit of exotic goods. That pursuit brought them into contact with strangers of varying languages, ethnicities, and religions, which in turn influenced their encounters with the native peoples of Africa and the Americas. In Africa, for example, European traders and explorers expected to discover kingdoms of great wealth, for they knew that the trans-Saharan trade supplied Muslim merchants in North Africa with their gold. The legend of Prester John, a Christian ruler surrounded by Muslim enemies, led European rulers to sponsor expeditions to West Africa in the hope of discovering a profitable new ally and trading partner. Columbus himself was a reader of

Marco Polo, whose famous thirteenth-century account of China and India shaped Columbus's mental picture of the people he expected to meet across the Atlantic. Numerous other medieval travel narratives describing faraway lands and the monstrous peoples that inhabited them influenced European attitudes about the world beyond the Mediterranean.

If such accounts encouraged flights of fantasy, brutal encounters with foreign peoples closer to home taught lessons about conquest and expansion. During the fifteenth and sixteenth centuries, the Spanish, Portuguese, and English gained such firsthand experience in the Canary Islands, São Tomé, and Ireland, respectively. These eastern Atlantic islands became the laboratories of European overseas colonization, and the fate of indigenous peoples there—forced labor, displacement, and religious conversion—foreshadowed what waited for Native Americans on the other side of the Atlantic.

The readings in this chapter offer differing perspectives on these early encounters between the peoples of Europe, Africa, and the Americas. In the first selection, a Portuguese ship captain describes meeting Africans along the coast of West Africa. His purpose is trade, but he is also willing to employ force when he encounters resistance. In the second selection, a French colonist in sixteenth-century Brazil describes the natives he met there with the same sense of the fantastic that Marco Polo brought to his portrayal of China. In the last selection, a North American Indian recounts his people's version of the Europeans' arrival. As you read these selections, look for similarities and differences in the ways that Africans, Native Americans, and Europeans reacted to each other. What motives brought them together? How did they attempt to overcome language and cultural barriers between them?

SELECTION 1: An Early Portuguese Encounter with West Africans

The Portuguese and Spanish pioneered Western Europe's navigation of the Atlantic. Merchants and monarchs in these countries were anxious to secure new trade routes to Asia and Africa that would bypass the Arab merchants who controlled overland access to those regions in North Africa and the Near East. In particular, Dom Henrique (Prince Henry the Navigator) of Portugal sponsored voyages of exploration to sub-Saharan Africa in hopes of finding a sea route to Asia and establishing direct contact with the African kingdoms that supplied gold, ebony, ivory, slaves, and other goods to the Mediterranean trade.

One of the adventurers he sponsored was a Venetian named Alvise da Cà da Mosto, who explored coastal West Africa in two voyages in 1455 and 1456. Cà da Mosto met a variety of peoples in his travels, some of whom expressed an interest in trading with him and others who were openly hostile. In the passages below, he describes two such encounters from his first voyage: a successful negotiation with a kingdom south of the Senegal River and an aborted attempt to sail up the Gambia River.

I passed beyond this river of Senega in my caravel and sailed to the country of Budomel, fifty miles by the coast from the said river: all this coast is low, without mountains. This name Budomel is the title of the ruler [not the name of the country]. It is called "Terra de Budomel," that is to say the land of that lord, or count.

At this place I made my caravel fast, in order to have converse with this ruler, for certain Portuguese who had had dealings with him had informed me that he was a notable and an upright ruler, in whom one could trust, and who paid royally for what was brought to him. Since I had with me some Spanish horses, which were in great demand in the country of Blacks, not to mention many articles such as woollen cloth, Moorish silk and other goods, I made up my mind to try my fortune with this lord.

Accordingly, I cast anchor at a place on the coast of this country, called "le Palme de Budomel," which is a roadstead, not a port. This done, I caused my negro interpreter to announce my arrival, with horses and goods for his service if he had need of them. To be brief, this lord, being informed of this, took horse and rode down to the sea-shore, accompanied by fifteen horsemen and one hundred and fifty footmen. He sent to me to say that it would please him if I would go ashore to see him, and that he would treat me with honour and esteem. Having heard of his high reputation I went thither. He entertained me to a great feast, and after much talk I gave him my horses, and all that he wished from me, trusting to his good faith. He besought me to go inland to his house, about two hundred and fifty [twenty-five] miles from the shore. There he would reward me richly, and I might remain for some days, for he had promised me 100 slaves in return for what he had received. I gave him the horses with their harness and other goods, which together had cost me originally about three hundred ducats. I therefore decided to go with him, but before I left he gave me a handsome young negress, twelve years of age, saying that he gave her to me for the service of my chamber. I accepted her and sent her to the ship. My journey inland was indeed more to see interesting sights and obtain information, than to receive my dues.

◆   ◆   ◆

Since it fell to me to spend many days on shore, I decided to go to see a market, or fair, at no great distance [from the spot where I was lodged]. This was held in a field, on Mondays and Fridays, and I went two or three times to it.

From *the Voyages of Cadamosto and Other Documents in Western Africa in the Second Half of the Fifteenth Century,* ed. G. R. Grone (London: Hakluyt Society, 1937), 35–36,48–49, 50–51, 58–61.

Men and Women came to it from the neighbourhood country within a distance of four or five miles, for those who dwelt farther off attended other markets. In this market I perceived quite clearly that these people are exceedingly poor, judging from the wares they brought for sale—that is, cotton, but not in large quantities, cotton thread and cloth, vegetables, oil and millet, wooden bowls, palm leaf mats, and all the other articles they use in their daily life. Men as well as women came to sell, some of the men offering their weapons, and others a little gold, but not in any quantity. They sold everything, item by item, by barter, and not for money, for they have none. They do not use money of any kind, but barter only, one thing for another, two for one, three for two.

These negroes, men and women, crowded to see me as though I were a marvel. It seemed to be a new experience to them to see Christians, whom they had not previously seen. They marvelled no less at my clothing than at my white skin. My clothes were after the Spanish fashion, a doublet of black damask, with a short cloak of grey wool over it. They examined the woollen cloth, which was new to them, and the doublet with much amazement: some touched my hands and limbs, and rubbed me with their spittle to discover whether my whiteness was dye or flesh. Finding that it was flesh they were astounded.

To this market I went to see further strange sights, and also to find out whether any came thither with gold for sale, but altogether, as I have said, there was little to be found.

❖　❖　❖

The women of this country are very pleasant and light-hearted, ready to sing and to dance, especially the young girls. They dance, however, only at night by the light of the moon. Their dances are very different from ours.

These negroes marvelled greatly at many of our possessions, particularly at our cross-bows, and, above all, our mortars. Some came to the ship, and I had them shown the firing of a mortar, the noise of which frightened them exceedingly. I then told them that a mortar would slay more than a hundred men at one shot, at which they were astonished, saying that it was an invention of the devil's. The sound of one of our country pipes, which I had played by one of my sailors, also caused wonderment. Seeing that it was decked out with trappings and ribbons at the head, they concluded that it was a living animal that sang thus in different voices, and were much pleased with it. Perceiving that they were misled, I told them that it was an instrument, and placed it, deflated, in their hands. Whereupon, recognising that it was made by hand, they said that it was a divine instrument, made by God with his own hands, for it sounded so sweetly with so many different voices. They said they had never heard anything sweeter.

They were also struck with admiration by the construction of our ship, and by her equipment—mast, sails, rigging, and anchors. They were of opinion that the portholes in the bows of ships were really eyes by which the ships saw whither they were going over the sea. They said we must be great wizards, almost the equal of the devil, for men that journey by land have difficulty in knowing the way from place to place, while we journeyed by sea, and, as they were given to understand, remained out of sight of land for many days, yet knew which direction to take, a thing only possible through the power of the devil. This appeared so to them because they do not understand the art of navigation [the compass, or the chart].

They also marvelled much on seeing a candle burning in a candlestick, for here they do not know how to make any other light than that of a fire. To them the sight of the candle, never seen before, was beautiful and miraculous. As, in this country, honey is found, they suck the honey from the comb, and throw away the wax. Having bought a little honeycomb, I showed them how to extract the honey from wax, and then asked whether they knew what it was that remained. They replied that it was good for nothing. In their presence, therefore, I had some candles made, and lighted. On seeing this, they showed much wonderment, exclaiming that we Christians had knowledge of everything.

In this country they have no musical instruments of any kind, save two: the one is a large Moorish "tanbuchi," which we style a big drum; the other is after the fashion of a viol; but it has, however, two strings only, and is played with the fingers, so that it is a simple rough affair and of no account.

◆　◆　◆

The following morning, at about the third hour, we on the other two ships, made sail with a favourable wind and tide to seek our consort and in God's name to enter the river, hoping that in the country farther upstream we might find more civilized people than those we had seen in the canoes. Having joined our consort, she made sail in company and we began to enter the river: the small caravel led the way over the shallows, we following one behind the other.

Having sailed about four miles upstream, we suddenly perceived several canoes coming up behind us (I do not know from whence they came) as fast as they were able. Seeing this, we turned upon them, and being dubious of their poisoned arrows of which we had been informed we protected our ships as best we could, and stood to arms at our stations, although we were poorly equipped. In a short time they reached us. I, being in the leading ship, split the canoes into two sections, and thrust into the midst of them: on counting the canoes, we found they numbered seventeen, of the size of considerable boats. Checking their course and lifting up their oars, their crews lay gazing as upon a marvel. We estimated on examination that there might be about one hundred and fifty at most; they appeared very well-built, exceedingly black, and all clothed in white cotton shirts: some of them wore small white caps on their heads, very like the German style, except that on each side they had a white wing with a feather in the middle of the cap, as though to distinguish the fighting men. A negro stood in the prow of each canoe, with a round shield, apparently of leather, on his arm. They made no movement towards us, nor we to them; then they perceived the other two vessels coming up behind me, and advanced towards them. On reaching them, without any other salute, they all threw down their oars, and began to shoot off their arrows.

Our ships, seeing the attack, at once discharged four bombards: hearing these, amazed and confounded by the roar, they threw down their bows, and gazing some here, some there, stood in astonishment at the sight of the shots falling into the river about them. After watching thus for a considerable while, and seeing no more they overcame their fear [of the thunder claps after many shots had been fired], and taking up their bows, began afresh to shoot with much ardour, approaching to within a stone's throw of the ships. The sailors began to discharge their cross-bows at them: the first to do so was a bastard son of the Genoese, who hit a negro in the breast so that he immediately fell dead in the canoe. His companions perceiving this pulled out the arrow and examined it closely, in astonishment at such a weapon: but this did not restrain them from shooting vigorously at the ships, the crews of which replied in like fashion so that in a short space a great number of negroes were wounded. By the grace of God, however, not one of the Christians was hit.

When they saw the wounded and dead, all the canoes with one accord made for the stern of the small caravel, where a stiff fight was waged, for her crew were few and ill armed. Seeing this I made sail for the small vessel and towed her between our two larger ships amidst a discharge of bombards and cross-bows. At this, the negroes drew off: we, lashing our three ships together by chains, dropped anchor, which, [as the water was calm] held all three.

We then attempted to parley with the Negroes.

◆   ◆   ◆

After much gesticulating and shouting by our interpreters one of the canoes returned within bowshot. We asked of those in it the reason for their attack upon us notwithstanding that we were men of peace, and traders in merchandize, saying that we had peaceful and friendly relations with the negroes of the Kingdom of Senega, and that we wished to be on similar terms with them, if they were willing: further, that we had come from a distant land to offer fitting gifts to their king and lord on behalf of our king of Portugal, who desired peace and friendship with them. We besought them to tell us in what country we were, what lord ruled over it, and the name of the river, and told them they might come in peace and confidence to take our wares, for we were content that they should have as much or as little as they pleased.

They replied that they had had news of our coming and of our trade with the negroes of Senega, who, if they sought our friendship, could not but be bad men, for they firmly believed that we Christians ate human flesh, and that we only bought negroes to eat them: that for their part they did not want our friendship on any terms, but sought to slaughter us all, and to make a gift of our possessions to their lord, who they said was three days distant. Theirs was the country of Gambra, and to the river, which was very large, they gave a name which I do not recall.

At this moment the wind freshened; realizing the ill will they bore us, we made sail towards them. They, anticipating this move, scattered in all directions for the land, and thus ended our engagement with them.

Thereupon, we debated [took the advice of our chief men, who formed the ship's council] whether we should proceed farther up the river, if possible for at least one hundred miles, in the hope of finding better disposed peoples. But our sailors, who wished to return home and not to essay further dangers, began with one accord to murmur, declaring that they would not consent to such a course, and that what had been done was sufficient for the voyage.

When we saw that this was their general desire we agreed to give way in order to avoid dissention, for they were pig-headed and obstinate men. Accordingly on the following day, we departed thence, shaping our course for Cape Verde to return, in God's name, to Spain.

SELECTION 2: First Impressions in South America

One of the earliest regions of European colonization in the New World was coastal Brazil. The Portuguese arrived first, but they faced challenges from the French and Dutch during the sixteenth and seventeenth centuries. The natives these colonizers encountered were Tupinamba Indians, and stories and pictures of them published in Europe gave many Europeans their first notions of what Indians were like. Travelers portrayed the Tupinamba as inhabitants of a tropical paradise, often naked or dressed only in feathered skirts. These images of a New World Eden, however, were countered in the same pages by descriptions of native savagery and cannibalism.

Jean de Léry participated in a failed French attempt to colonize Brazil in the 1550s. Léry was a Huguenot, or French Protestant, who came to the New World to establish a refuge for his fellow believers and to convert Indians to his faith. He lived in Brazil from September 1556 until January 1558, during which time he traveled and traded with the Tupinamba. He published his narrative of this adventure twenty years later. In the passages reproduced below, Léry describes the Indians' physical appearance, his first encounter with cannibalism, and an exchange between himself and a native that almost went wrong.

In the first place then (so that I begin with the chief subject, and take things in order), the savages of America who live in Brazil, called the *Tupinamba*, whom I lived among and come to know for about a year, are not taller, fatter, or smaller in stature than we Europeans are; their bodies are neither monstrous nor prodigious with respect to ours. In fact, they are stronger, more robust and well filled-out, more nimble, less subject to disease; there are almost none among them who are lame, one-eyed, deformed, or disfigured.

Furthermore, although some of them reach the age of a hundred or a hundred twenty years (for they know how to keep track of their ages and count them by moons), few of the elderly among them have white or gray hair. Now this clearly shows not only the benign air and temperature of their country (in which, as I have said elsewhere, there are no frosts or great cold, and the woods, plants, and fields are always greening), but also—for they all truly drink at the Fountain of Youth—the little care or worry that they have for the

From Jean de Léry, *History of a Voyage to the Land of Brazil, Otherwise Called America* translated by Janet Whately (Berkeley and Los Angeles: University of California Press, 1990), 56–58, 64–68, 161–164, 169–171.

things of this world. And indeed, as I will later show in more detail, since they do not in any way drink of those murky, pestilential springs, from which flow so many streams of mistrust, avarice, litigation, and squabbles, of envy and ambition, which eat away our bones, suck out our marrow, waste our bodies, and consume our spirits—in short, poison us and kill us off before our due time—nothing of all that torments them, much less dominates or obsesses them.

As for their natural color, considering the hot region where they live, they are not particularly dark, but merely of a tawny shade, like the Spanish or Provençals.

Now this next thing is no less strange than difficult to believe for those who have not seen it: the men, women, and children do not hide any parts of their bodies; what is more, without any sign of bashfulness or shame, they habitually live and go about their affairs as naked as they come out of their mother's womb. And yet, contrary to what some people think, and what others would have one believe, they are by no means covered with hair; in fact, they are not by nature any hairier than we are over here in this country. Furthermore, as soon as the hair begins to grow on any part of the body, even the beard and eyelashes and eyebrows, it is plucked out, either with their fingernails, or, since the arrival of the Christians, with tweezers that the latter have given them—which makes their gaze seem wall-eyed, wandering, and wild. It has been written that the inhabitants of the island of Cumana in Peru do the same. As for our Tupinamba, they make an exception only of the hair on the head, which on all the males, from their youth onward, is shaved very close from the forehead to the crown, like the tonsure of a monk; behind, in the style of our forefathers or of those who let their hair grow, they have it trimmed on the neck.

To leave nothing out (if that is possible), I will also add this. There are certain grasses in that land with leaves about two fingers wide, which grow slightly curved both around and lengthwise, something like the sheath that covers the ear of the grain that we call "Saracen wheat." I have seen old men (but not all of them, and none of the young men or children) take two leaves of these grasses and arrange them together and bind them with cotton thread around their virile member; sometimes they wrapped it with handkerchiefs and other small pieces of cloth that we gave them. It would seem, on the face of it, that there remains in them some spark of natural shame, if indeed they did this on account of modesty, but, although I have not made closer inquiry, I am still of the opinion that it is rather to hide some infirmity that their old age may cause in that member.

To go on, they have the custom, which begins in the childhood of all the boys, of piercing the lower lip just above the chin; each of them usually wears in the hole a certain well-polished bone, as white as ivory, shaped like one of those little pegs that we play with over here, that we use as tops to spin on a table. The pointed end sticks out about an inch, or two fingers' width, and is held in place by a stop between the gums and the lip; they can remove it and put it back whenever they please. But they only wear this bodkin of white bone during their adolescence; when they are grown, and are called *conomi-ouassou* (that is, big or tall boy), they replace it by mounting in the lip-hole a green stone (a kind of false emerald), also held in place inside by a stop, which appears on the outside to be of the roundness and width of a testoon [a silver coin], with twice its thickness. There are some who wear a stone as long and round as a finger (I brought one such stone back to France). Sometimes when these stones are removed, our Tupinamba amuse themselves by sticking their tongues through that slit in the lip, giving the impression to the onlooker that they have two mouths; I leave you to judge whether it is pleasant to see them do that, and whether that deforms them or not. What is more, I have seen men who, not content with merely wearing these green stones in their lips, also wore them in both cheeks, which they had likewise had pierced for the purpose.

As for the nose: our midwives over here pull on the noses of newborn babies to make them longer and more handsome; however, our Americans, for whom the beauty of their children lies in their being pug-nosed, have the noses of their children pushed in and crushed with the thumb as soon as they come out of their mothers' wombs (just as they do in France with spaniels and other puppies). Someone else has said that there is a certain part of Peru where the Indians have such outlandishly long noses that they set in them emeralds, turquoises, and other white and red stones with gold thread.

❖   ❖   ❖

But for now let us leave a little to one side our Tupinamba in all their magnificence, frolicking and enjoying the good times that they know so well how to have, and see whether their wives and daughters, whom they call *quoniam* (and in some part, since the arrival of the Portuguese, *Maria*) are better adorned and decked out.

First, besides what I said at the beginning of this chapter—that they ordinarily go naked as well as the men—they also share with them the practice of pulling out all body hair, as well as the eyelashes and eyebrows. They do not follow the men's custom regarding the hair of the head: for while the latter, as I have said above, shave their hair in front and clip it in the back, the women not only let it grow long, but also (like the women over here), comb and wash it very carefully; in fact, they tie it up sometimes with a red-dyed cotton string. However, they more often let it hang on their shoulders, and go about wearing it loose.

They differ also from the men in that they do not slit their lips or cheeks, and so they wear no stones in their faces. But as for their ears, they have them pierced in so extreme a fashion for wearing pendants that when they are removed, you could easily pass a finger through the holes; what is more, when they wear pendants made of that big scallop shell called *vignol* which are white, round, and as long as a medium-sized tallow candle, their ears swing on their shoulders, even over their breasts; if you see them from a little distance, it looks like the ears of a bloodhound hanging down on each side.

As for their faces, this is how they paint them. A neighbor woman or companion, with a little brush in hand, begins a small circle right in the middle of the cheek of the one who is having her face painted; turning the brush all around to trace a scroll or the shape of a snail-shell, she will continue until she has adorned and bedizened the face with various hues of blue, yellow, and red; also (as some shameless women in France likewise do), where the eyelashes and eyebrows have been plucked, she will not neglect to apply a stroke of the brush.

Moreover, they make big bracelets, composed of several pieces of white bone, cut and notched like big fish-scales, which they know how so closely to match and so nicely to join—with wax and a kind of gum mixed together into a glue—that it could not be better done. When the work is finished, it is about a foot and a half long; it could be best compared to the cuff used in playing ball over here. Likewise, they wear the white necklaces (called *boüre* in their language) that I have described above, but they do not wear them hung around the neck, as you have heard that the men do; they simply twist them around their arms. That is why, for the same use, they find so pretty the little beads of glass that they call *mauroubi*, in yellow, blue, green, and other colors, strung like a rosary, which we brought over there in great number for barter. Indeed, whether we went into their villages or they came into our fort, they would offer us fruits or some other commodity from their country in exchange for them, and with their customary flattering speech, they would be after us incessantly, pestering us and saying *"Mair, deagatorem, amabé mauroubi"*: that is, "Frenchman, you are good; give me some of your bracelets of glass beads." They would do the same thing to get combs from us, which they call *guap* or *kuap*, mirrors, which they call *aroua*, and all the other goods and merchandise we had that they desired.

But among the things doubly strange and truly marvelous that I observed in these Brazilian women, there is this: although they do not paint their bodies, arms, thighs, and legs as often as the men do, and do not cover themselves with feathers or with anything else that grows in their land, still, although we tried several times to give them dresses and shifts (as I have said we did for the men, who sometimes put them on), it has never been in our power to make them wear clothes: to such a point were they resolved (and I think they have not changed their minds) not to allow anything at all on their bodies. As a pretext to exempt themselves from wearing clothes and to remain always naked, they would cite their custom, which is this: whenever they come upon springs and clear rivers, crouching on the edge or else getting in, they throw water on their heads with both hands, and wash themselves and plunge in with their whole bodies like ducks—on some days than a dozen times; and they said that it was too much trouble to get undressed so often. Is that not a fine and pertinent excuse? But whatever it may be, you have to accept it, for to contest it further with them would be in vain, and you would gain nothing by it.

This creature delights so much in her nakedness that it was not only the Tupinamba women of the mainland, living in full liberty with their husbands, fathers, and kinsmen, who were so obstinate in refusing to dress themselves in any way at all; even our women prisoners of war, whom we had bought and whom we held as slaves to work in our fort—even they, although we forced clothing on them, would secretly strip off the shifts and other rags, as soon as night had fallen, and would not be content unless, before going to bed, they could promenade naked all around our island. In short, if it had been up to these poor wretches, and if they had not been compelled by great strokes of the whip to dress themselves, they would choose to bear the heat and burning of the sun, even the continual skinning of their arms and shoulders carrying earth and stones, rather than to endure having any clothes on.

And there you have a summary of the customary ornaments, rings, and jewelry of the American women and girls. So, without any other epilogue here, let the reader, by this narration, contemplate them as he will.

When I treat the marriage of the savages, I will recount how their children are equipped from birth. As for the children above the age of three or four years, I especially took great pleasure in watching the little boys, whom they call *conomimiri*; plump and chubby (much more so than those over here), with their bodkins of white bone in their split lips, the hair shaved in their style, and sometimes with their bodies painted, they never failed to come dancing out in a troop to meet us when they saw us arrive in their villages. They would tag behind us and play up to us, repeating continually in their babble, "*Contoüassat, amabé pinda*"; that is, "My friend and my ally, give me some fishhooks." If thereupon we yielded (which I have often done), and tossed ten or twelve of the smallest hooks into the sand and dust, they would rush to pick them up; it was great sport to see this swarm of naked little rascals stamping on the earth and scratching it like rabbits.

During that year or so when I lived in that country, I took such care in observing all of them, great and small, that even now it seems to me that I have them before my eyes, and I will forever have the idea and image of them in my mind. But their gestures and expressions are so completely different from ours, that it is difficult, I confess, to represent them well by writing or by pictures. To have the pleasure of it, then, you will have to go see and visit them in their own country. "Yes," you will say, "but the plank is very long." That is true, and so if you do not have a sure foot and a steady eye, and are afraid of stumbling, do not venture down that path.

We have yet to see more fully, as the matters that I treat present themselves, what their houses are like, and to see their household utensils, their ways of sleeping, and other ways of doing things.

Before closing this chapter, however, I must respond both to those who have written and to those who think that the frequenting of these naked savages, and especially of the women, arouses wanton desire and lust. Here, briefly, is what I have to say on this point. While there is ample cause to judge that, beyond the immodesty of it, seeing these women naked would serve as a predictable enticement to concupiscence; yet, to report what was commonly perceived at the time, this crude nakedness in such a woman is much less alluring than one might expect. And I maintain that the elaborate attire, paint, wigs, curled hair, great ruffs, farthingales, robes upon robes, and all the infinity of trifles with which the women and girls over here disguise themselves and of which they never have enough, are beyond comparison the cause of more ills than the ordinary nakedness of the savage women—whose natural beauty is by no means inferior to that of the others. If decorum allowed me to say more, I make bold to say that I could resolve all the objections to the contrary, and I would give reasons so evident that no one could deny them. Without going into it further, I defer concerning the little that I have said about this to those who have made the voyage to the land of Brazil, and who, like me, have seen both their women and ours.

I do not mean, however, to contradict what the Holy Scripture says about Adam and Eve, who, after their sin, were ashamed when they recognized that they were naked, nor do I wish in any way that this nakedness be approved; indeed, I detest the heretics who have tried in the past to introduce it over here, against the law of nature (which on this particular point is by no means observed among our poor Americans).

But what I have said about these savages is to show that, while we condemn them so austerely for going about shamelessly with their bodies entirely uncovered, we ourselves, in the sumptuous display, superfluity, and excess of our own costume, are hardly more laudable. And, to conclude this point, I would to God that each of us dressed modestly, and more for decency and necessity than for glory and worldliness.

◆　　◆　　◆

Although the Tupinamba receive very humanely the friendly strangers who go to visit them, nevertheless the Frenchmen and others from over here who do not understand their language find themselves at first marvelously disconcerted in their midst. The first time that I myself frequented them was three weeks after we arrived at Villegagnon's island, when an interpreter took me along to four or five villages on the mainland. The first one—called *Yabouraci* in the native language and "Pepin" by the French (because of a ship that loaded there once, whose master had that name)—was only two leagues from our fort. When we arrived there, I immediately found myself surrounded by savages, who were asking me "*Marapé-derere, marapé derere?*" meaning "What is your name? What is your name?" (which at that time I understood no better than High German). One of them took my hat, which he put on his head; another my sword and my belt, which he put around his naked body; yet another my tunic, which he donned. Deafening me with their yells, they ran through the village with my clothing. Not only did I think that I had lost everything, but I didn't know what would become of me. As experience has shown me several times since, that was only from ignorance of their way of doing things; for they do the same thing to everyone who visits them, and especially those they haven't seen before. After they have played around a little with one's belongings, they carry them all back and return them to their owners.

The interpreter had warned me that they wanted above all to know my name; but if I had said to them Pierre, Guillaume, or Jean, they would have been able neither to retain it nor to pronounce it (in fact, instead of saying "Jean," they would say "Nian"). So I had to accommodate by naming something that was known to them. Since by a lucky chance my surname, "Léry," means "oyster" in their language, I told them that my name was "*Léry-oussou*," that is, a big oyster. This pleased them greatly; with their "*Teh!*" of admiration, they began to laugh, and said, "That is a fine name; we have not yet seen any *Mair* (that is, a Frenchman) of that name." And indeed, I can say with assurance that never did Circe metaphorphose a man into such a fine oyster, nor into one who could converse so well with Ulysses, as since then I have been able to do with our savages.

One must note that their memory is so good that as soon as someone has told them his name, if they were to go a hundred years (so to speak) without seeing him, they will never forget it. Presently I will tell about the other ceremonies they observe when they receive friends who go to see them.

But for the moment I will continue to recount some of the noteworthy things that happened to me during my first journey among the Tupinamba. That same day the interpreter and I were going on to spend the night in another village called *Euramiri* (the French called it "Goset," because of an interpreter of that name who stayed there). Arriving at sunset, we found the savages dancing and finishing up the *caouin* [a fermented drink] of a prisoner whom they had killed only six hours earlier, the pieces of whom we saw on the *boucan* [a wooden grill for cooking meat]. Do not ask whether, with this beginning, I was astonished to see such a tragedy; however, as you will hear, that was nothing compared to the fright that I had soon after.

We had entered one of the village houses, where each of us sat, according to custom, in a cotton bed hung in the air. After the women had wept (in a manner that I will describe in a moment) and the old man, the master of the house, had made his speech of welcome, the interpreter—who was not new to the customs of the savages and who, moreover, liked to drink and *caouiner* [get intoxicated] as much as they did—without saying a single word to me, nor warning me of anything, went over to the big crowd of dancers and left me there with some of the savages. So after eating a little root flour and other food they had offered us, I, weary and asking only for rest, lay down in the cotton bed I had been sitting on.

Not only was I kept awake by the noise that the savages made, dancing and whistling all night while eating their prisoner; but, what is more, one of them approached me with the victim's foot in hand, cooked and *boucané* [grilled] asking me (as I learned later, for I didn't understand at the time) if I wanted to eat some of it. His countenance filled me with such terror that you need hardly ask if I lost all desire to sleep. Indeed, I thought that by brandishing the human flesh he was eating, he was threatening me and wanted to make me understand that I was about to be similarly dealt with. As one doubt begets another, I suspected straight away that the interpreter, deliberately betraying me, had abandoned me and delivered me into the hands of these barbarians. If I had seen some exit through which to flee, I would not have hesitated. But seeing myself surrounded on all sides by those whose intentions I failed to understand (for as you will hear, they had not the slightest thought of doing me harm), I firmly expected shortly to be eaten, and all that night I called on God in my heart. I will leave it to those who understand what I am saying, and who put themselves in my place, to consider whether that night seemed long.

At daybreak my interpreter (who had been off carousing with those rascals of savages all night long in other village houses) came to find me. Seeing me, as he said, not only ashen-faced and haggard but also feverish, he asked me whether I was sick, or if I hadn't rested well. Distraught, I answered wrathfully that they had well and truly kept me from sleeping, and that he was a scoundrel to have left me among these people whom I couldn't understand at all; still as anxious as ever, I urged that we get ourselves out of there with all possible speed. Thereupon he told me that I should have no fear, and that it wasn't us they were after. When he recounted the whole business to the savages—who, rejoicing at my coming, and thinking to show me affection, had not budged from my side all night—they said that they had sensed that I had been somewhat frightened of them, for which they were very sorry. My one consolation was the hoot of laughter they sent up—for they are great jokers—at having (without meaning to) given me such a scare.

◆   ◆   ◆

Now you may want to know whether we felt safe among the savages of America. Just as they hate their enemies so mortally (as you have already heard) that when they have captured them, without any discussion of terms, they slay and eat them, so, on the contrary, they love so dearly their friends and confederates (as we were to the Tupinamba nation) that to keep them safe and spare them any hardship they would have had themselves cut into a hundred thousand pieces. Having had experience of them, I would entrust myself to them, and in fact felt myself safer among this people we call savage, than I would now in some parts of our France, among disloyal and degenerate Frenchmen (I speak only of those who are such: as for worthy people, of whom by the grace of God the kingdom is not yet empty, I would be very sorry to taint their honor.)

However, so that I give both sides, I will recount an event containing the greatest apparent danger I ever found myself in among them. Having met up unexpectedly with six Frenchmen in that fine big village of *Ocarentin*, which I have already mentioned, ten or twelve leagues from our fort, and having decided to spend the night there, we made up a bow-and-arrow shooting match, three against three, to get some wild turkey and other fowl for our supper. As it happened, I was one of the losers. As I was looking through the village for poultry to buy, I came across one of those little French boys whom we had brought along in the ship Rosée to learn the language of the country, and who was now living in this village. "Here is a fine big duck," he said. "Kill it, and you will be quits by paying for it." I had no compunction about doing just that, because we had often killed chickens in other villages, which did not anger the savages since we could content them with a few knives as payment.

The dead duck in my hand, I went into a house where nearly all the savages of the place were assembled to *caouiner*. When I asked who the duck belonged to, so that I might pay him, an old man with a fairly disagreeable mug came forward and said, "It's mine." "What do you want me to give you for it?" I asked him. "A knife," he replied. I offered him one at once; when he saw it, he said, "I want a better one." Which, making no reply, I presented to him; he said he didn't want that one either. "Then what do you want me to give you?" I said. "A pruning hook," he answered. Now aside from the fact that in that country a pruning hook was too much to pay for a duck, I didn't even have one; I told him to content himself with the second knife I was offering him, and that he would have nothing more from me. But thereupon the interpreter, who knew their ways of doing things better than I did (although on this point, as I shall tell you, he was as mistaken as I) said to me, "He is very angry; somehow a pruning hook must be found." I borrowed one from the boy I mentioned, but when I tried to give it to this savage, he refused it more emphatically than he had previously done with the knives. Now I was getting angry, and for the third time I said to him: "What do you want from me?" To which he answered in a rage that he wanted to kill me as I had killed his duck; for, he said, "since it belonged to a brother of mine who is dead, I loved it more than anything else I have in my possession." And indeed, this lout went off to find a sword, or rather a big wooden club five or six feet long; suddenly advancing on me again, he kept repeating that he wanted to kill me. I was dumbfounded; still, I knew that one must not seem to knuckle under or show any fear among these people.

Thereupon the interpreter, seated in a cotton bed suspended between the quarreler and me, and warning me about what I didn't understand, said to me: "Hold your sword in your fist, and show him your bow and arrow, and let him know just who he is dealing with; as for you, you are strong and valiant, and will not let yourself be killed as easily as he thinks." So I bluffed my way through, and after a few more exchanges between this savage and me (without any attempt from the others to reconcile us), he left to sleep off the *caouin* that he had been drinking all day. The interpreter and I went off to dine on the duck with our companions, who were waiting for us in the village and knew nothing of our quarrel.

However, as it turned out, the Tupinamba knew perfectly well that, already having the Portuguese for enemies, if they had killed a Frenchman an irreconcilable war would have been declared between them and that they would be forever deprived of our merchandise; so everything that my man had done was in jest. And in fact, when he woke up about three hours later, he sent a message to me saying that I was his son, and that what he had done to me was only to test me, and to see by my countenance whether I would be valiant in war against the Portuguese and the Margaia, our common enemies. For my part, in order to deprive him of the chance to do the same another time, either to me or to another of our men—for such jokes are not very pleasant—I sent word to him that I would have nothing to do with him, and that I did not want a father who would test me with a sword in his hand. What is more, so as to make him find some better away of dealing with me, and to show him that such a game displeased me, the next day I gave little knives and fishhooks to the others right in front of him, who got nothing.

One can gather, then, as much from this example as from the other I have recounted about my first sojourn among the savages (where, out of ignorance of the standing that our nation had among them, I thought I was in danger), that what I have said about their loyalty toward their friends remains true and firm; that is, they would be very grieved to cause them displeasure.

For a conclusion on this point, I will add that the elders especially, who in the past lacked axes, pruning hooks and knives—which they now find useful for cutting their wood and making their bows and arrows—not only treat visiting Frenchmen very well, but also exhort their young people to do the same in the future.

SELECTION 3: An Indian Perspective on the Europeans' Arrival in North America

The Iroquois (also known as the Six Nations) were a powerful confederacy of Indian peoples who inhabited the region south of Lake Ontario in modern day New York. During the seventeenth and eighteenth centuries, they encountered

Dutch, French, and English colonizers and became adept at using the commercial and imperial rivalries between these newcomers to extend their own power in northeastern America. At first with the Dutch and then with the English, the Iroquois established an alliance known as the Covenant Chain, which preserved peace and trade between Indians connected to their confederacy and their colonial neighbors. According to Iroquois custom, this "chain" was "brightened" by colonial officials and Indians who met at periodic conferences to exchange presents, settle differences, and renew their friendship.

One such conference convened in the frontier town of Lancaster, Pennsylvania in 1744. Delegations from Pennsylvania, Maryland, and Virginia met with the Iroquois to discuss trade and to acquire land. One of the Iroquois speakers at this conference was Canasatego, who in a speech addressed to the Maryland governor, recounted the arrival of the Europeans to his people's homelands. Canasatego's version of this story is an excellent example of how Indians incorporated their version of the European-Indian encounter into their own oral traditions.

The spelling has been modernized.

"**B**rother, the *Governor of* Maryland,
"When you mentioned the Affair of the Land Yesterday, you went back to old Times, and told us, you had been in Possession of the Province of *Maryland*, above One Hundred Years; but what is a Hundred Years, in Comparison of the Length of Time since our Claim began? Since we came out of this Ground? For we must tell you, that long before a Hundred Years, our Ancestors came out of this very Ground, and their Children have remained here ever since.

"You came out of the Ground in a Country that lies beyond the Seas; there you may have a just Claim, but here you must allow us to be your elder Brethren, and the Lands to belong to us long before you knew any Thing of them.

"It is true, that above One Hundred Years ago the *Dutch* came here in a Ship, and brought with them several Goods, such as Awls, Knives, Hatchets, Guns, and many other Particulars, which they gave us: And when they had taught us how to use their Things, and we saw what Sort of People they were, we were so pleased with them, that we tied their Ship to the Bushes on the Shore; and afterwards, liking them still better the longer they stayed with us, and thinking the Bushes too slender, we removed the Rope and tied it to the Trees; and as the Trees were liable to be blown down by high Winds, or to decay of themselves, from the Affection we bore them, again removed the Rope, and tied it to a strong and big Rock: [*Here, the Interpreter said, they mean the* Oncido

From *A Treaty, Held at the Town of Lancaster, in Pennsylvania, by the Honourable the Lieutenant-Governor of the Province, and the Honourable the Commissioners for the Provinces of Virginia and Maryland, with the Indians of the Six Nations, in June, 1744*. (Philadelphia: B. Franklin, 1744), 11–13.

(Oneida) *Country*.] And not content with this, for its further Security, we removed the Rope to the big Mountain, [*Here, the Interpreter says, they mean the* Onondago *Country*.] and there we tied it very fast, and rolled *Wampum* [shell beads] about it; and to make it still more secure, we stood upon the *Wampum*, and sat down upon it, to defend it, and to prevent any Hurt coming to it, and did our best Endeavors, that it might remain uninjured for ever.

"During all this Time, the New-comers the *Dutch*, acknowledged our Right to the Lands and solicited us from time to time, to grant them part of our Country, to enter into League and Covenant with us, and to become one People with us.

"After this, the *English* came into the Country, and as we were told, became one People with the *Dutch*: About two Years after the Arrival of the *English*, an *English* Governor came to *Albany*; and finding what great Friendship subsisted between us and the *Dutch*, he approved it mightily, and desired to make as strong a League, and to be upon as good Terms with us, as the *Dutch* were, with whom he was united, and to become one People with us; and by his further Care in looking into what had passed between us, he found, That the Rope which tied the Ship to the great Mountain, was only fastened with *Wampum*, which was liable to break and rot, and to perish in a Course of Years: He therefore told us, that he would give us a Silver Chain, which would be much stronger, and would last for ever: This we accepted, and fastened the Ship with it, and it has lasted ever since.

"Indeed, we have had some small Differences with the *English*, and during these Misunderstandings, some of their young Men would, by way of Reproach, be every now and then telling us, that we should have perished, if they had not come into the Country, and furnished us with Strouds [a type of woolen cloth], Hatchets, Guns, and other Things necessary for the Support of Life: But we always gave them to understand, that they were mistaken; that we lived before they came amongst us, and as well or better, if we may believe what our Forefathers have told us: We had then Room enough, and Plenty of Deer, which was easily caught; and though we had not Knives and Hatchets, and Guns, such as we have now, yet we had Knives of Stone, and Hatchets of Stone, and Bows and Arrows, and these served our Uses as well then, as the *English* ones do now: We are now straightened, and sometimes in want of Deer, and liable to many more Inconveniences, since the *English* came among us. . . ."

∼ Discussion Questions ∼

1. Compare Cà da Mosto's description of Africans with Léry's description of Indians: can you find similarities between them that suggest a common approach Europeans took toward strangers they encountered in the Atlantic World? What differences between these accounts suggest potentially different paths for the European-African and European-Indian encounters that would follow?

2. Compare the Africans' reactions to Cà da Mosto with the Indians' reactions to Léry. According to these two narratives, what did native peoples find impressive about Europeans? What did they find suspect?

3. According to Canasatego, what first attracted the Iroquois to the Dutch ship that arrived in their homelands? How has that relationship changed since the arrival of the English? On what grounds does Canasatego challenge the colonists' claim to the land?

4. In all three of these selections, trade provides a common context for encounter between natives and newcomers. What commercial objectives are evident in Cà da Mosto's and Léry's accounts? What prejudices are revealed in their descriptions of trade with these strangers? How does Canasatego's description of the European-Indian encounter reflect a different perspective on this exchange?

Suggested Readings

For overviews of European society on the eve of Columbus's voyage, see William D. Phillips, Jr. and Carla Rahn Phillips, *The Worlds of Christopher Columbus* (Cambridge, England: Cambridge University Press, 1992), and Janet L. Abu-Lughod, *Before European Hegemony: The World System A.D. 1250–1350* (New York: Oxford University Press, 1989). For European reactions to the New World, see J. H. Elliott, *The Old World and the New, 1492–1650* (Cambridge, England: Cambridge University Press, 1970), and Stephen Greenblatt, *Marvelous Possessions: The Wonder of the New World* (Chicago: University of Chicago Press, 1991). For early encounters between Europeans and sub-Saharan Africans, see John Thornton, *Africa and Africans in the Making of the Atlantic World, 1400–1680* (Cambridge, England: Cambridge University Press, 1992), and Donald R. Wright, *The World and a Very Small Place in Africa* (Armonk, N.Y.: M. E. Sharpe, 1997). For European encounters with the Tupinamba Indians of Brazil, see John Hemmings, *Red Gold: The Conquest of the Brazilian Indians* (Cambridge, Mass.: Harvard University Press, 1978). For the Iroquois-European encounter described by Canasatego in his speech, see Daniel K. Richter, *Ordeal of the Longhouse: The Peoples of the Iroquois League in the Era of European Colonization* (Chapel Hill, N.C.: University of North Carolina Press, 1992).

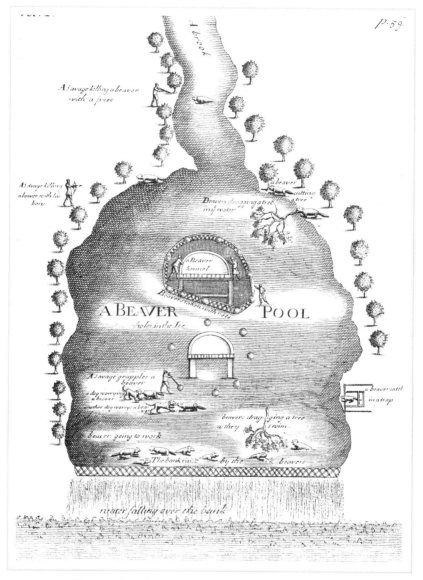

Beaver Hunting in Seventeenth-Century Canada

This image is indicative of the Europeans' fascination with the animal life they encountered in the New World (see Selection 3). Note the attention the artist paid to the beavers' engineering skill in building dams. How does this image illustrate the Indians' hunting techniques, and what evidence do you see here of the impact European trade has had on that hunting?

Source: Dechert Collection/Anneneberg Rare Book and Manuscript Library/University of Pennsylvania

The Columbian Exchange

Introduction

The passage of human beings between the Old World and the New led to a much wider transfer of plant and animal life commonly known as the Columbian Exchange. Some of this exchange occurred by design, such as when Old World farmers planted American crops in their fields; other times, the exchange was inadvertent, such as when colonists unwittingly introduced new diseases to Native American populations. Whether purposeful or accidental, such exchanges forever altered the nature of plant, animal, and human life on both sides of the Atlantic. Formerly isolated ecosystems became intertwined and transformed in the process. Some species experienced extinction or near extinction, while others flourished in new surroundings unchecked by natural enemies. While scholars have typically studied the human actors involved in this drama, we cannot appreciate the full impact of the Columbian Exchange without considering the other forms of life it affected.

The most profound changes wrought by the Columbian Exchange resulted from the transmission of microbes from the Old World to the New. European sailors, explorers, traders, and colonists brought to the Americas a number of diseases to which Native Americans had no previous exposure, and therefore, no natural immunities. Smallpox, measles, influenza, bubonic plague, and others broke out in "virgin-soil epidemics" among these new host populations. Estimating the impact that these diseases had on Native Americans has become a contentious business among scholars, involving debates over the pre-Columbian population of the Americas and the fatality rates associated with virgin-soil epidemics. On the high end, some scholars estimate that as many as eighteen million Indians lived in North America prior to 1492, and that Old World microbes reduced that number by as much as 95 percent. More conservative estimates place the pre-Columbian population of North America at four to seven million, with a 60 to 70 percent reduction in that number by 1700.

Arriving at a consensus figure is difficult because the record is so fragmentary and the methodologies used to interpret it differ significantly. Any estimates recorded by European observers of native populations were local in nature and did not account for earlier epidemics that may have gone unrecorded. Furthermore, the fatality rates associated with such epidemics varied considerably depending upon the diseases and the regions and cultures involved. Factors of climate and population density influenced how quickly a disease spread among a new population. Generally speaking, sedentary Indian populations were more vulnerable because they came into sustained contact with the newcomers and had difficulty quarantining the infected. Those Indians who lived in hunter-gatherer societies were more isolated and mobile, factors that impeded the spread of epidemics.

The Columbian Exchange also affected plant and animal life in the Atlantic World. Early European explorers were awestruck by the flora and fauna they encountered in the Americas, the sheer variety of which called into question the biblical stories that informed their understanding of the natural world. The existence of different species in the Americas suggested that life in the Western Hemisphere might be the product of a separate creation, not related to the human and animal descendants of Noah's ark. The tropical climate, lush landscape, and naked peoples encountered by Columbus and other explorers in the American tropics called to mind the Garden of Eden, only in this version, humankind still lived in innocence and bounty.

Such impressions of America as an unspoiled Eden were countered by an impulse to profit from its abundant resources. Forests became lumber and naval supplies. The codfish that teemed in the Grand Banks off of New England and Canada became a staple of Old World diets. Furbearing animals, most famously the beaver, were transformed into hats, coats, and gloves for the wealthy. The addictive properties of tobacco made this plant a wildly popular consumer good in Atlantic markets. Everywhere Europeans looked in the Americas, they found plants and animals that they could turn into commodities at home. Colonists also introduced new plants and animals to the American landscape for the same purpose. Sugar, rice, and coffee were Old World crops that became staples of colonial plantation economies. European livestock flourished on American farms and ranches, and these animals carried in their bellies and dung the seeds of plants such as bluegrass and dandelions that spread quickly in American ecosystems.

This invasion of new species transformed Native American subsistence patterns. Pigs damaged unfenced Indian cornfields, and grazing by cattle caused soil erosion. Some Native American peoples became sheep and cattle ranchers, and the horse revolutionized the transportation and hunting of Indians on the Great Plains. Indians who had long used beaver, deer, and buffalo for a variety of purposes—food, clothing, tools, shelter—now hunted them to trade in a transatlantic marketplace. The demands of this market challenged taboos that governed Indian-animal relations and led to overhunting of some species, while Indians themselves became increasingly dependent on European-manufactured firearms, clothing, and metal wares.

Much of what has been said thus far about the Columbian Exchange would suggest that it was one-sided: Old World microbes, plants, and animals invaded and reshaped the ecological balance of the New World. While it is true that the most obvious environmental changes in the Atlantic World occurred in the Americas, the exchange of organisms did have a significant impact on life in the Old World as well. Most important was the introduction of New World crops to Old World agriculture. American maize, potatoes, peanuts, and manioc diversified and enriched diets in Europe and Africa, making possible a population boom in the Old World that continued well into the twentieth century.

The transmission of microbes across the Atlantic had a much less devastating impact on Old World populations than New. In the wake of Columbus, only one disease ravaged Europe's population with the ferocity of a virgin-soil epidemic. Epidemiologists debate the exact origins of syphilis, but there is no doubt that this sexually transmitted disease, first reported in Europe in the 1490s, spread quickly and with devastating consequences in its new host population. For this reason, some scholars contend that it originated in the Americas and was carried back to the Old World by sailors who had sexual contact with Native American women. It is harder to find evidence of other Native American illnesses that crossed the Atlantic. In part, this is because no significant number of Indians resettled in the Old World, either voluntarily or as a result of enslavement. Thus, Europeans and Africans who stayed at home never faced prolonged exposure to illnesses that may have been endemic to the Americas. Also, infectious diseases in human history have typically evolved in farming societies that rely on domesticated animals for food and milk. Over thousands of years, microbes carried by cows, pigs, sheep, and horses have mutated and adapted to human hosts. At the time of Columbus, the only large animals Native Americans had domesticated were dogs, chiefly for hunting and companionship, and llamas, chiefly as beasts of burden and for their wool. This limited experience with livestock meant that Indians simply had fewer germs to offer to Columbus than he had to offer them.

While the Columbian Exchange continues even today (consider for example the spread of the AIDS virus), its historical legacy for the Atlantic World is quite clear. Old World species derived considerable benefit from contact with the New, by way of access to new land and resources, but the species of the New World suffered considerably. Europeans and Africans displaced Native Americans, while the Old World's demand for American fish, pelts, timber, and other goods tested the sustainability of many American species. Overall, the mixing of species from both sides of the Atlantic has diversified and expanded the world's food supplies and trade, but at the cost of disrupting local ecosystems and human populations.

The readings in this chapter focus on the role microbes, plants, and animals played in encounters between the Old World and the New.

The first selection presents an early description of Indian farming, including the "three sisters" (corn, beans, and squash) that were staples of the Indian diet, and tobacco. The second selection focuses on the clash between European and Native American conceptions of human-animal relations and disease transmission. The third selection provides an example of the European fascination with the animal life encountered in the Americas. As you read these sources, think about how the Columbian Exchange challenged the mental and physical worlds of the people it involved. How did the collision of microbes, plants, and animals in the Atlantic World shape human experience there?

SELECTION 1: An Elizabethan Scientist Admires Indian Agriculture

During the 1580s, the English tried twice to establish a colony on Roanoke Island off the coast of modern-day North Carolina. Both ventures failed, but they did give the English their first prolonged interaction with Indians and the American environment. Thomas Hariot was a scientist and mathematician who participated in the first Roanoke expedition of 1585. After returning to England, he published a description of his experiences there to promote further colonization of Virginia.

While he shared many of the prejudices of his Elizabethan contemporaries about America's native inhabitants, Hariot was nevertheless a careful observer of their culture and society. He expressed great admiration for their agriculture and described in detail their crops and methods of planting. His glowing descriptions of the Indian diet and the fertility of the land must have appealed mightily to English farmers accustomed to eking meager livings out of spent soil and backbreaking labor.

The spelling has been modernized.

Such commodities as Virginia is known to yield for victual and sustenance of man's life, usually fed upon by the natural inhabitants, as also by us, during the time of our abode, and first of such as are sowed and husbanded [cultivated]:

Pagatowr, a kind of grain so called by the inhabitants; the same in the West Indies is called Maize. English men call it Guinea Wheat or Turkey wheat, according to the names of the countries from whence the like has been brought. The grain is about the bigness of our ordinary English peas and not much dif-

From Thomas Hariot, *A briefe and true report of the new found land of Virginia*, in Richard Hakluyt, *The Principall Navigations, Voiages, and Discoveries of the English Nation* (London: George Bishop, 1589), 753–757.

ferent in form and shape, but of diverse colors, some white, some red, some yellow, and some blue. All of them yield a very white and sweet flower, being used according to this kind, it makes a very good bread. We made of the same in the country some malt, whereof was brewed as good Ale as was to be desired. So likewise by the help of hops thereof may be made as good Beer. It is a grain of marvelous great increase; of a thousand, fifteen hundred, and some two thousand fold. . . .

Okingíer, called by us Beans, because in greatness and partly in shape they are like the Beans in England; saving that they are flatter, of more diverse colors, and some pied. The leaf also of the stem is much different. In taste they are altogether as good as our English peas.

Wickonzówr, called by us Peas, in respect of the beans, for distinction sake, because they are much less [in size], although in form they little differ, but in goodness of taste much, and are far better than our English peas. Both the beans and peas are ripe in ten weeks after they are set. They make them victual either by boiling them all to pieces into a broth, or boiling them whole until they be soft and begin to break as is used in England, either by themselves or mixed together. Sometimes they mingle of the wheat with them. Sometime also being whole sodden, they bruise or pound them in a mortar, and therefore make loaves or lumps of doughish bread, which they use to eat for variety.

Macócqwer [pumpkins and squash], according to their several forms, called by us Pompions, Melons, and Gourds, because they are of the like forms as those kinds in England. In Virginia such of several forms are of one taste and very good, and do also spring from one seed. There are two sorts: one is ripe in the space of a month, and the other in two months.

There is also an herb which in Dutch is called *Melden*. Some of those that I describe it onto take it to be a kind of Orach [spinach or beets]. It grows about four or five foot high; of seeds thereof they make a thick broth and pottage of a very good taste; of the stalk by burning into ash they make a kind of salt earth, where withal many use sometimes to season their broths. Other salt they know not. We ourselves used the leaves for pot-herbs.

There is also another great herb, in form of a Marigold, about six foot in height, the head with the flower is a span in breadth. Some take it to be *Planta Solis* [sunflowers]; of the seeds hereof they make both a kind of bread and broth.

All the aforesaid commodities for victual are set or sowed, sometimes in grounds apart and severally by themselves, but for the most part together in one ground mixedly, the manner thereof, with the dressing and preparing of the ground, because I will note unto you the fertility of the soil, I think good briefly to describe.

The ground they never fatten with muck, dung, or any other thing, neither plow nor dig it as we in England, but only prepare it in sort as follows. A few days before they sow or set, the men with wooden instruments, made also in form of mattocks or hoes with long handles, with women with short peckers or parers, because they use them sitting, of a foot long and about five inches in breadth, do only break the upper part of the ground to raise up the weeds, grass, and old stubs of corn stalks with their roots, which after a day or two drying in the sun, being scraped up into many small heaps, to save them labor for carrying them away, they burn into ashes. . . . And this is all the husbanding of their ground that they use.

Then their setting or sowing is after this manner. First for their corn, beginning in one corner of the plot, with a pecker they make a hole, wherein they put four grains, with that care they touch not one to another (about an inch asunder) and cover them with the mold again, and so throughout the whole plot, making such holes and using them after such manner, but with this regard, that they be made in ranks, every rank differing from the other half a fathom or a yard, and the holes also in every rank, as much. By this means there is a yard spare ground between every hole, where according to discretion here and there, they set as many Beans and Peas, and in diverse places also among the seeds of *Macócqwer, Melden,* and *Planta Solis.*

The ground being thus set . . . doth there yield in crop of . . . corn, beans, and peas, at the least two hundred London bushels, besides the *Macócqwer, Melden,* and *Planta Solis;* when as in England, forty bushels of our wheat yielded out of such an acre is thought to be much.

I thought also good to note this unto you, that you which shall inhabit and plant there, may know how specially that country corn is there to be preferred before ours. Besides the manifold ways of applying it to victual, the increase is so much that small labor and pains is needful in respect that must be used for ours. For this I can assure you, that according to the rate we have made proof of, one man may prepare and husband so much ground (having once borne corn before) with less than four and twenty hours labor, as shall yield him victual in a large proportion for twelve months. . . .

There is an herb which is sowed apart by itself and is called by the inhabitants *uppówoc.* In the West Indies it has diverse names, according to the several places and countries where it grows and is used. The Spaniards generally call it Tobacco. The leaves thereof being dried and brought into powder, they use to take the fume or smoke thereof by sucking it through pipes made of clay, into their stomach and head, from whence it purges superfluous phlegm and other gross humors, opens all the pores and passages of the body, by which means the use thereof, not only preserves the body from obstructions, but also, if any be, so that they have not been of too long continuance, in short time breaks them, whereby their bodies are notably preserved in health and know not many grievous diseases wherewithal we in England are oftentimes afflicted.

This *uppówoc* is of so precious estimation among them, that they think their gods are marvelously delighted therewith. Whereupon sometime they make hallowed fires and cast some of the powder therein for a sacrifice. Being in a storm upon the waters, to pacify their gods, they cast some up into the air and into the water. So a weir for fish being newly set up, they cast some therein into the air likewise, but all done with strange gestures, stamping, sometime dancing, clapping of hands, holding up of hands, and staring up into the heavens, uttering therewithal and chattering strange words and noises.

We ourselves during the time we were there used to suck it after their manner, as also since our return, and have found many rare and wonderful experiments of the virtues thereof, of which the relation would require a volume by itself; the use of it by so many of late men and women of great calling as else and some learned physicians also, is sufficient witness.

SELECTION 2: The Exchange of Furs and Microbes in New France

The Society of Jesus was a Catholic religious order founded in the sixteenth century for the purpose of winning converts throughout the world. Jesuits, as its members were known, spearheaded the missionary effort in French Canada. Their annual reports, which were published in Paris to gain financial and political support for their cause, detailed their efforts to learn Indian languages, ingratiate themselves to Indian communities, and gain converts by persuasion and example. Collected and published in a series known as the *Jesuit Relations,* these reports are one of the most important sources on early contact and exchange between Europeans and Indians.

The Jesuits were most concerned with the Indians' spiritual beliefs, but in documenting those, they invariably described other aspects of native life, such as human-animal relations and medicine. In the first passage below, from 1634, Father Paul Le Jeune, S.J. reports on taboos that governed Indian hunting practices and one Indian's reaction to the fur trade. In the second, from 1653, Father Francesco Bressani, S.J. describes how the outbreak of new diseases affected the Hurons' reception of the Jesuits.

The Savages do not throw to the dogs the bones of female Beavers and Porcupines,—at least, certain specified bones; in short, they are very careful that the dogs do not eat any bones of birds and of other animals which are taken in the net, otherwise they will take no more except with incomparable difficulties. Yet they make a thousand exceptions to this rule, for it does not matter if the vertebrae or rump of these animals be given to the dogs, but the rest must be thrown into the fire. Yet, as to the Beaver which has been taken in a trap, it is best to throw its bones into a river. It is remarkable how they gather and collect these bones, and preserve them with so much care, that you would say their game would be lost if they violated their superstitions. As I was laughing at them, and telling them that Beavers do not know what is done with their bones, they answered me, "Thou does not know how to take Beavers, and thou wishest to talk about it." Before the Beaver was entirely dead, they told me, its soul comes to make the round of the Cabin of him who has killed it, and looks very carefully to see what is done with its bones; if they

From Reuben G. Thwaites, editor, *The Jesuit Relations and Allied Documents: Travels and Explorations of the Jesuit Missionaries in New France,* 1610–1791, 73 volumes (Cleveland: Burrows Brothers, 1896–1901), 6:211–213, 297–299; 39:125–135.

are given to the dogs, the other Beavers would be apprised of it and therefore they would make themselves hard to capture. But they are very glad to have their bones thrown into the fire, or into a river; especially the trap which has caught them is very glad of this. I told them that the Hiroquois [Iroquois], according to the reports of the one who was with us, threw the bones of the Beaver to the dogs, and yet they took them very often; and our Frenchmen captured more game than they did (without comparison), and yet our dogs ate these bones. "Thou hast no sense, "they replied, "dost thou not see that you and the Hiroquois cultivate the soil and gather its fruits, and not we, and that therefore it is not the same thing?" I began to laugh when I heard this irrelevant answer. The trouble is, I only stutter, I take one word for another, I pronounce badly; and so everything usually passes off in laughter. What great difficulty there is in talking with people without being able to understand them.

◆   ◆   ◆

The Castor or Beaver is taken in several ways. The Savages say that it is the animal well-beloved by the French, English and Basques,—in a word, by the Europeans. I heard my host say one day, jokingly, *Missi picoutau amissou*, "The Beaver does everything perfectly well, it makes kettles, hatchets, swords, knives, bread; and, in short, it makes everything." He was making sport of us Europeans, who have such a fondness for the skin of this animal and who fight to see who will give the most to these Barbarians, to get it; they carry this to such an extent that my host said to me one day, showing me a very beautiful knife, "The English have no sense; they give us twenty knives like this for one Beaver skin."

◆   ◆   ◆

[I]t was a common opinion that we were the authors of a kind of pestilence which was not usual in the country, and almost utterly ruined it. They founded their suspicion, or rather, certain belief, first, on the ground that the supposed magicians and the principal men of the country assured them of it, and the people easily believe without other examination; secondly, on the ground that although, at the beginning, almost all of ours had been attacked by the disease at the same time,—without a physician, or medicine, or convenience of provisions; without other refreshment than a little wild purslane [herb], boiled in clear water without salt; in extreme necessity and dearth of everything,—they had in a few days convalesced, and recovered perfect health; whereas the Barbarians, with all their remedies, both natural and superstitious, nearly all died. And, in truth, our cures in those countries were a singular grace of God. The Father who wrote the letter copied herein, a little above, being asked what remedy he had employed for the many and dangerous wounds he had received from the Hiroquois,—of which expert Physicians in Europe have said that they would not, without great fear, have undertaken the cure,—answered that he had used no other than a most austere but necessary diet, and his teeth,—with which, having no other instrument, he tore away even to the quick the putrid flesh, in order to eradicate the gangrene which was already forming in three several places of his lacerated hands. [B]ecause, although ours remained almost all the time with the diseased, and those the most filthy and dangerous ones, who were dying on our hands, no one caught the contagion; so that they accounted us Demons, and believed that we had made *fœdus cummorte, et pactum cum Inferno* [an agreement with death, and a pact with Hell]. There had been started at Kebek [Quebec] a Seminary for Huron Youths, which, we believed, would be of great use for propagating our Holy Faith in the country; but there the young men have not great influence, and more easily allow themselves to be perverted than to convert the others, so that, afterward, the mature men were preferred to the youths. To begin this, it was necessary to make great gifts to the parents of the Young men; and, besides that, to persuade them themselves to dwell with us. The Father who had charge of them told some one, in persuading him to remain at Kebek, that he warned him, indeed, that perhaps on returning to his own country he would die in the universal disease, which was ruining it. It is not certain whether the Father went so far; but it is not true that he might believe so, because many traders that year had been infected, as it was believed, with the contagion; and the malady had already assailed many of those Barbarians. Whether true or not, the young man having returned to that country, and seeing the spread of the disease, of course told the Captains that the Father who had wished to keep him at Kebek had predicted the same,—so that he concluded that he was an accomplice therein, and with his companions, the author. Some added that we had for this purpose brought from France a corpse, which we were carefully keeping in our house as something precious,—making allusion to the Most Holy Sacrament, which we kept in our Chapel; we had spoken of this to our Christians, on which account they wished to visit and seek everywhere this corpse, the origin of the pestilence. They said the same thing about some images, etc.; the prayers that we made, and the masses which we said at an early hour, with closed doors; the litanies; even walking abroad,—a new thing in those countries,—were superstitions which we practiced in order to destroy them. It was necessary to stop a small striking clock, which served to regulate our time,—for they regarded it as a Demon which, by striking, gave a sign to death for killing them. They found a superstition even in a little streamer hung at the crest of a pine, and believed that the disease was cast from that flag, wherever the wind drove it; and, because it turned about, now in one direction, now in another, they said therefore that there was no place untainted in the country; they supposed that we had enveloped the malady therein, so as to carry it into the country. "This disease," said many, "has not been engendered here; it comes from without; never have we seen Demons so cruel. The other maladies lasted two or three moons" (they reckon time by moons, like the Hebrews); "this has been persecuting us for more than a year. Ours are content with one or two in a family; this, in many, has left no more than that number,—and, in many, none at all. The loss from the old ones was repaired in a few years, of which we lost not the memory; this would require whole ages to repeople us." I omit the fables which they spread abroad about persons come to life again, who accused and condemned us, together with all the mysteries of the holy Faith, etc.

And this was not simply a popular opinion with people of small account, but it was that of the Captains themselves, and of the most intelligent men, who several times called a council to resolve upon the death of all of ours, and came to announce it to us. Father Brebeuf, the Superior, was repeatedly examined in the public councils, and harshly treated; and thinking the matter already decided, he made,—after the necessary preparations, and the vows made to God, appropriate to the time; and a letter written to Kebek, and consigned to one of our friends, who was already showing us compassion,—on the day when their execution was expected, and according to the usage of the country, a feast which they call "the Farewell." Every dying man makes this, whether he die naturally, or by a violent death, like the captives,—who, having received the news of their death, must say Farewell to their friends: and for this purpose the master of the captive prepares a feast, to which he invites the principal persons of the country, of whom the captive, already destined to the fire, takes leave; a dying man does the same. Ours did so in order to show themselves ready for death, which they did not fear; and they were expecting nothing else than the execution of the sentence which condemned them as sorcerers, and as the assassins of the entire country. Then an unlooked-for Ambassador came to invite Father Brebeuf to the council again, where the principal men of all those nations were assembled. After a very long examination, and a still longer discourse, though interrupted, by the Father,—who spoke more of the Faith than of the pestilence, warning them, with wonderful fearlessness, that not we, but the justice of the God whom we preach, provoked by their sins, was the sole cause of their troubles which would last until they appeased him with the requisite submission and penance,—they so changed their opinion that they sent him away, as it were absolved. Many— notwithstanding the replies of some Captains who called him "a troublesome fellow, who was always repeating the same thing," "one unworthy to live," etc.—requested of the Father, as he went out, to be instructed in the Faith; and, on leaving the same cabin, he saw killed at his feet, with a hatchet-blow, a barbarian who was most hostile to the Faith. Now, as it was getting late, the Father thought that the murderer had deceived himself, and had taken the dead man for him: and, having stopped, he said to him, "Was it not perhaps for me that this blow was intended?" "No," answered the other, "go on; this man was a sorcerer, and not thou." Let the reader imagine the thanks which were rendered to God at the sight of the Father, who regarded himself as a man risen from the dead; and at the hope of being able to continue the conversion of those wretched people in their extreme necessity.

❖   ❖   ❖

SELECTION 3: A Military Officer Contemplates Life in a Beaver Lodge

Thomas Anburey was an Anglo-Irish officer in the British Army who came to America in 1776. As a soldier and prisoner of war, he traveled extensively in Canada and the United States before returning home in 1781. His memoir, published in 1789, provides an engaging tour of the American landscape and its plant, animal, and human life.

Like many of his contemporaries, Anburey often described the new animal species he encountered by ascribing to them human attributes. Nowhere is this more evident than in his description of the beaver, an animal that many Europeans believed exhibited anthropomorphic social habits and engineering skills. Anburey described life in a beaver lodge as cozy, cooperative, and contented, its bliss interrupted only by human marauders who hunted these animals to satisfy their tastes for luxury and fashion. Anburey is a good example of the curiosity that the New World environment inspired in Europeans and the misgivings some of them expressed about its despoliation by profit-seekers.

[B]ut it was no sooner understood that Canada was stored with Beavers, than the savages, urged on by a more lucrative interest, directed their war against an animal the most harmless, who molests no living creature, and is neither carniverous nor sanguinary. This is, I am sorry to observe, become an object of man's most earnest pursuit, and the one that the savages hunt after with the greatest eagerness and cruelty; a circumstance entirely owing to the unmerciful rapaciousness which luxury has made necessary in skins, for all the polished nations of Europe.

This animal is by nature adapted for social life, being endowed with an instinct in the preservation and propagation of its species; it is generally about three or four feet long, mostly weighing from forty to sixty pounds; the hinder feet are webbed, which enables it to swim, and in the fore feet the toes are divided; its tail is oval, very flat, and covered with scales; the head resembles that of a rat, in which are four very sharp teeth, with these it will gnaw through trees of a great circumference.

This animal is divested of turbulent passions, without a desire of doing injury to any one, free from craft, scarcely defending itself, unless it lives in society; it never bites, except when caught, and as nature has not supplied it with any weapons of defence, by a natural instinct as it were, it forms societies, and has various contrivances to secure its ease, without fighting, and to live without committing, or suffering an injury; although this peaceable, and you may say almost tame animal, enters into society, it is nevertheless independent, every want being supplied by itself, and therefore it is a slave to none. It will not serve, nor does it pretend to command, every care seems directed by an instinct, that at the same time, as it labors for the general good, it lives for itself alone. To learn the nature of the societies of these animal, as it was related to me by my landlord, may afford you the same entertainment it did me.

In the month of June or July, they assemble from all quarters, to the number of two or three hundred, near some lake or pool of water, to build

From Thomas Anburey, *Travels Through the Interior Parts of America*, 2 volumes (London: William Lane, 1789), 1: 241–248, 251–253.

their habitations against winter, the construction of which, from the complication and manner of disposing the materials, one would be led to imagine to be beyond the capacity of any one but an intelligent being, and especially in their constructing of dams, when they cannot meet with a lake or pool; in this case they fix upon some river, when the first of their labour is to make a dam, which they generally do in the shallowest part of the stream, for that purpose felling trees with the four sharp teeth that I have already described; five or six of them will gnaw a large one through, and to mark to you the wonderful sagacity of these industrious brutes, they contrive it so that it always falls in the water: having laid this foundation, they fell smaller trees, which they roll to this great one, but what appears the most wonderful is, the manner they sink the piles in the water, to prevent the stream's carrying away the trees, they lay across. Their contrivance is this, with their nails they dig a hole in the ground, or at the bottom of the water, with their teeth they rest the stake against the bank of the river, or against the tree that lies across, and with their feet they raise the stake and sink it with the sharp end (which these sensible animals make to it) in the hole that they have made, where it stands up; and to render these stakes or piles more secure, they interweave branches of small trees, and with their tails wisk up a kind of mortar with clay, and fill the vacant space of the interwoven branches.

After this work is finished by the body at large, each one considers of some lodging for himself; an hut being built upon piles on the sides of the Lake, capable of containing from two or three to ten or fifteen, (for they divide themselves into companies, and build these huts accordingly;) which are formed with walls and partitions of about two feet thick and as many in height, arched over, and the whole so plaistered with clay, that the smallest breath of air cannot penetrate through them; each apartment is made large enough to contain two, a male and female; each hut has two entrances, one towards the land, and the other on the side towards the stream, the former for them to go into the woods to fetch provisions, and the latter to escape from their enemy, that is to say MAN, the destroyer of cities and commonwealths. The inside of their apartments has no other furniture than the flooring of grass covered with the boughs of the fir, and these animals are so cleanly, that no filth of any kind is ever seen in these apartments.

In each hut there are store houses proportionate to the number of its inhabitants; every one knows its own, and never steals from his neighbour. Each party, that is to say, the male and female, live in their own habitations; they have no jealousies or quarrels; the provisions of the community are collected and expended without any contest, and rest satisfied with the simple food that their labors procure them. The only passion they have is that of conjugal affection, wherein a most excellent example is held forth to that all-wise and all-sufficient man, who is led away by every gust of passion and vanity.

Two of these animals, in the course of their labours in the summer months, match together, unite by inclination and reciprocal choice, and agree to pass the winter, and like too many couple who hastily enter into matrimony with equally as good motives, but forgetting what should make the happiness lasting, that of laying up a stock to guard against an inclement season.

The happy couple retire to their hut about the end of autumn, which has been observed to be no less favorable to love than spring; for if the season of flowers invites the feathered tribe to propagate in the woods, the season of fruits as powerfully excites the inhabitants of the earth in the reproduction of their species; besides, as winter gives leisure for amorous pursuits, it compensates for the advantages of other seasons.

◆　◆　◆

If by chance a sun-shiny day should happen to enliven the gloomy melancholy of the season, the happy couple leave their huts to walk on the borders of the Lake, regaling themselves with some fresh bark, and breathing the salutary exhalations of the earth. At the conclusion of the winter, the mother brings forth the endearing pledges of their affection, while the father ranges the woods, allured by the sweets of the spring, leaving to his little family that portion of room which he took up in his narrow cell. The Beaver generally produces two or three, which the mother suckles, nurses and trains up, for when the father is absent, she takes out the young ones, in her excursions for cray and other fish, and green bark to recruit her own strength and to feed her young, till the season of labor returns; for although these animals are so industrious as to build themselves habitations that would last them a century, they are obliged to rebuild them every year, as the first thing the traders do when they meet with any of their works, is to break down their cabins and the dam, together with their dyke.

There are various methods of taking and destroying these animals, by draining the water from their dykes, and sometimes by snares; they are very seldom shot at, for unless killed on the spot, they are lost to the huntsman, by plunging into the water wounded, when they sink to the bottom and never rise. The most certain and general mode of catching them is by setting traps in the woods, where they perceive them to have been eating the bark of the young trees; they bait these traps with fresh slips of wood, which the Beaver no sooner touches, than a great weight falls and crushes its loins, when the huntsman, who lies concealed near the spot, hastens to kill it.

No doubt but by this time you are heartily tired with so long a detail of this animal; but if I have deviated from the common path of description, I can only say it has proceeded from these two causes, that I cannot sufficiently admire the many virtues it possesses, divested of all manner of vice, and have been lost in the contemplation of that Divine Being, who formed it with all these natural endowments.

➣ Discussion Questions ➣

1. According to Hariot, what accounts for the bounty of Indian agriculture? Why do you think his description of the Indians' diet and farming would appeal to potential colonists? What are some of the remarkable properties he attributes to tobacco and smoking?

2. According to the *Jesuit Relations*, how did Indians relate the arrival of epidemic diseases to the European newcomers? How does Bressani's description of Father Brebeuf's escape from execution reflect the Jesuits' interpretation of the meaning of these epidemics?

3. How did the spiritual and physical worlds interact in the Indians' hunting and healing practices? What was the Jesuits' opinion of these native beliefs, and how did the Indians respond to their criticism?

4. What human qualities does Anburey attribute to the beaver? How does he compare this animal's behavior to human nature? In what ways do you think Anburey may be using this account of the beaver to criticize human society?

Suggested Readings

The work of Alfred W. Crosby, Jr. has profoundly influenced the questions historians ask about the ecological consequences of the Atlantic World. See especially *The Columbian Exchange: Biological and Cultural Consequences of 1492* (Westport, Conn.: Greenwood Press, 1972), and *Germs, Seeds, and Animals: Studies in Ecological History* (Armonk, N.Y.: M. E. Sharpe, 1994). Two environmental histories of North American colonization are William Cronon, *Changes in the Land: Indians, Colonists, and the Ecology of New England* (New York: Hill and Wang, 1983), and Timothy Silver, *A New Face on the Countryside: Indians, Colonists, and Slaves in South Atlantic Forests, 1500–1800* (Cambridge, England: Cambridge University Press, 1990). The effect of European diseases on Native American populations is described in Noble David Cook, *Born to Die: Disease and New World Conquest, 1492–1650* (Cambridge, England: Cambridge University Press, 1998). For a critical view of recent estimates of the pre-Columbian population of the Americas, see David P. Henige, *Numbers from Nowhere: The American Indian Contact Population Debate* (Norman, Okla.: University of Oklahoma Press, 1998). Jared Diamond offers a lucid and convincing explanation for the unequal nature of disease transmission between the Old World and the New in *Guns, Germs, and Steel: The Fates of Human Societies* (New York: W. W. Norton and Company, 1999).

Works that address how New World animal species became commodities in Atlantic World markets include Mark Kurlansky, *Cod: A Biography of the Fish that Changed the World* (New York: Penguin Books, 1997), and Calvin Martin, *Keepers of the Game: Indian-Animal Relationships and the Fur Trade* (Berkeley: University of California Press, 1978). For a comprehensive review of North American Indians' environmental attitudes and practices, see Sherpard Krech III, *The Ecological Indian: Myth and History* (New York: W.W. Norton and Company, 1999).

Readers interested in Hariot's Roanoke colony should refer to Karen Ordahl Kupperman, *Roanoke: The Abandoned Colony* (Savage, Md.: Rowland and Littlefield Publishers, Inc., 1984), and those interested in learning more about the Jesuits' interaction with the Indians of Canada should see Bruce G. Trigger, *The Children of Aataentsic: A History of the Huron People to 1660*, 2 volumes (Montreal: McGill-Queen's University Press, 1976).

Indian Converts Receiving Religious Instruction

This image, from an eighteenth-century Anglican prayer book published in the Mohawk language, presents an idealized version of the conversion process (see Selections 1 and 3). Two Mohawks kneel before an Anglican clergyman in the foreground, while another kneels and receives a Bible from the King and Queen of England. In the background, a minister preaches to his congregation from an elevated pulpit. Note how this image conflates themes of Christian conversion and Indian submission to European authority. Does anything about the appearance of the assembled Mohawks suggest that they have not embraced conversion entirely on the Europeans' terms?
Source: Dartmouth College Library

Captivity and Conversion: Religion and the European-Indian Encounter

Introduction

The European-Indian encounter had a profoundly spiritual dimension for both sides. European colonizers, though they were split into Protestant and Catholic camps, shared a perspective on the New World shaped by their Christian heritage and beliefs. They tried to fit the Americas into a cosmology that was rooted in biblical stories of creation and prophecy, even if the existence of Indians challenged such scriptural authority. Consider, for example, the conundrum posed by the nakedness of the Indians that Columbus met in the Caribbean. The Book of Genesis taught that after Adam and Eve had sinned, they clothed themselves; thereafter, they and their descendants equated nakedness with shame. Yet, the Indians Columbus met exhibited no shame in their lack of clothing. Did that mean they inhabited a prelapsarian Garden of Eden into which sin had not entered? European colonizers quickly put such speculation aside for the more practical task of converting Indians into proselytes and allies, initiating a spiritual struggle between native and newcomer that shaped the European-Indian encounter for centuries to come.

Every European nation that colonized the New World paid at least lip service to the notion of converting Indians to Christianity. The Catholic powers (Spain, Portugal, and France) devoted far more resources to this task than did the Protestant ones (England and the Netherlands), sponsoring missionaries and claiming spiritual and political authority over large populations of Indian converts. In those regions colonized by Protestant powers, missionary work was not nearly so well funded or organized, but the conversion of natives nevertheless remained a fundamental legal and political justification for seizing Indian land and labor.

Whether Catholic or Protestant, missionaries pursued a full-scale cultural conversion of Indians that involved much more than catechizing them in a new faith. Oftentimes, missionaries described their work as "reducing the Indians to civility": breaking down their old cultural habits and values so that they could be remade in a European image. Missionaries expected converts not only to pray like Christians, but also to eat, dress, and work like them. This process entailed separating converts from their unconverted kin, resettling them into communities (*reserves* in New France, praying towns in New England, *reducciones* in New Spain) under the missionaries' supervision, and reordering their family and gender roles on European models. These communities served as military buffers for colonial populations against their enemies and as pools from which to draw labor or military assistance when necessary.

Indian conversions were never as numerous or thorough as European missionaries wished they would be. Some elements of European religious culture appealed mightily to Indians. Many converts accepted the sacrament of baptism because they believed it would convey spiritual protection against disease and other types of misfortune that followed in the wake of European contact. The religious artifacts used by Catholic missionaries to teach their faith—saints' medals, rings, rosaries—resembled in color and shape native objects Indians already associated with spiritual well-being, such as wampum beads. Conversion also offered a variety of practical advantages when it came to dealing with the newcomers. Missionaries provided material support in times of need and worked as diplomatic go-betweens on behalf of their converts with colonial authorities. Indians who resettled in French *reserves*, English praying towns, and Spanish *reducciones* could also expect greater security of tenure in their lands than those Indians who spurned the missionaries. There were also elements of Christianity that Indians generally ignored or resisted. The biblical injunction against nakedness, which missionaries usually invoked to convince Indian men and women to dress like Europeans, held little sway among converts, who adopted European clothing in a selective manner that still left plenty of flesh exposed. Likewise, converts were not particularly interested in altering their family and sexual practices so that they were in accordance with Christian prohibitions against polygamy and divorce.

While Europeans relied on conversion to Christianity to render Indians more tractable, Indians used captivity and adoption to incorporate Europeans into their world. This process of conversion did not focus on the spiritual condition of the captive per se, but like the Europeans' missionary effort, the goals of Indian captivity and adoption were to render a stranger more predictable and useful. In a cultural practice that predated European contact, Indian war parties took captives to replace deceased loved ones. Adult male captives, whether Indian or European, were not good candidates for adoption, and so were more likely to suffer ritual torture and execution to assuage the grief of the bereaved. Captive women and children, on the other hand, were prime candidates for cultural conversion and adoption. Women could be married to male members of the community and produce children for it. Children captives were adept at quickly learning the language, manners, and customs that would make them productive adult members of the community. European captives, regardless of their age or sex, also presented another advantage. They could be ransomed to colonial governments in exchange for money and trade goods.

Indians generally had more success converting European captives into "white Indians" than Europeans had in transforming Indians into "red Christians." Indian converts to Christianity never achieved a social or political equality with their colonial contemporaries, and the physical segregation of Indian converts into *reserves*, praying towns, and *reducciones* did not encourage the sustained contact between natives and colonists necessary to knit Christian Indians into the fabric of colonial society. By contrast, an adopted captive gradually became a full-fledged family member, marriage partner, and neighbor within an Indian community. Indian children sent to missionary schools often ran away at their first opportunity; European captive children, on the other hand, were often reluctant to leave their adopted kin and had difficulty returning to colonial life.

The readings in this chapter present captivity and conversion from two different vantage points. The first two selections are from narratives—one by a French priest and the other by a Scots-Irish woman—that illustrate the cultural practices involved in Indian captivity and adoption. The third selection, taken from the correspondence of a Christian Indian with his colonial mentor, illustrates the psychological tensions inherent in this relationship. As you read these sources, think about what they tell you about the spiritual collision between European and Indian worlds. How did captivity and conversion work as methods of cross-cultural adaptation, and what difficulties did people face when they tried to straddle native and colonial worlds?

SELECTION 1: A French Missionary's Captivity Among the Mohawks

Father Isaac Jogues, S.J. was a Jesuit missionary in New France, and his captivity narrative was first published in the 1647 edition of the *Jesuit Relations* (see Chapter 2, pp. 33–36). In 1642, while en route to the Huron nation, Jogues and his companions were waylaid by a war party of Mohawks, one of the five Iroquois nations south of Lake Ontario. Jogues lived among the Mohawks for several months until some of the villagers told him that others planned to kill him, at which point he escaped to the Dutch settlement at Fort Orange (modern Albany) and from there to France. He returned to Canada a few years later, and the French governor sent him on a diplomatic mission to the Mohawk village that had been the site of his captivity. While some of the Mohawks welcomed Jogues back, others suspected him of having caused a blight among their crops and murdered him. Jogues became the first French martyr in North America and was later canonized by the Catholic Church.

The passages below from Jogues's narrative describe his captivity at three different points: the capture of his party by the Mohawks, the captives' arrival at a Mohawk village, and the death of one of Jogues's associates several weeks later. Note that the narrative shifts between Jogues's voice and a third person narration provided by the priest who compiled the 1647 edition of the *Jesuit Relations.*

· · ·   ⁀⁀⁀⁀⁀   · · ·

The first day was favorable to us; the second caused us to fall into the hands of the Hiroquois [Iroguois]. We were forty persons, distributed in several canoes; the one which kept the vanguard, having discovered on the banks of the great river some tracks of men, recently imprinted on the sand and clay, gave us warning. A landing was made; some say that these are footprints of the enemy, others are sure that they are those of Algonquins, our allies. In this dispute, Eustache Ahatsistari [an Indian convert], to whom all the others deferred on account of his exploits in arms and his virtue, exclaimed: "Be they friends or enemies, it matters not; I notice by their tracks that they are not in greater number than we; let us advance, and fear nothing." We had not yet made a half-league, when the enemy, concealed among the grass and brushwood, rises with a great outcry, discharging at our canoes a volley of balls. The noise of their arquebuses [muskets] so greatly frightened a part of our Hurons that they abandoned their canoes and weapons, and all their supplies, in order to escape by flight into the depth of the woods. This discharge did us no great hurt, and no one lost his life; one Huron alone had his hand pierced through, and our canoes were broken in several places. We were four French,—one of whom, being in the rear, escaped with the Hurons, who abandoned him before approaching the enemy. Eight or ten, both Christians and Catechumens [converts in training], joined us; having been made to say a brief prayer, they oppose a courageous front to the enemy; and although the latter were thirty men against twelve or fourteen, our people valiantly sustained their effort. But, having perceived that another band—of forty Hiroquois, who were in ambush on the other shore of the river—was coming to attack them, they lost courage; insomuch that those who were least entangled fled, abandoning their comrades in the fight. A Frenchman named René Goupil, whose death is precious before God, being no longer sustained by those who followed him, was surrounded and captured, along with some of the most courageous Hurons. "I was watching this disaster," says the Father, "from a place very favorable for concealing me from the sight of the enemy, being able to hide myself in thickets and

From Reuben G. Thwaites, editor, *The Jesuit Relations and Allied Documents: Travels and Explorations of the Jesuit Missionaries in New France, 1610–1791*, 73 volumes (Cleveland: Burrows Brothers, 1896–1901), 31:21–25, 29–31, 39–45, 53–57.

among very tall and dense reeds; but this thought could never enter my mind. 'Could I, indeed,' I said to myself. 'abandon our French and leave those good Neophytes and those poor Catechumens, without giving them the help which the Church of my God has entrusted to me?' Flight seemed horrible to me; 'It must be,' I said in my heart, 'that my body suffer the fire of earth, in order to deliver these poor souls from the flames of Hell; it must die a transient death, in order to procure for them an eternal life.' My conclusion being reached without great opposition from my feelings, I call the one of the Hiroquois who had remained to guard the prisoners. This man, having perceived me, dared not approach me, fearing some ambush. 'Come on,' I say to him; 'be not afraid; lead me to the presence of the Frenchman and the Hurons whom you hold captive.' He advances and, having seized me, puts me in the number of those whom the world calls miserable. I tenderly embraced the Frenchman, and said to him: 'My dear brother, God treats us in a strange manner, but he is the master, and he has done what has seemed best in his sight; he has followed his good pleasure. May his holy Name be blessed forever.'"This good young man at once made his confession; having given him absolution, I approach the Hurons, and instruct and baptize them; and, as at every moment those who were pursuing the fugitives brought back some of them, I heard these in confession, making Christians those who were not so. Finally, they brought that worthy Christian Captain named Eustache, who, having perceived me, exclaimed: 'Ah! my Father, I had sworn and protested to you that I would live or die with you.' The sight of him piercing my heart, I do not remember the words that I said to him.

＊　＊　＊

"All their men being assembled, and the runners having come back from their hunt for men, those barbarians divided among themselves their booty, rejoicing in their prey with great shouts of mirth. As I saw them engrossed in examining and distributing our spoils, I sought also for my share. I visit all the captives; I baptize those who were not yet baptized; I encourage those poor wretches to suffer with constancy, assuring them that their reward would far exceed the severity of their torments. I ascertained, on this round of visits, that we were twenty-two captives, without counting three Hurons killed on the spot. An old man, aged eighty years, having just received holy Baptism, said to the Hiroquois who were commanding him to embark: 'It is no more for an old man like me to go and visit foreign countries; I can find death here, if you refuse me life.' Hardly had he pronounced these words when they beat him to death.

"So there we were, on the way to be led into a country truly foreign. Our Lord favored us with his Cross. It is true that, during thirteen days that we spent on that journey, I suffered in the body torments almost unendurable, and, in the soul, mortal anguish; hunger, the fiercely burning heat, the threats and hatred of those Leopards, the pain of our wounds—which, for not being dressed, became putrid even to the extent of breeding worms,—caused us, in truth, much distress. But all these things seemed light to me in comparison with an inward sadness which I felt at the sight of our earliest and most ardent Christians of the Hurons. I had thought that they were to be the pillars of that rising Church, and I saw them become the victims of death. The ways closed for a long time to the salvation of so many peoples, who perish every day for want of being succored, made me die every hour, in the depth of my soul. It is a very hard thing, or rather very cruel, to see the triumph of the Demons over whole nations redeemed with so much love, and paid for in the money of a blood so aborable."

❖   ❖   ❖

"After they had glutted their cruelty, they led us in triumph into that first village; all the youth were outside the gates, arranged in line,—armed with sticks, and some with iron rods, which they easily secure on account of their vicinity to the Dutch. Casting our eyes upon these weapons of passion, we re-membered what saint Augustin says, that those who turn aside from the scourges of God, turn aside from the number of his children; on that account, we offered ourselves with great courage to his fatherly goodness, in order to be victims sacrificed to his good pleasure and to his anger, lovingly zealous for the salvation of these peoples. Here follows the order which was observed at that funereal and pompous entry. They made one Frenchman march at the head, and another in the middle of the Hurons, and me the very last. We were following one another at an equal distance; and, that our executioners might have more leisure to beat us at their ease, some Hiroquois thrust themselves into our ranks in order to prevent us from running and from avoiding any blows. The procession beginning to enter this narrow way of Paradise, a scuf-fling was heard on all side; its was indeed then that I could say with my Lord and master, *Supra dorsum meum fabricaverunt peccatores*,—'Sinners have built and left monuments and marks of their rage upon my back.' I was naked to my shirt, like a poor criminal; the others were wholly naked, except poor René Goupil, to whom they did the same favor as to me. The more slowly the procession marched in a very long road, the more blows we received. One was dealt above my loins, with the pommel of a javelin, or with an iron knob, the size of one's first, which shook my whole body and took away my breath. Such was our entrance into that Babylon. Hardly could we arrive as far as the scaffold which was prepared for us in the midst of that village, so exhausted were we; our bodies were all livid, and our faces all stained with blood. But more disfigured than all was René Goupil, so that nothing white appeared in his face except his eyes. I found him all the more beautiful as he had more in common with him who, bearing a face most worthy of the regards and delight of the Angels, appeared to us, in the midst of his anguish, like a leper. Having ascended that scaffold, I exclaimed in my heart: '*Spectaculum facti sumus mundo et Angelis et hominibus propter Christum*'—We have been made a gazing-stock in the sight of the world, of Angels, and of men, for Jesus Christ.' We found some rest in that place of triumph and of glory. The Hiroquois no longer persecuted us except with their tongues,—filling the air and our ears with their insults, which did us no great hurt; but this calm did not last long. A Captain exclaims that the Frenchmen ought to be caressed. Sooner done than it is said,—one wretch, jumping on the stage, dealt three heavy blows with sticks, on each Frenchman, without touching the Hurons. Others, meanwhile drawing their knives and approaching us, treated me as a Captain,—that is to say, with more fury than the rest. The deference of the French, and the respect which the Hurons showed me, caused me this advantage. An old man takes my left hand and commands a captive Algonquin woman to cut one of my fingers; she turns away three or four times, unable to resolve upon this cruelty; finally, she has to obey, and cuts the thumb from my left hand; the same caresses are extended to the other prisoners. This poor woman having thrown my thumb on the stage, I picked it up and offered it to you, O my God! Remembering the sacrifices that I had presented to you for seven years past, upon the Altars of your Church, I accepted this torture as a loving vengeance for the want of love and respect that I had shown, concerning your Holy Body; you heard the cries of my soul. One of my two French companions, having perceived me, told me that, if those Barbarians saw me keep my thumb, they would make me eat it and swallow it all raw; and that, therefore, I should throw it away somewhere. I obey him instantly. They used a scallop or an oyster-shell for cutting off the right thumb of the other Frenchman, so as to cause him more pain. The blood flowing from our wounds in so great abundance that we were likely to fall in a swoon, a Hiroquois—tearing off a little end of my shirt, which alone had been left to me—bound them up for us; and that was all the dressing and all the medical treatment applied to them."

◆   ◆   ◆

When those poor captives had recovered a little of their strength, the principal men of the country talked of conducting them back to Three Rivers [a French settlement], in order to restore them to the French; the affair made so much progress that it was considered as settled. But, as their captors could not agree, the Father and his companions endured, more than ever, the pangs of death. Those Barbarians are accustomed to give prisoners, whom they do not choose to put to death, to the families who have lost some of their relatives in war. These prisoners take the place of the deceased, and are incorporated into that family, which alone has the right to kill them, or to let them live. The others would not dare to offend them; but when they retain some public prisoner, like the Father, without giving him to any individual, this poor man is every day within two finger-lengths of death. If some rascal beat him to death, no one will trouble himself about it; if he drag out his poor life, it is by favor of some individuals who have love for him. In such condition was the Father, and one of the Frenchmen; for the other had been given to take the place of a Hiroquois killed in war.

The young Frenchman who was the Father's companion was accustomed to caress the little children and to teach them to make the sign of the Cross. An old man, having seen him make this scared sign upon the forehead of his grandson, and that he took the child's hand in order to teach him to form it, said to a nephew of his: "Go and kill that dog: the Dutch tell us that what he does is of no account; that act will cause some harm to my grandson." The nephew obeyed, as soon as possible; when he, accordingly, sought the opportunity to commit this murder outside the village, it presented itself thus: Father Jogues—having learned that their purpose to release the French was set aside, and that, in consequence, some young men had come to seek him even in his cabin, in order to torment him and to treat him as a victim destined to death—wished to forewarn and strengthen his poor companion. He leads him to a grove near the village, and explains to him the dangers in which they stood. They both offer prayers, and then recite the rosary of the Blessed Virgin; in a word, they cheerfully prepare themselves for death, encouraged by strength from him who never fails those who seek and love him. While they were returning toward their village, talking of the blessings of the other life, the nephew of that old man, and another Savage, armed with hatchets and watching for an opportunity, go to meet them. Having approached them, one of these men says to the Father, "March forward;" and at the same time he breaks the head of poor René Goupil, who, on falling and expiring, pronounced the Holy Name of Jesus. The Father, seeing him prostrate, falls upon him and embraces him; those Barbarians draw him away, and deal two more blows with the hatchet on that blessed body. "Give me a moment's time," the Father said to them, supposing that they would accord him the same favor as to his companion. He then falls on his knees, he offers himself in sacrifice to the divinity; then, turning toward those Barbarians, "Do," he said to them, "what you please; I fear not death." "Get up," they reply; "thou wilt not die this time." They drag the dead man through the streets of the village, and then go and throw him into a very sequestered place. The Father, wishing to render him the last duties, seeks him, everywhere; some children having informed him, he finds the corpse in a brook, and covers it with great stones in order to protect it from the claws and beaks of the birds, until he might come to bury it. But it rained all the following night, and this torrent became so violent and so deep that he could not find that blessed body. This death occurred on the twenty-ninth of September, in the year 1642.

SELECTION 2: A Pennsylvania Woman's Adoption into an Indian Family

Mary Jemison was born on the ship that carried her family from Ireland to North America in 1742. Like many Scots-Irish emigrants of that period, the Jemisons settled in the backcountry of Pennsylvania (see Chapter 9, pp. 179–185), on land that the Delaware and Shawnee Indians still claimed as their own. During the Seven Years' War (also known as the French and Indian War in North America), Mary, her parents, and three of her siblings were taken captive by a war party of Shawnee and Frenchmen. Her captors took her to an Indian village on the Ohio River, where she was adopted into a Seneca family, learned their language, and married an Indian husband. She eventually moved with her adopted family to the Genesee River Valley of New York, where she remarried after her first husband's death and bore six more children. In 1823 she told her life story to a newspaper writer, James E. Seaver, who published it the following year as *A Narrative of the Life of Mrs. Mary Jemison*. She died on the Senecas' Buffalo Creek Reservation in western New York in 1833, at age 91. The passages from her narrative describe her experience from the point of her capture until her marriage to her first husband.

The party that took us consisted of six Indians and four Frenchmen, who immediately commenced plundering, as I just observed, and took what they considered most valuable; consisting principally of bread, meal, and meat. Having taken as much provision as they could carry, they set out with their prisoners in great haste, for fear of detection, and soon entered the woods.

❖ ❖ ❖

Mother, from the time we were taken, had manifested a great degree of fortitude, and encouraged us to support our troubles without complaining; and by her conversation seemed to make the distance and time shorter, and the way more smooth. But father lost all his ambition in the beginning of our trouble, and continued apparently lost to every care—absorbed in melancholy. Here, as before, she insisted on the necessity of our eating; and we obeyed her, but it was done with heavy hearts.

As soon as I had finished my supper, an Indian took off my shoes and stockings and put a pair of moccasins on my feet, which my mother observed; and believing that they would spare my life, even if they should destroy the other captives, addressed me as near as I can remember in the following words:

"My dear little Mary, I fear that the time has arrived when we must be parted forever. Your life, my child, I think will be spared; but we shall probably be tomahawked here in this lonesome place by the Indians. O! how can I part with you my darling? What will become of my sweet little Mary? Oh! How can I think of your being continued in captivity without a hope of your being rescued? O that death had snatched you from my embraces in your infancy; the pain of parting then would have been pleasing to what it now is; and I should have seen the end of your troubles! Alas, my dear! My heart bleeds at the thoughts of what awaits you; but, if you leave us, remember my child your own name, and the name of your father and mother. Be careful and not forget your English tongue. If you shall have an opportunity to get away from the Indians, don't try to escape; for if you do, they will find and destroy you. Don't forget, my little daughter, the prayers that I have learned you—say them often; be a good child, and God will bless you. May God bless you my child, and make you comfortable and happy."

❖ ❖ ❖

My suspicions as to the fate of my parents proved too true; for soon after I left them they were killed and scalped, together with Robert, Matthew, Betsey [Jemison's siblings], and the woman and her two children [neighbors also taken captive], and mangled in the most shocking manner. . . .

From James E. Seaver, editor, *A Narrative of the Life of Mrs. Mary Jemison* (1824; New York: The American Scenic and Historic Preservation Society, 1918), 25–29, 32–40, 44–45.

In the afternoon we came in sight of Fort Pitt (as it is now called), where we were halted while the Indians performed some customs upon their prisoners which they deemed necessary. That fort was then occupied by the French and Indians, and was called Fort Du Quesne. It stood at the junction of the Monongahela, which is said to signify, in some of the Indian languages, the Falling-in-Banks, and the Alleghany rivers, where the Ohio river begins to take its name. The word O-hi-o, signifies bloody.

At the place where we halted, the Indians combed the hair of the young man [another captive in the war party], the boy, and myself, and then painted our faces and hair red, in the finest Indian style. We were then conducted into the fort, where we received a little bread, and were then shut up and left to tarry alone through the night. . . .

The morning at length arrived, and our masters came early and let us out of the house, and gave the young man and boy to the French, who immediately took them away. Their fate I never learned; as I have not seen or heard of them since.

I was now left alone in the fort, deprived of my former companions, and of everything that was near or dear to me but life. But it was not long before I was in some measure relieved by the appearance of two pleasant looking squaws of the Seneca tribe, who came and examined me attentively for a short time, and then went out. After a few minutes absence, they returned with my former masters, who gave me to them to dispose of as they pleased.

The Indians by whom I was taken were a party of Shawanees, if I remember right, that lived, when at home, a long distance down the Ohio.

My former Indian masters, and the two squaws, were soon ready to leave the fort, and accordingly embarked; the Indians in a large canoe, and the two squaws and myself in a small one, and went down the Ohio.

❖   ❖   ❖

At night we arrived at a small Seneca Indian town, at the mouth of a small river, that was called by the Indians, in the Seneca language, She-nan-jee, where the two Squaws to whom I belonged resided. There we landed, and the Indians [Jemison's captors] went on; which was the last I ever saw of them.

Having made fast to the shore, the Squaws left me in the canoe while they went to their wigwam or house in the town, and returned with a suit of Indian clothing, all new, and very clean and nice. My clothes, though whole and good when I was taken, were now torn in pieces, so that I was almost naked. They first undressed me and threw my rags into the river; then washed me clean and dressed me in the new suit they had just brought, in complete Indian style; and then led me home and seated me in the center of their wigwam.

I had been in that situation but a few minutes, before all the Squaws in the town came in to see me. I was soon surrounded by them, and they immediately set up a most dismal howling, crying bitterly, and wringing their hands in all the agonies of grief for a deceased relative.

Their tears flowed freely, and they exhibited all the signs of real mourning. At the commencement of this scene, one of their number began, in a voice somewhat between speaking and singing, to recite some words to the following purport, and continued the recitation till the ceremony was ended; the company at the same time varying the appearance of their countenances, gestures and tone of voice, so as to correspond with the sentiments expressed by their leader:

"Oh our brother! Alas! He is dead—he has gone; he will never return! Friendless he died on the field of the slain, where his bones are yet lying unburied! Oh, who will not mourn his sad fate? No tears dropped around him; oh, no! No tears of his sisters were there! He fell in his prime, when his arm was most needed to keep us from danger! Alas! he has gone! and left us in sorrow, his loss to bewail: Oh where is his spirit? His spirit went naked, and hungry it wanders, and thirsty and wounded it groans to return! Oh helpless and wretched, our brother has gone! No blanket nor food to nourish and warm him; nor candles to light him, nor weapons of war:—Oh, none of those comforts had he! But well we remember his deeds!—The deer he could take on the chase! The panther shrunk back at the sight of his strength! His enemies fell at his feet! He was brave and courageous in war! As the fawn he was harmless: his friendship was ardent: his temper was gentle: his pity was great! Oh! our friend, our companion is dead! Our brother, our brother, alas! he is gone! But why do we grieve for his loss? In the strength of a warrior, undaunted he left us, to fight by the side of the Chiefs! His war-whoop was shrill! His rifle well aimed laid his enemies low: his tomahawk drank of their blood: and his knife flayed their scalps while yet covered with gore! And why do we mourn? Though he fell on the field of the slain, with glory he fell, and his spirit went up to the land of his fathers in war! Then why do we mourn? With transports of joy they received him, and fed him, and clothed him, and welcomed him there! Oh friends, he is happy; then dry up your tears! His spirit has seen our distress, and sent us a helper whom with pleasure we greet. Dickewamis [Jemison's Indian name] has come: then let us receive her with joy! She is handsome and pleasant! Oh! she is our sister, and gladly we welcome her here. In the place of our brother she stands in our tribe. With care we will guard her from trouble; and may she be happy till her spirit shall leave us."

In the course of that ceremony, from mourning they became serene—joy sparkled in their countenances, and they seemed to rejoice over me as over a long lost child. I was made welcome amongst them as a sister to the two Squaws before mentioned, and was called Dickewamis; which being interpreted, signifies a pretty girl, a handsome girl, or a pleasant, good thing. That is the name by which I have ever since been called by the Indians.

I afterwards learned that the ceremony I at that time passed through, was that of adoption. The two squaws had lost a brother in Washington's war [Anglo-French-Indian hostilities in the Ohio Country], sometime in the year before, and in consequence of his death went up to Fort Pitt, on the day on which I arrived there, in order to receive a prisoner or an enemy's scalp, to supply their loss.

It is a custom of the Indians, when one of their number is slain or taken prisoner in battle, to give to the nearest relative to the dead or absent, a prisoner, if they have chanced to take one, and if not, to give him the scalp of an enemy. On the return of the Indians from conquest, which is always announced by peculiar shoutings, demonstrations of joy, and the exhibition of some trophy of victory, the mourners come forward and make their claims. If they receive a prisoner, it is at their option either to satiate their vengeance by taking his life in the most cruel manner they can conceive of; or, to receive and adopt him into the family, in the place of him whom they have lost. All the prisoners that are taken in battle and carried to the encampment or town by the Indians, are given to the bereaved families, till their number is made good. And unless the mourners have but just received the news of their bereavement, and are under the operation of a paroxysm of grief, anger, and revenge; or unless the prisoner is very old, sickly, or homely, they generally save him, and treat him kindly. But if their mental wound is fresh, their loss so great that they deem it irreparable, or if their prisoner or prisoners do not meet their approbation, no torture, let it be ever so cruel, seems sufficient to make them satisfaction. It is family, and not national, sacrifices amongst the Indians, that has given them an indelible stamp as barbarians, and identified their character with the idea which is generally formed of unfeeling ferocity, and the most abandoned cruelty.

It was my happy lot to be accepted for adoption; and at the time of the ceremony I was received by the two squaws, to supply the place of their brother in the family; and I was ever considered and treated by them as a real sister, the same as though I had been born of their mother.

During my adoption, I sat motionless, nearly terrified to death at the appearance and actions of the company, expecting every moment to feel their vengeance, and suffer death on the spot. I was, however, happily disappointed when at the close of the ceremony the company retired, and my sisters went about employing every means for my consolation and comfort.

Being now settled and provided with a home, I was employed in nursing the children, and doing light work about the house. Occasionally I was sent out with the Indian hunters, when they went but a short distance, to help them carry their game. My situation was easy; I had no particular hardships to endure. But still, the recollection of my parents, my brothers and sisters, my home, and my own captivity, destroyed my happiness, and made me constantly solitary, lonesome, and gloomy.

My sisters would not allow me to speak English in their hearing; but remembering the charge that my dear mother gave me at the time I left her, whenever I chanced to be alone I made a business of repeating my prayer, catechism, or something I had learned in order that I might not forget my own language. By practicing in that way I retained it till I came to Genesee flats, where I soon became acquainted with English people with whom I have been almost daily in the habit of conversing.

My sisters were diligent in teaching me their language; and to their great satisfaction, I soon learned so that I could understand it readily, and speak it fluently. I was very fortunate in falling into their hands; for they were kind, good natured women; peaceable and mild in their dispositions; temperate and gentle towards me. I have great reason to respect them, though they have been dead a great number of years. . . .

Not long after the Delawares came to live with us at Wiishto [an Indian village in the Ohio Country], my sisters told me that I must go and live with one of them, whose name was She-nin-jee. Not daring to cross them, or disobey their commands, with a great degree of reluctance I went; and Sheninjee and I were married according to Indian custom.

Sheninjee was a noble man; large in stature; elegant in his appearance; generous in his conduct; courageous in war; a friend to peace, and a great lover of justice. He supported a degree of dignity far above his rank, and merited and received the confidence and friendship of all the tribes with whom he was acquainted. Yet, Sheninjee was an Indian. The idea of spending my days with him, at first seemed perfectly irreconcilable to my feelings: but his good nature, generosity, tenderness, and friendship towards me, soon gained my affection; and, strange as it may seem, I loved him! To me he was ever kind in sickness, and always treated me with gentleness; in fact, he was an agreeable husband, and a comfortable companion. We lived happily together till the time of our final separation, which happened two or three years after our marriage, as I shall presently relate.

In the second summer of my living at Wiishto, I had a child at the time that the kernels of corn first appeared on the cob. When I was taken sick, Sheninjee was absent, and I was sent to a small shed, on the bank of the river, which was made of boughs, where I was obliged to stay till my husband returned. My two sisters, who were my only companions, attended me, and on the second day of my confinement my child was born; but it lived only two days. It was a girl: and notwithstanding the shortness of the time that I possessed it, it was a great grief to me to lose it.

After the birth of my child, I was very sick, but was not allowed to go into the house for two weeks; when to my great joy, Sheninjee returned, and I was taken in and as comfortably provided for as our situation would admit of. My disease continued to increase for a number of days; and I became so far reduced that my recovery was despaired of by my friends, and I was concluded that my troubles would soon be finished. At length, however, my complaint took a favorable turn, and by the time the corn was ripe I was able to get about. I continued to gain my health, and in the fall was able to go to our winter quarters, on the Sciota [a tributary of the Ohio], with the Indians.

From that time nothing remarkable occurred to me till the fourth winter of my captivity, when I had a son born, while I was at Sciota: I had a quick recovery, and my child was healthy. To commemorate the name of my much lamented father, I called my son Thomas Jemison.

SELECTION 3: A Christian Indian Challenges His Colonial Mentor

David Fowler was a Montauk Indian from eastern Long Island. By the time of his birth in 1735, the Montauks had lived among English colonists for over a century, and many of them had converted to Christianity. At age 24, Fowler attended Moor's Charity School, an Indian school established in Lebanon, Connecticut by Congregational minister Eleazar Wheelock. One of Wheelock's star pupils, Fowler conducted missionary work among the Oneida and Mohawk Indians of New York in the 1760s. He worked there with the Reverend Samuel Kirkland until his falling out with Kirkland and Wheelock led him back to Montauk, where he worked as a schoolmaster. During the Revolutionary Era, he returned to the Oneidas' country as part of a Christian Indian settlement known as Brothertown. He died in 1807.

Wheelock's missionary work, like Fowler's, met with disappointing results. In 1769, he established Dartmouth College in New Hampshire, nominally to serve as a seminary for Christian Indians. Wheelock, however, had grown discontented with his Indian students and shifted Dartmouth's priorities to educating Anglo-Americans.

Fowler's correspondence offers an interesting glimpse inside the relationship between Christian Indians and their European mentors. Note in particular Fowler's descriptions of the non-Christian Indians among whom he labored and his anger at Wheelock's and Kirkland's treatment of his ministry.

The spelling has been modernized.

David Fowler left Eleazar Wheelock's Indian School in Connecticut in the Fall of 1765, and moved to the New York frontier, to work as a schoolmaster and missionary among the Mohawks and Oneidas.

David Fowler to Eleazar Wheelock
Canajoharie [New York], January 21, 1766

Reverend and Honored Sir:

After much Worry and Fatigue about my House and Journeys, after also hungry Belly, I began to keep my School steadily sometime in November. My Scholars learn very well: I find it is impossible to keep the Children steadily to School. Let [Indian] Men labor and work as English do: They are lazy and inhuman pack of Creatures as I ever saw in the World; They have seen me working and tugging Day after Day and never offered to help in the least thing I had to do in my House, only finished covering it and left me. I was obliged to eat with Dogs near two Months. I say with Dogs because they are always licking Water out of the Pails and Kettles we use: Now I live like a Gentleman, I have a plantation of Corn, Flour, Meat and rotten Fish. I applied to Sir William [Johnson, a local Indian agent] for Provision; accordingly, he ordered the Commanding Officer at the Royal Block House to give me out Provision as long as I should want. . . .

From James Dow McCallum, editor, *Letters of Eleazar Wheelock's Indians* (Hanover, New Hampshire: Dartmouth College Publications, 1932), 87–113.

I never saw such general Disposition of hearing the Word of God amongst these poor People as I do now: most every one of the adults of this Place, have openly renounced their Liquor and said that they will devote themselves in hearing the Word of God. Now is the time for Ministers to come up whilst they are in such Disposition. Oh, for a Minister whose Heart is full of Love to God and Compassion to poor Sinners, one who is meek and lowly and crafty in winning Souls to Christ, who has a real Sense and worth of Immortal Souls, would greatly weaken the Strong Holds of Satan in this Place. Dear Sir, do all that is in your Power to get up a Minister early in the Spring, for the poor Creatures are really desirous to hear the Word of God; we have no Minister and yet we have a full Assembly every Sabbath. I have nothing New to acquaint you; I enjoy a good State of Health and am contented. . . .

Your affectionate and obedient Servant,

DAVID FOWLER

❖　❖　❖

David Fowler to Eleazar Wheelock
Canajoharie, February 17, 1766

Reverend Sir,

I received yours 25th of January which offered me much Pleasure, and also warned me against those things which I am so much addicted to. I hope your Admonition will not be entirely lost. I will try to take care mind what you wrote to me.

I wrote you a large Letter in the Month past which exhausted all the Matter that was in my Head; I now write you but a few Lines. I am pursuing my Business with all Courage and Resolution that lies in my Power or Capacity. Reverend Mr. Chamberlain can inform you what Progress my Scholars have made in learning to read as well as I can.

Sir, I am almost naked, my Cloths are coming all to pieces; I shall be very glad all the Cloth that is intended for me be in readiness against my coming. I design to come down [to Connecticut] the latter End of May or beginning June. I have nothing New to acquaint you, I am well and hearty also contented. I am . . .

your affectionate Indian Son,

DAVID FOWLER

P.S. Regards to Madam Sir Wheelock and to all the rest.

❖　❖　❖

Fowler returned to Connecticut to get supplies for himself and his wife, Hannah. His purchase of some clothing apparently caused Wheelock to reprimand him for being proud, which in turn caused Fowler to vent his anger at Wheelock.

David Fowler to Eleazar Wheelock
Lebanon [Connecticut], August 26, 1766

Reverend and Honored Sir,

I think it very hard that I must be blamed so much as I have been since my Return from home, and all for taking up those things at Mr. Breeds [a local trader], When I have Orders from you to get them, for which I am now accounted a Devil or Proud as the Devil, After you have repeatedly and manifestly told me that I should have whatsoever I wanted. If you denied me when I came to ask for them, I should not feel half so bad as I do now, or if you told me in a mild Manner when I got home, "those things which you got were too good and too costly, you must not have them," I should not resist you. You know, Sir, I have always been governed and advised by you with all ease imaginable.

This brings into my mind what Treatment I met since I came here. Yea it is shameful, when I have been so faithful to you as if I was your Negro, yea I have almost killed myself in Laboring. I have done hither to all what laid in my Power to help you; I think I can say and believe you too that I have done more Service to you than all the rest of the Indian Boys. And now I am too bad to live in the House for one of my missteps, therefore I must leave you and your School this very Day and go weeping in the Road homeward.

I am grieved that I have troubled you so much as I have. I am sorry those things were not denied me at first and then it would be all well and easy before now. But assure you, Sir, you shall receive Payment from me yearly till every Farthing be paid, it shall not be said all that Money and Pains which was spent for David Fowler on Indians was for naught. I can get Payment as well as white Man. O Dear me! I can't say no more, I am . . .

your unworthy Servant,

DAVID FOWLER

◆   ◆   ◆

Wheelock replied to Fowler's angry letter by chastising Fowler for the sin of pride.

Eleazar Wheelock to David Fowler
Lebanon [Connecticut], August 26, 1766

David Fowler,

I this Minute received Yours and [am] Sorry to find that you are not yet come to your right Temper of Mind. Who has called You a Devil, or Said you are as proud as the Devil since you came here? Who has ever said that you have not behaved well in the Main since you lived with me, or that I have not sat as much by You and expected as much benefit to the grand Design as by any Indian I ever Educated, or [that] there has been any Indian that I have been more friendly to than to you and your Character? Have I ever said you have not done more for my Benefit than all the Indians I ever had, and now you say, "I am too bad to live in the House for one of my missteps, therefore, I must leave you and your School this very day and go weeping in this Road Homeward."

Now, David, consider a little. Is this just, comely, and reasonable Treatment of me? Have I said worse of you or to you than that I was afraid that the Pride of your heart aspired after such Grandeur as was not for the glory of God and could not consist with the good of the general Design in view? That when I had given you leave to get every thing that you wanted for the Design and told you I begrudged you nothing that was necessary for you, that you should effect to cloth yourself and Hannah like Courtiers and that when you knew I had already been reproached through the Country, as I have been, only for letting you Wear an old velvet Coat that was given to you. I told you that the Eyes of all Europe and America were upon you and me too, and the Eyes of thousands who are unfriendly and will not fail to Catch at any occasion to reproach me and the Design. I told you it was no Interest of mine, but only the Honor and Interest of Christ that I was pleading for, and the Success of the Cause which has been so long an [?], and which I have so much labored and Worn out myself, and which certainly so nearly concerns you as me to Labor to promote. Did you not, when I was only Enquiring why it was prudent and best for you to have so many as 4 pairs of shoes at once, rise up and with very unbecoming air go out of the Room and Say "I will have no shoes, I'll wear Indian shoes," and how you and Hannah have Spent your precious Hours yesterday and today I know not. I wish your setting out were more in the Meekness and Humility of Christ.

As for my own part, great as the prospects of your Usefulness are (and they are very great if you will take God with you), I don't at all desire you should return to Oneida with your present Tempers. Nor am I at all afraid but I can fully vindicate my own Reputation, take what Course you will. I suppose you can't reasonably think it unjust if the Whole and Plain Truth comes to the Light of the World, if I am put upon my own Vindication. Nor do I think you can feel very Easy if you should go till you return to me again, which I promise myself you will do as Soon as you return to God. My heart is the same and as full of Kindness and Good Will toward you as ever it has been, and I am as ready to do any thing that will Honor Christ and promote the Salvation of the Souls of the poor Indians as I ever was, but I have no notion of sending any Man who is aiming to set up himself instead of Christ Jesus as the object of your Worship, and when you will appear the Same as you have heretofore done, you will find me the same. I am . . .

Your Sincere Well wisher,

ELEAZAR WHEELOCK

❖ ❖ ❖

David Fowler to Eleazar Wheelock
Canajoharie, February 26, 1767

Reverend and Honored Sir:

I think all that tender Affection which I used to have from you is quite gone: but when I consider my miscarriages I can't say anything for myself, only this: if I am unworthy to be looked upon, I should not be employed. I think it very strange that one who has done most should be forgotten for all those which have been sent into these [parts?], who have not done any thing worth mentioning. All what they have done is only roving abroad and making the Indians angry. I take it very hard that I have not received one Line when others have received Folios after Folios [sheets after sheets of letters]. But since I am forsaken, I now beg the Favor of you to bury my Name entirely and never mention no more to any one abroad, but bury into oblivion though you may hear of my good Behavior, my Managements, and my Prospects and whatsoever you may hear from me that is worthy to be reported, let it never go out of your Doors. But I shall always remember my obligations to you till the Day [of] my Death. . . .

Your affectionate though unworthy Servant,

DAVID FOWLER

❖   ❖   ❖

One of Fowler's difficulties in New York was his relationship with the Reverend Samuel Kirkland, an associate of Wheelock. Fowler considered himself a partner of Kirkland's mission to the Oneida Indians and grew discontented with Kirkland's treatment of him as a servant and laborer.

David Fowler to Eleazar Wheelock
Oneida [New York], March 17, 1767

Reverend and Honored Sir:

I suppose you have received my presumptuous Letter; which I believe has given you much Sorrow and Trouble of Mind. For I was in a very bad frame of Mind, occasioned by Mr. Kirkland's resuming too much of greatness before Company; he appeared to me, that he wanted to show what [a] great man he was that he could order us about where and how he pleased; this soon stuck in my Crop; and at this time Mr. Kirkland had letters come to hand and none for me; this increased my anger, and in the midst of my Passion I wrote your Letter. I indeed wrote whatsoever came out first; I hardly knew what I was writing about, nor can I now tell what I wrote, for as soon as I finished writing I sealed it up, but I remember some harsh Word in it.

. . . I now beg a Favor of you which will afford me Comfort and Ease, which is this: whensoever you write to Mr. Kirkland, charge him not to mention one Syllable of [it] to me, for [it] cuts me very much; though I see myself a mean and worthless Fellow and yet I am such [a] foolish Creature as to trouble myself when others receive a Letter.

I speak calmly and sincerely not in ruffle. Another Favor of Mr. Kirkland's Comfort, which is this: Don't try to give him so much authority as that he would persuade or take upon himself to govern me or order me about. As soon as he tries to do that, he won't be so comfortable here; for he can't order me, nor no Missionary that shall come into these parts. As I am an Instructor I am able to act for myself, without having a master over me. . . .

Your affectionate and unworthy servant,

DAVID FOWLER

❖   ❖   ❖

By 1767, Fowler had grown discontented with his missionary work in New York. He had difficulty keeping Indian students in his school, and the labor of keeping his family housed and fed on the frontier proved too burdensome to continue. He returned to his native Montauk on Long Island to work as a schoolmaster there.

David Fowler to Eleazar Wheelock
Canajoharie, May 28, 1767

Reverend and Honored Sir:
I am really sorry that I have molested you again in my last letter to you, and now I sincerely ask your forgiveness of all my past ungrateful and undutiful behavior to You; I am ashamed of my haughty talk to you; for I have seen the Baseness of [it] since I [have] given you that undutiful treatment. Again, I ask your forgiveness and [that you] no longer think hard of me. I determine to show such Haughtiness to you no more.
I am quite sorry to inform you of my Discouragement here. I can't see what I can do here as long as these Indians don't labor, for they are continually going from Place to Place and when they are at home in some Business [or] another which will take them from the School. I find it too hard to tarry with my wife at my present circumstances, for instead of keeping School, I have been at work almost ever since my arrival here, for I have not kept the School this two Months. I don't know when I have so much to do. The Indians are unwilling to help us in our outward Business [i.e., farming].
I think as soon as my wife gets over her trial [sickness] to come down and go over to Long Island where they are sincerely desirous for a School Master to come amongst them; Jacob [Fowler's younger brother] is too young to manage a School there and our Parents.
Sir, it is too hard for one to carry farming for two Families in a new Country. I can't no more for the Boys are awaiting. Only much Love and Duty from,

Your unworthy Servant,

DAVID FOWLER

⇜ Discussion Questions ⇝

1. What characteristics distinguish good Indians from bad Indians in Jogues's captivity narrative? How does his spiritual identity as a Christian and missionary shape his interpretation of his captivity? How can you use his narrative to retell the story of his captivity from his captors' perspective?

2. Briefly describe the process by which Mary Jemison was transformed from a captive into an adopted member of her Seneca family. Compare her narrative with that of Jogues. Why did Jogues choose to be taken captive when he could have fled, and why did Jemison choose to remain with her captors for the rest of her life? What do these two narratives tell you about the role gender played on both sides (Indian and European) of the captivity experience?

3. Why did David Fowler find his missionary work among the Oneidas so frustrating? How did his background and education as a Christian Indian affect his approach to this work? What do his letters tell you about the prejudices and ostracism that Christian Indians faced in both native and colonial worlds?

4. Where in these three sources do you see evidence that experiences of captivity and conversion created common ground between Indian and European worlds? Who was most likely to inhabit this common ground, and what advantages or disadvantages did it give them in passing between these worlds?

Suggested Readings

James Axtell's essay collections on the European-Indian encounter include numerous pieces on captivity and conversion; see especially *The European and the Indian: Essays in the Ethnohistory of Colonial North America* (New York: Oxford University Press, 1981), and *Beyond 1492: Encounters in Colonial North America* (New York: Oxford University Press, 1992). Also useful in this regard are Neal Salisbury, *Manitou and Providence: Indians, Europeans, and the Making of New England, 1500-1643* (New York: Oxford University Press, 1982), and John Demos, *The Unredeemed Captive: A Family Story from Early America* (New York: Random House, 1994). Two books noteworthy for their attention to the spiritual dimensions of the European-Indian encounter in Early America are Daniel K. Richter, *Facing East from Indian Country: A Native History of Early America* (Cambridge, Mass.: Harvard University Press, 2001), and Colin G. Calloway, *New Worlds for All: Indians, Europeans, and the Remaking of Early America* (Baltimore: Johns Hopkins University Press, 1997).

Collections of captivity narratives include Alden T. Vaughan and Edward W. Clark, editors, *Puritans Among the Indians: Accounts of Captivity and Redemption, 1676–1724* (Cambridge, Mass.: Harvard University Press, 1981), which focuses on colonial New England, and Kathryn Zabelle

Derounian-Stodola, editor, *Women's Indian Captivity Narratives* (New York: Penguin Books, 1998), which focuses on the female captivity experience. Deborah Larsen's novel *The White* (New York: Alfred A. Knopf, 2002) offers a dramatic retelling of Mary Jemison's captivity, and Brian Moore's novel *Black Robe* (New York: Dutton, 1985) owes much to Isaac Jogues's captivity narrative. The film adaptation of *Black Robe* (dir. Bruce Beresford, 1991) depicts the spiritual clash between Indian and European cultures in stunning detail.

Fort des **Maures** *sur l'Isle* **Moyella.**

Slave Trading at Fort des Maures, Moyella Island, West Africa

This engraving from the late eighteenth century depticts Africans and Europeans involved in the fur trade. At the center of the image, a European merchant meets with an African chief, each of whom is accompanied by armed guards. In the background, African and European workers carry goods back and forth from the ships in the harbor. Note the walled fort or "factory" in the background, where slaves would be confined until their departure for the Americas.
Source: © CORBIS

West Africa and the Atlantic Slave Trade

Introduction

Even before Columbus's voyages to America, Portuguese and Spanish ships were exploring the West African coast, engaging in trade with the people they encountered there, and bringing slaves back to their homeports. Once the Portuguese began cultivating sugar in Brazil, African slaves became an important part of the transatlantic trade with the New World. Between 1492 and 1870, approximately ten million Africans came to the Americas as a result of the Atlantic Slave Trade, making them the largest immigrant group to the New World during that time. Of those ten million, about 60 percent went to the Caribbean, 35 percent to Latin America, and 5 percent to North America; the majority arrived between 1700 and 1800, with the peak years of the trade occurring around 1780. African slaves provided labor for plantation colonies that produced sugar, tobacco, rice, cotton, and coffee, and they worked as miners, domestic servants, and urban craftsmen. Regardless of its location, climate, geography, or nationality, each colony in the New World recognized the legitimacy of slavery and used the labor of African slaves.

Throughout the Americas, European colonists came to equate slavery with sub-Saharan Africans and the color of their skin. Slavery had been an important part of the social and economic orders of the ancient Roman and medieval Islamic worlds, but in both of those cases, people of various ethnicities, religions, and races were eligible for enslavement, most typically as a result of warfare and captivity. In the Atlantic World, slavery acquired a distinctive racial designation: It became a lifelong, hereditary status most often justified by the use of racial classifications that defined Africans as inherently unequal and best suited to serve whites. Thus, while using a form of labor as old as history itself, the colonization of the Americas created an entirely new kind of slavery that would have profound ramifications for the intellectual and social development of the Western World.

The Atlantic Slave Trade was also a business involving the exchange of manufactured goods for human beings. The bulk of this trade took place along the West African coast, near the mouths of four major river systems: the Senegal, the Gambia, the Niger, and the Congo (also known as the Zaire) (see Figure 4.1). European powers competed against each other to establish diplomatic and commercial relations with African states and kingdoms in these regions. The merchant companies that conducted the trade lacked the manpower and resources to conquer and colonize West Africa. Instead, they entered into agreements with local rulers who allowed them to maintain coastal forts or "factories" from which to conduct their business, in return for tribute and duties paid on their trade. In exchange for slaves, West Africans demanded items of European manufacture, including cloth, iron bars, metal wares, firearms, jewelry, and liquor. Iron bars, which African blacksmiths could work into a variety of goods, became a common means of reckoning prices for slaves in the trade. West Africans had the ability to produce iron and cloth for themselves, but for coastal peoples in the era of the Atlantic Slave Trade, it was cheaper to acquire such items from Europeans. Furthermore, West Africans valued European cloth, swords, and firearms as prestige goods that exhibited the wealth and power of their owners. Europeans did not force this trade upon Africans; nor did they hoodwink Africans into exchanging slaves for trinkets. Rather, Africans participated in the Atlantic Slave Trade because it offered them goods at a lower cost and in greater varieties than they could produce at home.

Of course, describing the Atlantic Slave Trade strictly in terms of economics overlooks the enormous human cost incurred by the slaves themselves. Slavery was not unfamiliar to Africans prior to the Atlantic Slave Trade, but the particular type of slavery bred by this exchange was. In West Africa, a person might be enslaved as a result of war, debt, or criminal behavior, and slaves did all kinds of work, including farming, craft production, and domestic and military service. In short, there were many ways to be enslaved and many types of slavery.

When Europeans began dealing directly with sub-Saharan Africans, the slaves involved in this exchange encountered a type of slavery previously unknown in Africa. They had to endure long journeys from the interior to the coast, moving farther and farther away from familiar people and surroundings. Time spent in coastal forts and on slave ships waiting to depart for America exposed them to malnutrition and diseases that often proved fatal. Slave traders also relied on brutal discipline to maintain order over their human cargoes. The shock of this kind of enslavement was compounded by the difficulties of the Middle Passage, the transatlantic voyage to the Americas, which involved still more physical abuse, malnourishment, and sickness, as well as the deplorable crowding and sanitation of the ship's hold.

The readings in this chapter offer two different perspectives on the operation of the Atlantic Slave Trade in West Africa. In the first, an African recounts the ordeal by which he was enslaved in the interior of West Africa and eventually carried aboard a slave ship. In the second, a European describes the operations of a slave-trading post and the people who worked there. As you read these passages, compare and con-

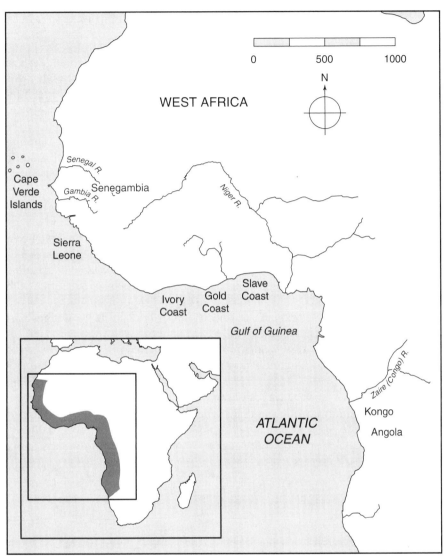

Figure 4.1   Coastal West Africa
Coastal West Africa, showing major rivers and trading regions.
Source: Adapted from W. Jeffrey Bolster, *Black Jacks: African American Seamen in the Age of Sail* (Cambridge, Mass.: Harvard University Press, 1997), 46.

trast how the slave trade worked from African and European perspectives. If high rates of mortality were involved on both sides, why did the trade thrive for more than three hundred years? Who profited from this trade? Where in both selections do you find evidence of cultural exchange and adaptation between the persons involved in trading slaves?

SELECTION 1: **An African Experiences Enslavement**

Very few firsthand accounts by Africans of the Atlantic Slave Trade exist, and even fewer provide detailed descriptions of the process by which a slave passed from African to European masters. The narrative written by Gustavus Vassa, also known as Olaudah Equiano, is important on both counts. First published in 1789, this autobiography told the remarkable story of a West African who had been enslaved as a boy in the mid-1750s and transported to the Americas, where he managed to educate himself and buy his freedom. Earning his living as a seaman and trader, Equiano traveled throughout the Atlantic World and eventually settled in London, where he became active in the anti-slavery movement of the late eighteenth century.

In the selection from his narrative, Equiano describes how he was enslaved and his passage from African to European masters. Equiano's family and village were part of the Ibo people, who inhabited modern-day Nigeria. As a young boy, he was familiar with the African practice of slavery, but he had not previously encountered Europeans or the Atlantic Slave Trade. The passage below offers readers a chance to compare and contrast the nature of slavery within West Africa with the larger, intercontinental traffic in human beings that shaped the Atlantic World. Equiano's perspective is important for understanding how and why Africans participated in this trade and the human toll it took on those who were enslaved.

As you read the passage, you should also bear in mind that there exists some confusion about Equiano's origins. While Admiralty records from the British Public Records Office corroborate Equiano's story about his seafaring life aboard British vessels, a baptismal record and naval muster book describe him as born in South Carolina. If that was indeed the case, then he fabricated his story of enslavement in Africa, perhaps relying on information he gathered from other slaves. How should that uncertainty over Equiano's origins affect your use of his narrative as a source?

* · · ·   · · ·

My father, besides many slaves, had a numerous family of which seven lived to grow up, including myself and a sister who was the only daughter. As I was the youngest of the sons I became, of course, the greatest favourite with my mother and was always with her; and she used to take particular pains to form my mind. I was trained up from my earliest years in the art of war, my daily exercise was shooting and throwing javelins, and my mother adorned me with emblems after the manner of our greatest warriors. In this way I grew up till I was turned the age of 11, when an end was put to my happiness in the following manner. Generally when the grown people in the neighbourhood were gone far in the fields to labour, the children assem-

From Olaudah Equiano, *The Interesting Narrative of the Life of Olaudah Equiano, or Gustavus Vassa, the African* (1789; Halifax: J. Nicholson, 1813), 38–64.

bled together in some of the neighbours' premises to play, and commonly some of us used to get up a tree to look out for any assailant or kidnapper that might come upon us, for they sometimes took those opportunities of our parents' absence to attack and carry off as many as they could seize. One day, as I was watching at the top of a tree in our yard, I saw one of those people come into the yard of our next neighbour but one to kidnap, there being many stout young people in it. Immediately on this I gave the alarm of the rogue and he was surrounded by the stoutest of them, who entangled him with cords so that he could not escape till some of the grown people came and secured him. But alas! ere long it was my fate to be thus attacked and to be carried off when none of the grown people were nigh. One day, when all our people were gone out to their works as usual and only I and my dear sister were left to mind the house, two men and a woman got over our walls, and in a moment seized us both, and without giving us time to cry out or make resistance they stopped our mouths and ran off with us into the nearest wood. Here they tied our hands and continued to carry us as far as they could till night came on, when we reached a small house where the robbers halted for refreshment and spent the night. We were then unbound but were unable to take any food, and being quite overpowered by fatigue and grief, our only relief was some sleep, which allayed our misfortune for a short time. The next morning we left the house and continued travelling all the day. For a long time we had kept to the woods, but at last we came into a road which I believed I knew. I had now some hopes of being delivered, for we had advanced but a little way before I discovered some people at a distance, on which I began to cry out for their assistance: but my cries had no other effect than to make them tie me faster and stop my mouth, and then they put me into a large sack. They also stopped my sister's mouth and tied her hands, and in this manner we proceeded till we were out of the sight of these people. When we went to rest the following night they offered us some victuals, but we refused it, and the only comfort we had was in being in one another's arms all that night and bathing each other with our tears. But alas! we were soon deprived of even the small comfort of weeping together. The next day proved a day of greater sorrow than I had yet experienced, for my sister and I were then separated while we lay clasped in each other's arms. It was in vain that we besought them not to part us; she was torn from me and immediately carried away, while I was left in a state of distraction not to be described. I cried and grieved continually, and for several days I did not eat anything but what they forced into my mouth. At length, after many days' travelling, during which I had often changed masters, I got into the hands of a chieftain in a very pleasant country. This man had two wives and some children, and they all used me extremely well and did all they could to comfort me, particularly the first wife, who was something like my mother. Although I was a great many days' journey from my father's house, yet these people spoke exactly the same language with us. This first master of mine, as I may call him, was a smith, and my principal employment was working his bellows, which were the same kind as I had seen in my vicinity. They were in some respects not unlike the stoves here in gentlemen's kitchens, and were covered over with leather; and in the middle of that leather a stick was fixed, and a person stood up and worked it in the same manner as is done to pump water out of a cask with a hand pump. I believe it was gold he worked, for it was of a lovely bright yellow colour and was worn by the women on their wrists and ankles. I was there I suppose about a month, and they at last used to trust me some little distance from the house. This liberty I used in embracing every opportunity to inquire the way to my own home: and I also sometimes, for the same purpose, went with the maidens in the cool of the evenings to bring pitchers of water from the springs for the use of the house. I had also remarked where the sun rose in the morning and set in the evening as I had travelled along, and I had observed that my father's house was towards the rising of the sun. I therefore determined to seize the first opportunity of making my escape and to shape my course for that quarter, for I was quite oppressed and weighed down by grief after my mother and friends, and my love of liberty, ever great, was strengthened by the mortifying circumstance of not daring to eat with the free-born children, although I was mostly their companion. While I was projecting my escape, one day an unlucky event happened which quite disconcerted my plan and put an end to my hopes. I used to be sometimes employed in assisting an elderly woman slave to cook and take care of the poultry, and one morning, while I was feeding some chickens, I happened to toss a small pebble at one of them, which hit it on the middle and directly killed it. The old slave, having soon after missed the chicken, inquired after it; and on my relating the accident (for I told her the truth, because my mother would never suffer me to tell a lie) she flew into a violent passion, threatened that I should suffer for it, and, my master being out, she immediately went and told her mistress what I had done. This alarmed me very much and I expected an instant flogging, which to me was uncommonly dreadful, for I had seldom been beaten at home. I therefore resolved to fly, and accordingly I ran into a thicket that was hard by and hid myself in the bushes. Soon afterwards my mistress and the slave returned, and not seeing me they searched all the house, but not finding me, and I not making answer when they called to me, they thought I had run away and the whole neighbourhood was raised in the pursuit of me. In that part of the country (as in ours) the houses and villages were skirted with woods or shrubberies, and the bushes were so thick that a man could readily conceal himself in them so as to elude the strictest search. The neighbours continued the whole day looking for me and several times many of them came within a few yards of the place where I lay hid. I then gave myself up for lost entirely, and expected every moment, when I heard a rustling among the trees, to be found out and punished by my master: but they never discovered me, though they were often so near that I even heard their conjectures as they were looking about for me; and I now learned from them that any attempts to return home would be hopeless. Most of them supposed I had fled towards home, but the distance was so great and the way so intricate that they thought I could never reach it, and that I should be lost in the woods. When I heard this I was seized with a violent panic and abandoned myself to despair. Night too began to approach and aggravated all my fears. I had before entertained hopes of getting home and I had determined when it should be dark to make the attempt, but I was now convinced it was fruitless and began to consider that, if possibly I could escape all other animals, I could not those of the human kind; and that, not knowing the way, I must perish in the woods. Thus was I like the hunted deer:

> Ev'ry leaf and ev'ry whisp'ring breath
> Convey'd a foe, and ev'ry foe a death.

I heard frequent rustlings among the leaves, and being pretty sure they were snakes I expected every instant to be stung by them. This increased my anguish and the horror of my situation became now quite insupportable. I at length quitted the thicket, very faint and hungry for I had not eaten or drank anything all the day, and crept to my master's kitchen from whence I set out at first, and which was an open shed, and laid myself down in the ashes with an anxious wish for death to relieve me from all my pains. I was scarcely awake in the morning when the old woman slave, who was the first up, came to light the fire and saw me in the fireplace. She was very much surprised to see me and could scarcely believe her own eyes. She now promised to intercede for me and went for her master, who soon after came, and, having slightly reprimanded me, ordered me to be taken care of and not ill-treated.

Soon after this my master's only daughter and child by his first wife sickened and died, which affected him so much that for some time he was almost frantic, and really would have killed himself had he not been watched and prevented. However, in a small time afterwards he recovered and I was again sold. I was now carried to the left of the sun's rising, through many different countries and a number of large woods. The people I was sold to used to carry me very often when I was tired either on their shoulders or on their backs. I saw many convenient well-built sheds along the roads at proper distances, to accommodate the merchants and travellers who lay in those buildings along with their wives, who often accompany them; and they always go well armed.

From the time I left my own nation I always found somebody that understood me till I came to the sea coast. The languages of different nations did not totally differ, nor were they so copious as those of the Europeans, particularly the English. They were therefore easily learned, and while I was journeying thus through Africa I acquired two or three different tongues. In this manner I had been travelling for a considerable time, when one evening, to my great surprise, whom should I see brought to the house where I was but my dear sister! As soon as she saw me she gave a loud shriek and ran into my arms—I was quite overpowered: neither of us could speak, but for a considerable time clung to each other in mutual embraces, unable to do anything but weep. Our meeting affected all who saw us, and indeed I must acknowledge, in honour of those sable destroyers of human rights, that I never met with any ill treatment or saw any offered to their slaves except tying them, when necessary, to keep them from running away. When these people knew we were brother and sister they indulged us to be together, and the man to whom I supposed we belonged lay with us, he in the middle while she and I held one another by the hands across his breast all night; and thus for a while we forgot our misfortunes in the joy of being together: but even this small comfort was soon to have an end, for scarcely had the fatal morning appeared when she was again torn from me for ever! I was now more miserable, if possible, than before. The small relief which her presence gave me from pain was gone, and the wretchedness of my situation was redoubled by my anxiety after her fate and my apprehensions lest her sufferings should be greater than mine, when I could not be with her to alleviate them. Yes, thou dear partner of all my childish sports! thou sharer of my joys and sorrows! happy should I have ever esteemed myself to encounter every misery for you, and to procure your freedom by the sacrifice of my own. Though you were early forced from my arms, your image has been always riveted in my heart, from which neither *time nor fortune* have been able to remove it; so that, while the thoughts of your sufferings have damped my prosperity, they have mingled with adversity and increased its bitterness. To that Heaven which protects the weak from the strong I commit the care of your innocence and virtues, if they have not already received their full reward and if your youth and delicacy have not long since fallen victims to the violence of the African trader, the pestilential stench of a Guinea ship, the seasoning in the European colonies, or the lash and lust of a brutal and unrelenting overseer.

I did not long remain after my sister. I was again sold and carried through a number of places till, after travelling a considerable time, I came to a town called Tinmah in the most beautiful country I had yet seen in Africa. It was extremely rich, and there were many rivulets which flowed through it and supplied a large pond in the centre of the town, where the people washed. Here I first saw and tasted coconuts, which I thought superior to any nuts I had ever tasted before; and the trees, which were loaded, were also interspersed amongst the houses, which had commodious shades adjoining and were in the same manner as ours, the insides being neatly plastered and whitewashed. Here I also saw and tasted for the first time sugar-cane. Their money consisted of little white shells the size of the finger-nail. I was sold here for 172 of them by a merchant who lived and brought me there. I had been about two or three days at his house when a wealthy widow, a neighbour of his, came there one evening, and brought with her an only son, a young gentleman about my own age and size. Here they saw me; and, having taken a fancy to me, I was bought of the merchant, and went home with them. Her house and premises were situated close to one of those rivulets I have mentioned, and were the finest I ever saw in Africa: they were very extensive, and she had a number of slaves to attend her. The next day I was washed and perfumed, and when meal-time came I was led into the presence of my mistress, and ate and drank before her with her son. This filled me with astonishment; and I could scarce help expressing my surprise that the young gentleman should suffer me, who was bound, to eat with him who was free; and not only so, but that he would not at any time either eat or drink till I had taken first, because I was the eldest, which was agreeable to our custom. Indeed, everything here, and all their treatment of me, made me forget that I was a slave. The language of these people resembled ours so nearly that we understood each other perfectly. They had also the very same customs as we. There were likewise slaves daily to attend us, while my young master and I with other boys sported with our darts and bows and arrows, as I had been used to do at home. In this resemblance to my former happy state I passed about two months; and I now began to think I was to be adopted into the family, and was beginning to be reconciled to my situation, and to forget by degrees my misfortunes, when all at once the delusion vanished; for without the least previous knowledge, one morning early, while my dear master and companion was still asleep, I was wakened out of my reverie to fresh sorrow, and hurried away even amongst the uncircumcised.

Thus at the very moment I dreamed of the greatest happiness, I found myself most miserable; and it seemed as if fortune wished to give me this taste of joy only to render the reverse more poignant. The change I now experienced was as painful as it was sudden and unexpected. It was a change indeed from a state of bliss to a scene which is inexpressible by me, as it discovered to me an element I had never before beheld and till then had no idea of, and wherein such instances of hardship and cruelty continually occurred as I can never reflect on but with horror.

All the nations and people I had hitherto passed through resembled our own in their manner, customs, and language: but I came at length to a country the inhabitants of which differed from us in all those particulars. I was very much struck with this difference, especially when I came among a people who did not circumcise and ate without washing their hands. They cooked also in iron pots and had European cutlasses and crossbows, which were unknown to us, and fought with their fists amongst themselves. Their women were not so modest as ours, for they ate and drank and slept with their men. But above all, I was amazed to see no sacrifices or offerings among them. In some of those places the people ornamented themselves with scars, and likewise filed their teeth very sharp. They wanted sometimes to ornament me in the same manner, but I would not suffer them, hoping that I might some time be among a people who did not thus disfigure themselves, as I thought they did. At last I came to the banks of a large river, which was covered with canoes in which the people appeared to live with their household utensils and provisions of all kinds. I was beyond measure astonished at this, as I had never before seen any water larger than a pond or a rivulet: and my surprise was mingled with no small fear when I was put into one of these canoes and we began to paddle and move along the river. We continued going on thus till night, and when we came to land and made fires on the banks, each family by themselves, some dragged their canoes on shore, others stayed and cooked in theirs and laid in them all night. Those on the land had mats of which they made tents, some in the shape of little houses: in these we slept, and after the morning meal we embarked again and proceeded as before. I was often very much astonished to see some of the women, as well as the men, jump into the water, dive to the bottom, come up again, and swim about. Thus I continued to travel, sometimes by land, sometimes by water, through different countries and various nations, till at the end of six or seven months after I had been kidnapped I arrived at the sea coast.

❖   ❖   ❖

The first object which saluted my eyes when I arrived on the coast was the sea, and a slave ship which was then riding at anchor and waiting for its cargo. These filled me with astonishment, which was soon converted into terror when I was carried on board. I was immediately handled and tossed up to see if I were sound by some of the crew, and I was now persuaded that I had gotten into a world of bad spirits and that they were going to kill me. Their complexions too differing so much from ours, their long hair and the language they spoke (which was very different from any I had ever heard) united to confirm me in this belief. Indeed such were the horrors of my views and fears at the moment that, if ten thousand worlds had been my own, I would have freely parted with them all to have exchanged my condition with that of the meanest slave in my own country. When I looked round the ship too and saw a large furnace or copper boiling and a multitude of black people of every description chained together, every one of their countenances expressing dejection and sorrow, I no longer doubted of my fate; and quite overpowered with horror and anguish, I fell motionless on the deck and fainted. When I recovered a little I found some black people about me, who I believed were some of those who had brought me on board and had been receiving their pay; they talked to me in order to cheer me, but all in vain. I asked them if we were not to be eaten by those white men with horrible looks, red faces, and loose hair. They told me I was not, and one of the crew brought me a small portion of spirituous liquor in a wine glass, but being afraid of him I would not take it out of his hand. One of the blacks therefore took it from him and gave it to me, and I took a little down my palate, which instead of reviving me, as they thought it would, threw me into the greatest consternation at the strange feeling it produced, having never tasted such any liquor before. Soon after this the blacks who brought me on board went off, and left me abandoned to despair.

I now saw myself deprived of all chance of returning to my native country or even the least glimpse of hope of gaining the shore, which I now considered as friendly; and I even wished for my former slavery in preference to my present situation, which was filled with horrors of every kind, still heightened by my ignorance of what I was to undergo. I was not long suffered to indulge my grief; I was soon put down under the decks, and there I received such a salutation in my nostrils as I had never experienced in my life: so that with the loathsomeness of the stench and crying together, I became so sick and low that I was not able to eat, nor had I the least desire to taste anything. I now wished for the last friend, death, to relieve me; but soon, to my grief, two of the white men offered me eatables, and on my refusing to eat, one of them held me fast by the hands and laid me across I think the windlass, and tied my feet while the other flogged me severely. I had never experienced anything of this kind before, and although, not being used to the water, I naturally feared that element the first time I saw it, yet nevertheless could I have got over the nettings I would have jumped over the side, but I could not; and besides, the crew used to watch us very closely who were not chained down to the decks, lest we should leap into the water: and I have seen some of these poor African prisoners most severely cut for attempting to do so, and hourly whipped for not eating. This indeed was often the case with myself. In a little time after, amongst the poor chained men I found some of my own nation, which in a small degree gave ease to my mind. I inquired of these what was to be done with us; they gave me to understand we were to be carried to these white people's country to work for them. I then was a little revived, and thought if it were no worse than working, my situation was not so desperate: but still I feared I should be put to death, the white people looked and acted, as I thought, in so savage a manner; for I had never seen among my people such instances of brutal cruelty, and this not only shewn towards us blacks but also to some of the whites themselves. One white man in particular I saw, when we were permitted to be on deck, flogged so unmercifully with a large rope near the foremast that he died in consequence of it; and they tossed him over the side as they would have done a brute. This made me fear these people the more, and I expected nothing less than to be treated in the same manner. I could not help expressing my fears and apprehensions to some of my countrymen: I asked them if these people had no country but lived in this hollow place (the ship): they told me they did not, but came from a distant one. 'Then,' said I, 'how comes it in all our country we never heard of them?' They told me because they lived so very far off. I then asked where were their women? had they any like themselves? I was told they had: 'and why,' said I, 'do we not see them?' They answered, because they were left behind. I asked how the vessel could go? They told me they could not tell, but that there were cloths put upon the masts by the help of the ropes I saw, and then the vessel went on; and the white men had some spell or magic they put in the water when they liked in order to stop the vessel. I was exceedingly amazed at this account and really thought they were spirits. I therefore wished much to be from amongst them for I expected they would sacrifice me: but my wishes were vain, for we were so quartered that it was impossible for any of us to make our escape. While we stayed on the coast I was mostly on deck, and one day, to my great astonishment, I saw one of these vessels coming in with the sails up. As soon as the whites saw it they gave a great shout, at which we were amazed; and the more so as the vessel appeared larger by approaching nearer. At last she came to an anchor in my sight, and when the anchor was let go I and my countrymen who saw it were lost in astonishment to observe the vessel stop, and were now convinced it was done by magic. Soon after this the other ship got her boats out, and they came on board of us, and the people of both ships seemed very glad to see each other. Several of the strangers also shook hands with us black people, and made motions with their hands, signifying I suppose we were to go to their country; but we did not understand them. At last, when the ship we were in had got in all her cargo, they made ready with many fearful noises, and we were all put under deck so that we could not see how they managed the vessel. But this disappointment was the least of my sorrow. The stench of the hold while we were on the coast was so intolerably loathsome that it was dangerous to remain there for any time, and some of us had been permitted to stay on the deck for the fresh air; but now that the whole ship's cargo were confined together it became absolutely pestilential. The closeness of the place and the heat of the climate, added to the number in the ship, which was so crowded that each had scarcely room to turn himself, almost suffocated us. This produced copious perspirations, so that the air soon became unfit for respiration from a variety of loathsome smells, and brought on a sickness among the slaves, of which many died, thus falling victims to the improvident avarice, as I may call it, of their purchasers. This wretched situation was again aggravated by the galling of the chains, now become insupportable, and the filth of the necessary tubs, into which the children often fell and were almost suffocated. The shrieks of the women and the groans of the dying rendered the whole a scene of horror almost inconceivable. Happily perhaps for myself I was soon reduced so low here that it was thought necessary to keep me almost always on deck, and from my extreme youth I was not put in fetters. In this situation I expected every hour to share the fate of my companions, some of whom were almost daily brought upon deck at the point of death, which I began to hope would soon put an end to my miseries. Often did I think many of the inhabitants of the deep much more happy than myself. I envied them the freedom they enjoyed, and as often wished I could change my condition for theirs. Every circumstance I met with served only to render my state more painful, and heighten my apprehensions and my opinion of the cruelty of the whites.

SELECTION 2: A European Describes a Slave-Trading Post

All of the European powers involved in the colonization of the Americas participated in the Atlantic Slave Trade. Even the Danes, whose sugar colonies in the Caribbean were among the last established there, engaged in a direct trade with West Africa to supply their New World labor needs. Following precedents established by other European powers, the Danes built coastal forts in the regions where they traded so that they could warehouse goods and the human cargoes destined for slave ships. These posts also housed European traders and laborers, as well as troops charged with protecting them from foreign competitors, pirates, and rebellious slaves. Mortality rates for Europeans living in West Africa during this period were staggering, ranging from 25 to 75 percent per year, and such posts needed to be resupplied constantly with fresh recruits.

Paul Erdmann Isert was a German-born surgeon sent by the Baltic Guinea Company, a Danish slave-trading venture, to work at its West African post Christiansborg in 1783. Isert remained in that position for three years, and then sailed to the West Indies to inspect the plantation colonies there. Upon returning to Copenhagen, he published a narrative based on letters he had written during his African and American sojourn. He was especially interested in the health problems Europeans experienced in West Africa, and his story also sheds light on the social and labor relations between Europeans and Africans working in the slave trade. In 1788 he returned to Africa to establish a plantation colony there, but the plan collapsed shortly after his death in 1789.

All of the Europeans who are staying in Guinea, regardless of what nation they come from, are in the service of either their king or a company. It was the Portuguese who first sailed along the Guinea Coast, in the mid-fifteenth century. Finding the people on the Gold Coast most courteous they built various fortified places, or forts, there, in which they kept their wares and carried on trade with the inhabitants. At first the articles that they took in barter from the Blacks as payment for their wares were limited principally to gold and ivory. But at the end of the century, after Columbia [America] was discovered, the sumptuousness of the products from there increased in Europe. However, since the Europeans, for their own safety, had exterminated most of the native Columbians, they began to lack workers to provide them with these products, so they turned to Africa which they knew was teeming with people at the time. Even though there were large numbers of people, the difficulty of travel and the climate in Africa would have made conquest too difficult for the Europeans. Thus they got this idea: buy Blacks and take them to their plantations in Columbia.

They had learned by experience that the Blacks were more robust by nature, and more suited to work, than the weaker Indians. For this reason, despite the cost of their transportation—during which many were to die on such a long trip—and other difficulties, they found that the transfer of these unhappy souls, which cost little or nothing at first, was a very profitable business. In this way began the Black slave trade which has been such an important undertaking during these last two centuries—to the shame of mankind.

◆　◆　◆

The fifth nation having possessions in Guinea is that of the Danes. At present we have four forts and six lodges, or trading stations. The forts are: Christiansburg, Friedensburg, Kønigstein and Prinzenstein, The lodges are: Labodei, Thessing [Teshi], Temma, Ponny, Aflahu and Popo. These establishments lie within a stretch of fifty miles along the coast. Along this stretch we alone are the masters of trade, except for an English fort, called Prampram, lying between Christiansburg and Friedensburg. Since I have already told you about each of these places, I shall not repeat myself now.

The supreme command over all our possessions is held by the Governor of Christiansburg, who exercises authority over all the other possessions as their Chief. A council made up of the commanders of the other forts has been established for him, without which he cannot treat any matter of importance.

From *Letters on West Africa and the Slave Trade: Paul Erdmann Isert's Journey to Guinea and the Caribbean Islands in Columbia (1788)*, translated and edited by Selena Axelrod Winsnes (New York: Oxford University Press, 1992), 147–153, 155–159.

The second in rank in the Council is the Chief Trader and Commander of Friedensburg. The other two commanders are called "Traders" and vote according to their length of service. At the more important lodges, command lies with the factor, and in the less important posts there are assistants, junior officers, or, in some places, only a soldier. The annual salary of the governor is not more than 1,000 *thalers*, plus 500 *thalers* for table allowance. The Chief Trader and Commandant of Friedensburg receives 500, and the other commanders 400 *thalers* each.

Commercial posts are held by assistants, under-assistants and reserve assistants. The factors and the two chief assistants, who take care of the bookkeeping and secretarial work, receive 400 *thalers*; the other chief assistants at the lodges and forts, 300; an under-assistant, 250; and a reserve assistant, 10 to 12 *thalers* a month.

The religious staff, when it is complete, consists of a clergyman and a catechist. The former is paid 400 *thalers* and the latter 250 *thalers* annually. The same conditions obtain in the medical service whose Chief Surgeon, stationed at Christiansburg, is paid 400 *thalers*, and the second one, stationed at Friedensburg, 300 *thalers*. But in addition they receive a bonus for each slave shipped out—an amount which can at times equal their salaries. Furthermore, the surgeon at Christiansburg is supplied with a Mulatto who performs bandaging and other surgical tasks, for which he is paid 12 *thalers* monthly.

The military personnel at the main fort consists, at present, of a sergeant, two corporals, two drummers, two pipers, twenty musketeers, one chief gunner, one assistant gunner, two constables, and two assistant constables, the last mentioned being Blacks. The other forts have one sergeant, one corporal, one drummer, one piper, ten musketeers, and, to man the cannon, two constables and a few Company slaves. A gunner is paid 20 *thalers*, a seargeant 16, a corporal 14, and the European soldiers 10 *thalers* monthly. But the Mulatto soldiers receive only 8 *thalers*.

There are also a number of artisans here in the service of the King. The person who is in charge of these and of the Company slaves is called the *Baas*, and receives 20 *thalers* a month. Masons, smiths, joiners and coopers are usually paid 14 *thalers* a month, or more if they are particularly skillful. The total number of Europeans here, at the time of writing this, amounts to not more than 38 people, and the posts are fairly well filled.

In addition there are 200–250 slaves in service who are not sent out of the country. The male slaves are given one *thaler* monthly and the females one-half *thaler*. Indeed, some of the younger girls are paid only one-quarter *thaler*. These wretched souls are most poorly paid for their work, and if they were not able to supplement their pay by one means or another, they could not possibly manage. Admittedly the free Black is not paid any better when his services are hired, but there is this difference, that he has his family in town and they have to feed him. The English have already recognized the drawbacks of the system and give their slaves twice as much as we give ours.

For the administration of all the establishments, the King pays 25,000 *thalers* annually to the Company which, if that is insufficient, is forced to supplement it from its own coffers.

All trade undertaken here is the monopoly of the Company which, to encourage that trade, pays the chiefs of the forts and offices considerable commissions.

On the whole, the Europeans here seldom live in a manner suitable to the nature of the climate. Instead of becoming accustomed to the fruits of the land, they prefer the products of their own lands and do not take into account that they have left their northern stomachs behind in their fatherlands. It is common knowledge that the stomach, as well as all the other organs of the body, becomes sluggish in a hot climate, and thus has not the strength to digest the foods for which it was designed. The extraordinary amount of meat which it is customary to serve at the tables of the rich here is veritable poison to the Europeans, if they do not take it in moderation. They ought to go to the natives of the land and see how four people relish one dish containing not more than one pound of meat or fish, with quantities of grain or other foodstuffs from the plant kingdom. Therefore they are healthy, while the Europeans are constantly plagued by illness.

In fact, it appears that certain northern Europeans, especially Norwegians, are totally unsuited to this climate. When they arrive in this land, even though they have never before in their lives been ill, they are like a fresh-water fish that has been placed in salt water. They become misanthropic, fretful, and do not know why. First they complain of a headache, usually accompanied by vomiting; after 24 hours often follow convulsions; after 36 hours a pustule-like rash appears on the forehead and the calves, and the patient dies—a man who had been perfectly healthy 48 hours earlier.

◆　◆　◆

The illness which, for the older Coastmen, usually blazes the trail to Elysium [death] is dysentery. From the heat of the atmosphere, and from eating meat, drinking, and using too much Spanish pepper, they have not rarely weakened their viscera in such a way that if they first get diarrhoea it very soon becomes dysentery. The surgeon does himself a disfavour if he is an adversary of astringent medicines. On the contrary, if the fever is not perceptible and the intestines have been cleaned out by a purgative, one might administer a mild astringent mixture (which I tried here) made of a decoction of the bark of a young mangrove in which gum arabic has been dissolved. However, one must be much on one's guard against puddings and meat. The most harmless food is a panada [a flour paste] accompanied by wine. The most important part of the cure is a strict diet, something to which the patient seldom cares to adhere.

◆　◆　◆

The Europeans' entertainment in this land is limited. He who has not learned to enjoy his own resources comes off the loser, since society here is so limited that one has not much choice. And because each person is acquainted with all the behaviour or manners of the others, and sees in them, regrettably, so little of merit, one seldom finds another with whom one wishes to keep company. Since public diversions are totally lacking, the refuge of such gentlemen is usually Bacchus [drinking], gaming, and Venus [sex], in all of which a number of our former citizens have so excelled that they have had to pay prematurely with their lives for their debauchery.

One of the most peculiar customs here is the marriage of the Europeans to the daughters of the country. It is called *cassare*, a word which comes from the Portuguese and means to set up house. When a European arrives here one of his first considerations is to acquire one of these bed-fellows, in spite of the fact that I give each one the well-meant advice not to enter into such an arrangement, at least for the first year, since I have often been struck by the harm that results. If he has now chosen one to his taste (a rejection has seldom to be feared) he then sends a humble memorandum to the High Council wherein he announces the name of his chosen future half and asks that he may be given permission to take her as his (*quasi*) wife. The Council, which looks very positively on such a connection, because the European would not then be so easily plagued by homesickness, answers that he is so permitted, but that he must immediately pay one-half month's salary into the Mulatto treasury, and an equal amount when he leaves, as well as four percent monthly during his stay. When this has been acknowledged, the celebration takes place, a celebration which is no different from the one I described to you in an earlier letter about the Blacks, except that the bridegroom in this case usually gives a dinner party where the bride, probably for the first time, eats at table among the Europeans. It is understood here, however, that neither an engagement nor a marriage ceremony has taken place here, and the new husband can send his wife packing the next day if he feels like it.

The children who are born to such a pair are always christened and instructed in Christianity. If the child is a boy he will be employed as a soldier in the king's service as soon as he is ten years old, and thus will enjoy a monthly wage of eight *thalers*. Poor girls and boys, as long as they are not otherwise supported, are given one *thaler* from the Mulatto treasury for their sustinence, a sum which is ample for them.

The property of the man is not held in common with that of the woman, but each keeps his own privately. A Black woman is paid one *thaler* monthly and a Mulatto woman two *thalers* monthly by their husbands, and they are given clothing twice a year. They have the right to demand this, and if the husband refuses they have the right to complain to the Council. In such a case they would be paid the sum, which would then be deducted from the husband's salary. Sometimes there are among the soldiers such ne'er-do-wells that they cannot manage their wages themselves. In such cases the wages are often paid to the Black wife who then has to provide the European with food.

The happiness of all those in service in the country is dependent, for the most part, on the nature of the Governor's temperament. Everyone tries to emulate him, even, indeed, in inconsequential things. If he is excellent, all the others are courteous; miserly, the others will outdo one another in that respect and so it goes through all the ranks. And, "as Heaven is high and Europe far way" (as they say here) at times a governor rules here more despotically than the most absolute monarch in Europe. Unfortunate are those who are in service when a bad man rises to the governorship. And since the mortality rate is usually so high in this country, and everyone gains promotion, it has often happened that people from the lowest ranks, such as soldiers, artisans or cabin boys have risen to the rank of governor. Since these people usually have lacked the opportunity of training their reasoning abilities, their government is often a mixture of petty arrogance and cruelty. This falls not a little tediously on those men (perhaps of greater insight) who because of less seniority in service must be subordinates. It has often cost them their lives. There have been instances where some men to whom it was necessary to give a flogging one day were given the supreme command the next day.

◆　　◆　　◆

The extraordinarily high mortality rate of the Europeans in this land has caused people in Europe to believe that the climate alone is to blame. But they are mistaken in this. From experience alone one could judge the opposite. In this land from which the Europeans have been able, by a moderate reckoning, to export 60,000 people annually who would never return, the population is still very high, even after 200 years of such export. This fact alone is proof enough that the climate is harmless. According to these calculations, it is clear that during this last hundred years six million people were exported, and one can, without stretching the truth, easily assume that in the preceding centuries, from the beginning of the Black trade, at least twice as many were exported. This makes 18 million in all who were exported. What a figure! In fact, this figure by itself equals the population of a fairly large and populous land, namely, France. It is something other than the climate on the Coast which is unhealthy. It is rather the perverse way of life of those who come to this land that is more the cause of the mortality than is the country itself. Some die from the preconceived idea that it is impossible to live in a land where so many die such a short time after their arrival. Still others become homesick and grieve themselves to death, probably because they have contracted to stay here a certain number of years. As for others, alas! a great many bring such a host of primordial illnesses with them that when these are activated by the hot climate, death is certain.

Those people who, in my experience, are best suited to the climate are young people, of from 25 to 30 years of age. Whoever is over this age should stay away from here since he will seldom reach a higher age. Moreover, the climate is less salubrious for apparently very healthy, sanguine persons than it is for the person who is thin and weak by nature. People who are very sanguine and who come here should not let themselves be deceived by prejudgment. In this hot climate they must not neglect to be well bled, and this should be done immediately upon arrival. They should keep an extremely lean diet during the first year, drink great amounts of cold water, and bathe daily. If all these things are faithfully observed, barring any damage to the character, I can assure them that their bodies will adjust to the climate and even in the unhealthful air of the coast, they can become as old as they would have done in their fatherland.

⊜ Discussion Questions ⊜

1. What do Equiano's kidnapping and early captivity tell you about the role slavery and an internal slave trade played in West Africa? As Equiano was passed from master to master, what evidence can you find that the circumstances of his enslavement were becoming increasingly unfamiliar to him?

2. Examine closely Equiano's first encounter with Europeans. How do these new masters differ from his previous African ones? What are his physical and emotional responses to the slave ship?

3. Using Isert's narrative, describe the European and African personnel that worked at a coastal slave factory. What is Isert's opinion of intermarriage between Europeans and Africans, and what role did such men and women and their children play in the coastal slave trade?

4. What evidence does Isert present against the argument that the West African climate is unhealthy? According to him, what are the causes of Europeans' high mortality there, and what does he recommend for improving their health?

Suggested Readings

For the distinctive nature of New World slavery and its significance in the intellectual development of the West, see David Brion Davis, *Slavery and Human Progress* (New York: Oxford University Press, 1984). For estimates of the numbers involved in the Atlantic Slave Trade, see Philip D. Curtin, *The Atlantic Slave Trade: A Census* (Madison, Wisc.: University of Wisconsin Press, 1969) and Paul E. Lovejoy, "The Volume of the Atlantic Slave Trade: A Synthesis," *Journal of African History* 23 (1982): 365–394. On the nature of slavery and the slave trade in Africa, see Paul E. Lovejoy, *Transformations in Slavery: A History of Slavery in Africa* (Cambridge, England: Cambridge University Press, 1983) and Patrick Manning, *Slavery and African Life: Occidental, Oriental, and African Slave Trades* (Cambridge, England: Cambridge University Press, 1990).

Studies of the Atlantic Slave Trade that emphasize its role in shaping the Atlantic World include David Eltis, *The Rise of African Slavery in the Americas* (Cambridge, England: Cambridge University Press, 1999), and Ira Berlin, *Many Thousands Gone: The First Two Centuries of Slavery in North America* (Cambridge, Mass.: Harvard University Press, 1998). Two good overviews of West Africa's role in shaping the Atlantic World are: David Northrup, *Africa's Discovery of Europe, 1450–1850* (New York: Oxford University Press, 2002), and John Thornton, *Africa and Africans in the Making of the Atlantic World, 1400–1800*, second edition (Cambridge, England: Cambridge University Press, 1998). An excellent compilation of first-person accounts from the African perspective is *Africa Remembered: Narratives of West Africans from the Era of the Slave Trade*, edited by Philip D. Curtin (Madison, Wisc.: University of Wisconsin Press, 1967). For the question of Equiano's origins, see Vincent Carretta, "Olaudah Equiano or Gustavus Vassa? New Light on an Eighteenth-Century Question of Identity," *Slavery and Abolition* 20 (1999): 96–105.

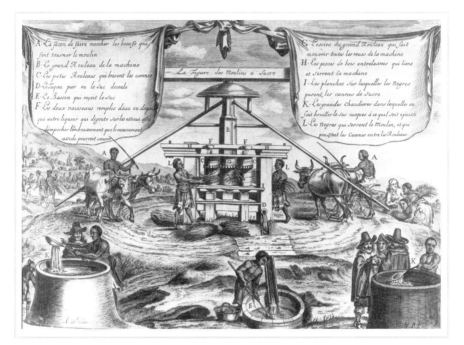

Sugar Making on a Caribbean Plantation

This early depiction of a sugar mill illustrates the steps involved in processing sugar cane. The three-roll mill (or *ingenio*), powered by oxen, crushes the cane and extracts the juice, which flows into a cistern and is then transferred into copper kettles, where it is boiled until it crystallizes. Byproducts of this process included the "trash," or crushed cane, which became fuel for the boiling fires; and molasses, which could be distilled into rum, also known as "kill-devil." What does this image tell you about the nature of labor relations on the sugar plantation? What hazards did slaves face in this process and what role did planters play in it?

Source: The Library Company of Philadelphia. From Charles de Rochefort, *Historie Naturelle et Morale des Iles Antilles de l'Amerique* (Rotterdam, 1665).

The Plantation Complex
in the Caribbean

Introduction

The islands of the Caribbean stretch in an eastern arc from the tip of Florida to the coast of South America. The four largest—Cuba, Hispaniola (modern Haiti and the Dominican Republic), Puerto Rico and Jamaica, known as the Greater Antilles—were colonized by the Spanish in the wake of Columbus. The Lesser Antilles are a string of much smaller islands that were colonized by the Dutch, French, and English during the seventeenth century, in part to serve as naval bases for raiding Spanish shipping and in part to cultivate cash crops that flourished in the tropical climate and rich volcanic soil these islands provided. (See Figure 5.1.)

By far, the most significant of those crops was sugar. Sugar cultivation originated in India and was carried eastward into the Mediterranean World by Arabic traders and colonizers. Europeans' taste for it increased during the Crusades, when the Mediterranean island of Cyprus became its chief supplier. Landowners there relied on a mixed labor force of servants and slaves from Eastern Europe, the Near East, and Africa to grow sugar cane and refine it. Gradually, sugar moved west, as Venetian merchants bankrolled plantations in Crete, Sicily, North Africa, and the southern Iberian Peninsula. In the fifteenth century, Spanish and Portuguese colonizers brought sugar to the Atlantic's Canary and Madeira Islands, respectively. In all of these places, the cultivation of sugar encouraged the development of what historians call the plantation complex: a method of cash crop production for international markets that relies on unfree labor controlled by a small, landowning elite. The profits from this trade motivated Columbus to carry sugar plants with him on his first voyage across the Atlantic, in hopes that he would find new regions suitable for this crop's cultivation.

Spanish attention in the Americas was quickly diverted by the pursuit of gold and silver, but the Portuguese successfully transplanted sugar along with their African slave trade to Brazil. The Dutch briefly

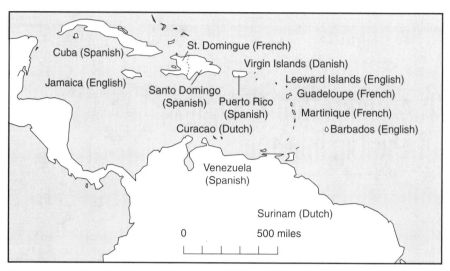

Figure 5.1   The Caribbean Islands, c. 1780
The major sugar islands of the Caribbean with northern coast of South America, not-
ing European possession.
Source: Adapted from Robin Blackburn, *The Making of New World Slavery* (London: Verso
Press, 1990), 372.

conquered Brazil in the early seventeenth century, but when the Portuguese regained control there, Dutch merchants and planters brought
their capital, expertise, and African slaves for sugar planting into the
Caribbean. So began a sugar revolution that transformed the Lesser
Antilles. The French and English had colonized a number of small islands, relying on white indentured servants to cultivate tobacco and
subsistence crops. Within a generation, the economy of these islands
shifted to sugar production, and the plantation complex took root. European immigration fell as a small planter class engrossed the arable
land and imported enslaved Africans to work it. Caught in this land
squeeze, former servants and other propertyless whites migrated elsewhere in search of opportunity.

Caribbean planters profited handsomely from the high demand for
sugar in Europe, and many became absentee landlords, living off their
fortunes in Paris or London. A typical plantation had fifty or more slaves
working in gangs under a handful of white managers and overseers. On
these sugar islands, Africans outnumbered Europeans by ratios ranging
from 3:1 to 25:1. For both races, men far outnumbered women and
tropical diseases took a heavy toll on new arrivals. Imbalanced sex ratios and high mortality rates meant that these colonies had to rely on a
constant influx of new workers to sustain their sugar production.

By the mid-eighteenth century, the Caribbean sugar economy
was in full flower. English production centered in Barbados and Jamaica, the latter of which had been won from Spain in 1655. The

French produced sugar on the islands of Martinique and Guadeloupe, but their most profitable Caribbean possession was St. Domingue, a colony established on the western half of Hispaniola, wrestled from the Spanish in the seventeenth century. Dutch sugar colonies included the islands of St. Maarten and St. Eustatius, as well as Surinam and Demerara on the northern coast of South America. The Spanish developed sugar plantations in Venezuela and Cuba, the latter of which would dominate the Caribbean's sugar industry in the nineteenth century. Even the Danes, latecomers to the scramble for empire, had established sugar colonies in the Lesser Antilles by the late eighteenth century (see Chapter 4, pp. 76–81). White and black migrants from the English and French sugar islands transplanted the plantation complex to the North American mainland, settling in the coastal lowlands of South Carolina and Georgia and in the lower Mississippi Valley of French Louisiana. In North America, tobacco and rice were the cash crops of the colonial era, but cotton and sugar production increased significantly as the plantation complex expanded west in the nineteenth century.

Plantation societies became cauldrons of adaptation and resistance by the slaves who lived and worked in them. African-American cultural patterns emerged in the slaves' language, diet, music, and religion, combining precedents from their African past with influences from the European and Native American peoples among whom they lived. Whenever possible, slave runaways established their own communities independent of white authority, often by retreating to mountainous interiors or dense jungles beyond the fringe of white settlement. These maroon communities, as they were known, varied in size and duration from region to region. One of the largest was Palmares, home to thousands of Africans in Brazil during the sixteenth and seventeenth centuries; in North America, runaway slaves from Georgia and South Carolina established a maroon settlement near the Spanish fortress of St. Augustine in Florida; maroon communities in Jamaica proved so difficult to defeat in battle that English planters negotiated peace treaties with them instead.

The plantation complex, embraced by every European colonial power in the Caribbean, became a model for colonization throughout the Americas, creating immense wealth for the European planters who owned the land and untold miseries for the African slaves who worked it. By 1776, there were 2.5 million slaves in the New World, most of them living on plantations that produced sugar, tobacco, coffee, cacao, rice, or cotton for export to the Old World. The plantation complex linked the fate of those slaves to the international market for the goods they produced. Indeed, the last New World society to abolish African slavery, Brazil, had been the first to use slaves for sugar production.

The readings in this chapter represent the Caribbean plantation complex at two different points in its history. In the first selection, an English colonist describes Barbados as it was undergoing the shift from

European servant labor to African slave labor in the mid-seventeenth century. In the second selection, a mercenary in Dutch Surinam describes a sugar colony of the late eighteenth century, with its white planter class dwarfed by a much larger population of rebellious slaves. As you read these passages, think about how they depict change in the colonization of the Caribbean over time. How does the shape of society in Barbados in the mid-seventeenth century anticipate the world of Surinam more than one hundred years later? What economic and social costs of producing sugar in the New World were exhibited in both of these societies?

SELECTION 1: Servants, Slaves, and Masters in Barbados

The English colony of Barbados was one of the first Caribbean islands to develop a plantation complex based on sugar cultivation. The English who colonized the island in the 1620s initially relied on a mixture of tobacco planting and subsistence agriculture to support themselves, and their labor force was made up mostly of European indentured servants. Between 1640 and 1660 they switched to sugar production, a transition that was accompanied by a shift in the labor force from white indentured servants to African slaves. By the latter part of the seventeenth century, Barbados was a prototypical sugar colony: Africans outnumbered Europeans by a ratio of 4:1, a small planter class controlled the land, and the island's population concentrated so much on producing sugar that it had to import foodstuffs from North America to feed itself.

Richard Ligon was a royalist exile from the English Civil Wars when he emigrated to Barbados in 1647. He lived there for several years before returning to England and publishing his description of the island in 1657. In addition to providing a detailed description of the social and economic order of Barbados, *A True & Exact History of the Island of Barbadoes* included a map of the island identifying the major plantations. The excerpt below is from the book's second edition, published in 1673. In it, Ligon describes the living and working conditions of the island's indentured servants, slaves, and planters.

The spelling has been modernized.

* · · * ~~~~~~~ * · · *

The Island is divided into three sorts of men, viz. Masters, Servants, and Slaves. The slaves and their posterity, being subject to their Masters forever, are kept and preserved with greater care than the servants, who are theirs but for five years, according to the law of the Island. So that for the time, the

From Richard Ligon, *A True & Exact History of the Island of Barbadoes*, second edition (London: Peter Parker and Thomas Guy, 1673), 43–51, 53–56.

servants have the worser lives, for they are put to very hard labor, ill lodging, and their diet very sleight. When we came first on the Island, some Planters themselves did not eat bone meat, above twice a week: the rest of the seven days, Potatoes, Loblolly [thick gruel], and Bonavist [a type of bean]. But the servants no bone meat at all, unless an Ox died: and then they were feasted, as long as that lasted. And till they had planted good store of Plantains, the *Negroes* were fed with this kind of food; but most of it Bonavist, and Loblolly, with some ears of Maize toasted, which food (especially Loblolly,) gave them much discontent: But when they had Plantains enough to serve them, they were heard no more to complain; for 'tis a food they take great delight in, and their manner of dressing, and eating it, is this: 'tis gathered for them (somewhat before it be ripe, for so they desire to have it,) upon *Saturday*, by the keeper of the Plantain grove; who is an able *Negro*, and knows well the number of those that are to be fed with this fruit; and as he gathers, lays them all together, till they fetch them away, which is about five a clock in the afternoon, for that day they break off work sooner by an hour: partly for this purpose, and partly for that the fire in the furnaces is to be put out, and the Ingenio [cylinders for crushing sugar cane] and the rooms made clean; besides they are to wash, shave and trim themselves against *Sunday*. But 'tis a lovely sight to see a hundred handsome *Negroes*, men and women, with every one a grass-green bunch of these fruits on their heads, every bunch twice as big as their heads, all coming in a train one after another, the black and green so well becoming one another. Having brought this fruit home to their own houses, and pilling off the skin of so much as they will use, they boil it in water, making it into balls, and so they eat it. One bunch a week is a *Negro's* allowance. To this, no bread nor drink, but water. Their lodging at night a board, with nothing under, nor any thing a top of them. They are happy people, whom so little contents. Very good servants, if they be not spoiled by the *English*. But more of them hereafter.

As for the usage of the Servants, it is much as the Master is, merciful or cruel. Those that are merciful, treat their Servants well, both in their meat, drink, and lodging, and give them such work, as is not unfit for Christians to do. But if the Masters be cruel, the Servants have very wearisome and miserable lives. Upon the arrival of any ship, that brings servants to the Island, the Planters go aboard; and having bought such of them as they like, send them with a guide to his Plantation; and being come, commands them instantly to make their Cabins, which they not knowing how to do, are to be advised by other of their servants, that are their Seniors; but, if they be churlish, and will not show them, or if materials be wanting, to make them Cabins, then they are to lye on the ground that night. These Cabins are to be made of sticks, withes [twigs], and Plantain leaves, under some little shade that may keep the rain off; Their suppers being a few Potatoes for meat, and water or Mobbie [an alcoholic beverage made from sweet potatoes] for drink. The next day they are rung out with a Bell to work, at six a clock in the morning, with a severe Overseer to command them, till the Bell ring again, which is at eleven a clock; and then they return, and are set to dinner, either with a mess of Loblolly, Bonavist, or Potatoes. At one a clock, they are rung out again to the field, there to work till six, and then home again, to a supper of the same. And if it chance to rain, and wet them through, they have no shift, but must lie so all night. If they put off their cloths, the cold of the night will strike into them; and if they be not strong men, this ill lodging will put them into a sickness: if they complain, they are beaten by the Overseer; if they resist, their time is doubled, I have seen an Overseer beat a Servant with a cane about the head, till the blood has followed, for a fault that is not worth the speaking of, and yet he must have patience, or worse will follow. Truly, I have seen such cruelty there done to Servants, as I did not think one Christian could have done to another. But, as discreeter and better natured men have come to rule there, the servants lives have been much bettered; for now, most of the servants lie in Hammocks, and in warm rooms, and when they come in wet, have shift of shirts and drawers, which is all the cloths they wear, and are fed with bone meat twice or thrice a week.

◆   ◆   ◆

A little before I came from thence, there was such a combination amongst them [servants], as the like was never seen there before. Their sufferings being grown to a great height, and their daily complainings to one another (of the intolerable burdens they labored under) being spread throughout the Island; at the last, some amongst them, whose spirits were not able to endure such slavery, resolved to break through it, or die in the act; and so conspired with some others of their acquaintance, whose sufferings were equal, if not above theirs; and their spirits no way inferior, resolved to draw as many of the discontented party into this plot, as possibly they could; and those of this persuasion, were the greatest numbers of Servants in the Island. So that a day was appointed to fall upon their Masters, and cut all their throats, and by that means, to make themselves not only freemen, but Masters of the Island. And so closely was this plot carried, as no discovery was made, till the day before they were to put it in act: And then one of them, either by the failing of his courage, or some new obligation from the love of his Master, revealed this long plotted conspiracy; and so by this timely advertisement, the Masters were saved: Justice *Hetersall* (whose servant this was) sending Letters to all his friends, and they to theirs, and so to one another, till they were all secured; and by, examination, found out the greatest part of them; whereof eighteen of the principal men in the conspiracy, and they the first leaders and contrivers of the plot, were put to death, for example to the rest. And the reason why they made examples of so many, was, they found these so haughty in their resolutions, and so incorrigible, as they were like enough to become Actors in a second plot, and so they thought good to secure them; and for the rest, to have a special eye over them.

It has been accounted a strange thing, that the *Negroes*, being more than double the numbers of the Christians that are there, and they accounted a bloody people, where they think they have power or advantages; and the more bloody, by how much they are more fearful than others: that these should not commit some horrid massacre upon the Christians, thereby to enfranchise themselves, and become Masters of the Island. But there are three reasons that take away this wonder; the one is, They are not suffered to touch or handle

any weapons: The other, That they are held in such awe and slavery, as t₁
are fearful to appear in any daring act; and seeing the mustering of our me
and hearing their Gun-shot, (than which nothing is more terrible to then ,
their spirits are subjugated to so low a condition, as they dare not look up to
any bold attempt. Besides these, there is a third reason, which stops all designs
of that kind, and that is, They are fetched from several parts of *Africa*, who
speak several languages, and by that means, one of them understands not another: For, some of them are fetched from *Guinny* [Guinea] and *Binny*
[Benin], some from *Cutchew* [?], some from *Angola*, and some from the River
of *Gambia*. And in some of these places where petty Kingdoms are, they sell
their Subjects, and such as they take in Battle, whom they make slaves; and
some mean men sell their Servants, their Children, and sometimes their Wives;
and think all good traffic, for such commodities as our Merchants send them.

When they are brought to us, the Planters buy them out of the Ship, where
they find them stark naked, and therefore cannot be deceived in any outward
infirmity. They choose them as they do Horses in a Market; the strongest,
youthfullest, and most beautiful, yield the greatest prices. Thirty pound sterling
is a price for the best man *Negroe*; and twenty-five, twenty-six, or twenty-seven
pound for a Woman; the Children are at easier rates. And we buy them so, as
the sexes may be equal; for, if they have more Men than Women, the men who
are unmarried will come to their Masters, and complain, that they cannot live
without Wives, and desire him, they may have them Wives, which satisfies
them for the present; and so they expect the good time: which the Master per-
forming with them, the bravest fellow is to choose first, and so in order, as they
are in place, and every one of them knows his better, and gives him the precedence, as Cows do one another, in passing through a narrow gate; for, the most
of them are as near beasts as may be, setting their souls aside. Religion they
know none; yet most of them acknowledge a God, as appears by their motions
and gestures: For, if one of them do another wrong, and he cannot revenge himself, he looks up to Heaven for vengeance, and holds up both his hands, as if
the power must come from thence, that must do him right.

❖   ❖   ❖

On *Sunday* they [slaves] rest, and have the whole day at their pleasure; and
the most of them use it as a day of rest and pleasure; but some of them who
will make benefit of that days liberty, go where the Mangrove trees grow, and
gather the bark, of which they make ropes, which they truck away for other
Commodities, as Shirts and Drawers.

In the afternoons on *Sundays*, they have their Music, which is of kettle
drums, and those of several sizes; upon the smallest the best Musician plays,
and the other come in as Choruses: the drum all men know, has but one tone;
and therefore variety of tunes have little to do in this music; and yet so
strangely they vary their time, as 'tis a pleasure to the most curious ears, and it
was to me one of the strangest noises that ever I heard made of one tone; and
if they had the variety of tune, which gives the greater scope in Music, as they
have of time, they would do wonders in that Arts. And if I had not fallen sick
before my coming away, at least seven months in one sickness, I had given

them some hints of tunes, which being understood, would have served as a great addition to their harmony; time without tune, is not an eighth part of the Science of Music.

I found *Macow* [a slave Ligon knew] very apt for it of himself, and one day coming into the house, (which none of the *Negroes* use to do, unless an Officer, as he was,) he found me playing on a Theorbo [a large stringed instrument], and singing to it, which he hearkened very attentively to; and when I had done, he took the Theorbo in his hand, and stroked one string, stopping it by degrees upon every fret, and finding the notes to vary, till it came to the body of the instrument; and that the nearer the body of the instrument he stopped, the smaller or higher the sound was, which he found was by the shortening of the string, considered with himself, how he might make some trial of this experiment upon such an instrument as he could come by; having no hope ever to have any instrument of this kind to practice on. In a day or two after, walking in the Plantain grove . . . I found this *Negro* (whose office it was to attend there) being the keeper of that grove, sitting on the ground, and before him a piece of large timber, upon which he had laid cross, six Billets, and having a handsaw and a hatchet by him, would cut the billets by little and little, till he had brought them to the tunes, he would fit them to; for the shorter they were, the higher the Notes, which he tried by knocking upon the ends of them with a stick, which he had in his hand. When I found him at it, I took the stick out of his hand, and tried the sound, finding the six billets to have six distinct notes, one above another, which put me in a wonder, how he of himself, should without teaching do so much. I then showed him the difference between flats and sharps, which he presently apprehended, as between *Fa*, and *Mi*: and he would have cut two more billets to those tunes, but I had then no time to see it done, and so left him to his own enquiries. I say thus much to let you see that some of these people are capable of learning Arts.

❖   ❖   ❖

On *Sundays* in the afternoon, their Music plays, and to dancing they go, the men by themselves, and the women by themselves, no mixed dancing. Their motions are rather what they aim at, than what they do; and by that means, transgress the less upon the *Sunday*; their hands having more of motion than their feet, and their heads more than their hands. They may dance a whole day, and never heat themselves; yet, now and then, one of the activest amongst them will leap bolt upright, and fall in his place again, but without cutting a caper. When they have danced an hour or two, the men fall to wrestle, (the Music playing all the while) and their manner of wrestling is, to stand like two Cocks, with heads as low as their hips; and thrusting their heads one against another, hoping to catch one another by the leg, which sometimes they do: But if both parties be weary, and that they cannot get that advantage, then they raise their heads, by pressing hard one against another, and so having nothing to take hold of but their bare flesh, they close, and grasp one another about the middle, and have one another in the hug, and then a fair fell is given on the back. And thus two or three couples of them are engaged at once, for an hour together, the women leave off their dancing, and come to be spectators of the sport.

When any of them die, they dig a grave, and at evening they bury him, clapping and wringing their hands, and making a doleful sound with their voices. They are a people of a timorous and fearful disposition, and consequently bloody, when they find advantages. If any of them commit a fault, give him present punishment, but do not threaten him; for it you do, it is an even lay, he will go hang himself, to avoid punishment.

What their other opinions are in the matter of Religion, I know not; but certainly, they are not altogether of the sect of the *Sadduces* [Jewish priests of ancient times]. For, they believe a Resurrection, and that they shall go into their own Country again, and have their youth renewed. And lodging this opinion in their hearts, they make it an ordinary practice, upon any great fright, or threatening of their Masters, to hang themselves.

But Colonel *Walrond* [a sugar planter] having lost three or four of his best *Negroes* this way, and in a very little time, caused one of their heads to be cut off, and set upon a pole a dozen foot high; and having done that, caused all his *Negroes* to come forth, and march round about this head, and bid them look on it, whether this were not the head of such an one that hanged himself. Which they acknowledging, he then told them, that they were in a main error, in thinking they went into their own Countries, after they were dead; for, this man's head was here, as they all were witnesses of; and how was it possible, the body could go without a head. Being convinced by this sad, yet lively spectacle, they changed their opinions; and after that, no more hanged themselves.

❖   ❖   ❖

Though there be a mark set upon these people [slaves], which will hardly ever be wiped off, as of their cruelties when they have advantages, and of their fearfulness and falseness; yet no rule so general but has its exception: for I believe, and I have strong motives to cause me to be of that persuasion, that there are as honest, faithful, and conscionable people amongst them, as amongst those of *Europe*, or any other part of the world.

A hint of this, I will give you in a lively example; and it was in a time when Victuals were scarce, and Plantains were not then so frequently planted, as to afford them enough. So that some of the high spirited and turbulent amongst them, began to mutiny, and had a plot, secretly to be revenged on their Master; and one or two of these were Firemen that made the fires in the furnaces, who were never without store of dry wood by them. These villains, were resolved to make fire to such part of the boiling-house [for refining sugar], as they were sure would fire the rest, and so burn all, and yet seem ignorant of the fact, as a thing done by accident. But this plot was discovered, by some of the others who hated mischief, as much as they loved it; and so traduced them, as they were forced to confess, what they meant should have been put in act the next night: so giving them condign [deserved] punishment, the Master gave order to the overseer that the rest should have a day's liberty to themselves and their wives, to do what they would; and withal to allow them a double proportion of victual for three days, both which they refused: which we all wondered at, knowing well how much they loved their liberties, and their meat, having been lately pinched of the one, and not having overmuch of the other; and therefore being doubtful what their meaning was in this, suspecting some discontent amongst them, sent for three or four of the best of them, and desired to know why they refused this favor that was offered them, but received such an answer: as we little expected; for they told us, it was not sullenness, or slighting the gratuity their Master bestowed on them, but they would not accept any thing as a recompense for doing that which became them in their duties to do, nor would they have him think, it was hope of reward, that made them to accuse their fellow servants, but an act of Justice, which they thought themselves bound in duty to do, and they thought themselves sufficiently rewarded in the Act. The substance of this, in such language as they had, they delivered, and poor *Sambo* [a slave leader] was the Orator; by whose example the others were led both in the discovery of the Plot, and refusal of the gratuity. And withal they said, that if it pleased their Master, at any time, to bestow a voluntary boon upon them, be it never so sleight, they would willingly and thankfully accept it: and this act might have beseemed the best Christians, though some of them were denied Christianity, when they earnestly sought it. Let others have what opinion they please, yet I am of this belief; that there are to be found amongst them, some who are as morally honest, as Conscionable, as humble, as loving to their friends, and as loyal to their Masters, as any that live under the Sun; and one reason they have to be so, is, they set on great value upon their lives: And this is all I can remember concerning the *Negroes*, except of their games, which I could never learn, because they wanted language to teach me.

❖   ❖   ❖

Now for the Masters, I have yet said but little, nor am able to say half of what they deserve. They are men of great abilities and parts, otherwise they could not go through, with such great works as they undertake; the managing of one of their Plantations, being a work of such a latitude, as will require a very good head-piece, to put in order, and continue it so.

I can name a Planter there, that feeds daily two hundred mouths, and keeps them in such order, as there are no mutinies amongst them; and yet of several nations. All these are to be employed in their several abilities, so as no one be idle. The first work to be considered, is Weeding, for unless that be done, all else (and the Planter too) will be undone, and if that be neglected but a little time, it will be a hard matter to recover it again, so fast will the weeds grow there. But the ground being kept clean, 'tis fit to bear any thing that Country will afford. After weeding comes Planting, and they account two seasons in the year best, and that is, *May* and *November*; but Canes are to be planted at all times, that they may come in, one field after another; otherwise, the work will stand still. And commonly they have in a field that is planted together, at one time, ten or a dozen acres. This work of planting and weeding, the Master himself is to see done; unless he have a very trusty and able Overseer; and without such a one, he will have too much to do. The next thing he is to consider, is the Ingenio [sugar mill], and what belongs to that; as, the Ingenio itself, which is the *Primum Mobile* of the whole work, the Boiling-house, with the Coppers and Furnaces, the Filling room, the Still-house, and Curing-house; and in all these, there are great casualties. If any thing in the Rollers, as the Gouges, Sockets, Sweeps, Cogs, or Braytrees, be at fault, the whole work stands still; or in the Boiling-house, if the Frame which holds the Coppers, (and is made of Clinkers, fastened with plaster of *Paris*) if by the violence of the heat from the Furnaces, these Frames crack or break, there is a stop in the work, till that be mended. Or if any of the Coppers have a mischance, and be burnt, a new one must presently be had, or there is a stay in the work. Or if the mouths of the Furnaces, (which are made of a sort of stone, which we have from *England*, and we call it there, high gate stone) if that, by the violence of the fire, be softened, that it molder away, there must new be provided, and laid in with much art, or it will not be. Or if the bars of Iron, which are in the floor of the Furnace, when they are red hot (as continually they are) the fire-man, throw great sides of wood in the mouths of the Furnace, hard and carelessly, the weight of those logs, will bend or break those bars, (though strongly made) and there is no repairing them, without the work stand still; for all these depend upon one another, as wheels in a Clock. Or if the Stills be at fault, the *kill-devil* [rum] cannot be made. But the main impediment and stop of all, is the loss of our Cattle, and amongst them there are such diseases, as I have known in one Plantation, thirty that have died in two days. And I have heard, that a Planter, an eminent man there, that cleared a dozen acres of ground, and railed it about for pasture, with intention, as soon as the grass was grown to a great height, to put in his working Oxen; which accordingly he did, and in one night fifty of them died; so that such a loss as this, is able to undo a Planter, that is not very well grounded. What it is that breeds these diseases, we cannot find, unless some of the Plants have a poisonous quality; nor have we yet found out cures for these diseases; Chickens guts being the best remedy was then known, and those being chopped or minced, and given them in a horn, with some liquor mixed to moisten it, was thought the best remedy: yet it recovered very few.

SELECTION 2: A Description of African Maroon Communities

Surinam, a colony on the northeastern shore of South America, was infamous for its slave rebellions and maroon communities. The English ceded Surinam to the Dutch in the 1660s in exchange for New Netherland (renamed New York by its new owners). Surinam's proximity to the Lesser Antilles and its sugar economy made it a part of the Caribbean plantation complex. The average sugar estate there was home to more than 200 slaves, and Africans outnumbered Europeans twenty-five to one. Maroon communities spawned by rebels and runaways from these plantations constantly harassed the colony's Dutch proprietors.

John Gabriel Stedman was a Scottish military officer who served in the Netherlands during the latter eighteenth century. Between 1773 and 1777, he lived in Surinam as part of an expeditionary force sent by the Dutch to fight rebellious slaves and to disperse the maroon communities that sheltered them.

That Stedman lived to tell his tale was no small feat; less than 15 percent of the European soldiers involved in this war returned home. Stedman eventually settled in England, where he published his narrative of the Surinam expedition in 1796. In the excerpts that follow, he describes the maroon communities he was sent to subdue and the system of sugar production they were rebelling against.

No sooner was this unfortunate colony delivered from its outward enemies than it was attacked by inward ones of a more fierce and desperate nature. In former times, the Carib and other Indians had often disturbed this settlement, but ever since a peace was established after the arrival of Governor Sommelsdyck in this colony, they have inviolably kept it, living in the greatest harmony and friendship with the Europeans.

The revolted Negro slaves are the foes I now intend to speak of, who may with truth be called the terror of this settlement, if not the total loss of it. From the earliest remembrance, some runaway Negroes had skulked in the woods of Surinam, but these were of very small consideration till about the year 1726 or 1728, when with their hostile numbers increasing, and mostly being armed with (in addition to bows and arrows) lances and firelocks which they had pillaged from the estates, they committed continual outrages and depredations upon the coffee and sugar plantations. These they did both from a spirit of revenge for the barbarous and inhuman treatment which they had formerly received from their masters and with a view toward carrying away plunder such as gunpowder, balls, hatchets, etc., in order to provide for their subsistence and defense. These Negroes were mostly settled in the upper parts of the rivers Coppename and Saramacca, from which last they take the name of the Saramaka Rebels, which distinguishes them from other gangs that have since revolted.

Several commands of military and plantation people were now sent out against them but were of very small effect in bringing them to reason by promises, or in getting them rooted out by blows. In 1730, a most shocking execution of eleven poor captives was experimented—to terrify, if possible, their companions, and thus to make them return to their duty. One man was hanged alive upon a gibbet with an iron hook struck through his ribs, and two others, being chained to stakes, were burnt to death by slow fire. Six women were broken alive upon the rack, and two girls were decapitated, through which tortures they went without uttering a sigh. In 1733, three Indians were also decapitated, for having killed three French deserters, which shows how far the civil law now extends in this country.

But I must return to the Negroes, on whom it appears the inhuman carnage that I have mentioned above had very little effect, indeed quite the reverse, since

From John Gabriel Stedman, *Stedman's Surinam: Life in an Eighteenth-Century Slave Society*, edited by Richard Price and Sally Price (Baltimore: The Johns Hopkins University Press, 1992), 25–32, 140–142.

it enraged the Saramaka Rebels to such a degree that they became dreadful to the colonists. This lasted for several years successively until the colonists—no longer being able to support the expense and fatigue of sallying out against them in the woods, besides the great losses and terrors which they so frequently sustained by their invasions—at last resolved to treat for peace with their sable enemies.

Governor Mauricius, who was at this period at the head of the Colony, accordingly sent out a strong detachment to the rebel settlement on the Saramacca River for the purpose of effecting, if possible, the so much wished-for peace. After some skirmishing with the struggling Rebel parties, the detachment at last arrived at their headquarters, where they demanded and obtained a parley. At this time, in 1749, a treaty of peace consisting of ten or twelve articles was actually concluded between them, as had been done before in 1739 with the rebels on the island of Jamaica.

The chief of the Saramaka Rebels was a Creole Negro called Captain Adu, who now received from the Governor as a present a fine large cane with a massive silver pommel, on which were engraved the arms of Surinam, as a mark of their further independence and as preliminary to the other presents that were to be sent out the following year, as stipulated by the treaty, particularly arms and ammunition, once the peace was finally concluded. To the Governor, Adu then returned a handsome bow with a complete case of arrows, which had been manufactured by his own hands, as a token that during that time, on his side, all enmity was ceased and at an end.

This affair gave great satisfaction to some, indeed to most of the inhabitants of Surinam, who now thought themselves and their effects perfectly secure, while others looked on this treaty as a most hazardous resource, nay, as a sure step to the Colony's inevitable ruin. Be that as it may, I cannot help thinking, with the latter, that regardless of Governor Mauricius' good intentions, nothing can be more dangerous than making a forced friendship with people who, by the most abject slavery and bad usage, were provoked to break their chains and shake off the yoke to seek revenge and liberty, and who by this trust being put in them have it in their power to become from day to day more formidable. Nor can I help thinking, on the contrary, that the insurrection having already risen to such a pitch, the colonists ought to have continued fighting against it while they had a nerve to strain, or a hand left to draw a trigger—not from a motive of cruelty, but for the political good of so fine a settlement. After all, if taken at the worst, it is still better to lose one's life with one's fortune, sword in hand, than to live in the perpetual dread of losing both by one general massacre.

That the best of all would be never to have driven these poor creatures to such extremities by constant ill treatment speaks for itself. At the same time, it is certainly true that to govern the Coast-of-Guinea Negroes well, nay, even for their own benefit, the strictest discipline is absolutely necessary. But I ask: Why in the name of humanity should they undergo the most cruel racks and tortures, entirely depending upon the despotic caprice of their proprietors and overseers, which it is well known is too generally the case throughout the West Indies? And why should their bitter complaints be never heard by the magistrate that has it in his power to redress them? Because His Worship himself is a planter and scorns to be against his own interest. Such is most truly the case, and such is no less truly lamentable, not only for the sake of the master and the man, but also and chiefly for that of one of the finest colonies in the West Indies being, by such unfair proceedings, put in the utmost danger and difficulty. However, it is to be supposed that exceptions do here take place, as they do in all other circumstances—God forbid they should not—and I myself have seen and even at different times been eyewitness where plantation slaves were treated with the utmost humanity, where the hand of the master was seldom lifted but to caress them, and where the eye of the slave sparkled with gratitude and affection.

Let us now step forward and see what were the fruits of making peace with the Saramaka Rebels. In 1750, which was the year thereafter, the promised presents were dispatched to Captain Adu, but the detachment that carried them was attacked on their march and every soul of them murdered on the spot by a desperate Negro called Zamzam who, not having been consulted at the peacemaking, had since put himself at the head of a strong party. He now carried off the whole stock (consisting of arms and ammunition, checked linens, canvas cloth, hatchets, saws and other carpenter's tools, besides salt beef, pork, spirits, etc.) as his own private property. Moreover, Adu, not having received his presents, suspected that the delay was intended to cut their throats, by means of a new supply of troops which he was told was coming from Europe.

By this accident the peace was immediately broken, cruelties and ravages increased more than ever, and death and destruction once more raged throughout the Colony. In 1757, things were come from bad to worse (while one Mr. Crommelin was Governor of this colony), a new revolt having broken out in the Tempaty Creek among the Negroes, owing to nothing but their being so cruelly treated by their masters. This fresh insurrection was of such serious consequence—they having joined themselves to 1600 other runaway Negroes already settled in eight different villages between the Tempaty and the River Marawina, along the banks of the Djuka Creek—that after repeated battles and skirmishes (they being all well armed, as I have mentioned) without much success for the colonists or any hopes of quelling it, they saw themselves once more reduced to suing for peace with their own slaves, as they had done in 1749 with the Rebels of Saramaka (but which peace was, as I have said, broken in 1750 by the irascible conduct of the Rebel Negro Zamzam).

To let the whole world now see that black men are not such brutes as the generality of white ones imagine, I must beg leave to mention a few of the principal ceremonies that attended the ratification of this peace. In 1760, the first thing was another parley, proposed by the colonists. This was, to be sure, agreed to by the Rebels, and these latter not only desired but absolutely insisted that the Dutch should send them yearly (among a great variety of other articles) a handsome quantity of firearms and ammunition, as specified in a long list made up in broken English by a Negro whose name was Boston and who was one of their captains.

Next, Governor Crommelin sent two commissioners, Mr. Sober and Mr. Abercrombie, who marched through the woods escorted by a few military etc., to carry some presents to the Rebels preliminary to the ratification of the peace. At the arrival of the above gentlemen in the Rebel camp at the Djuka Creek, they were introduced to a very handsome Negro called Araby who was the chief of them all, and born in the forest among the last 1600 that I have mentioned. He received them very politely, and taking them by the hand, desired they would sit down by his side upon the green, at the same time assuring them they needed not be under any apprehensions of evil, since coming in so good a cause, no one intended or even dared to hurt them.

But when the above-mentioned Captain Boston perceived that they had brought a parcel of trinkets—such as knives, scissors, combs, and small looking-glasses—and had forgotten the principal articles in question, viz., gunpowder, firearms, and ammunition, he resolutely stepped up to the commissioners and asked in a thundering voice if the Europeans imagined that the Negroes could live on combs and looking-glasses, adding that one of each was fully sufficient to let them all see their faces with satisfaction, while a single gallon of *mansanny*, viz., gunpowder, should have been accepted as a proof of their trust. But since that had been omitted, they should, with his will, never more return to their countrymen till every article of his list should be fulfilled. A Negro captain called Quacoo now interfered, saying that these gentlemen were only the messengers of their Governor and Court, and as they could not be answerable for their masters' proceedings they should certainly go back to where they came from without hurt or molestation, and not even he, Captain Boston, should dare to oppose them.

The chief of the Rebels then ordered silence and desired Mr. Abercrombie to make up a list himself of such articles as he, Araby, should name him, which that gentleman having done, the Rebels not only gave him and his companions leave peaceably to return with it to town, but their Governor and Court a whole year to deliberate on what they were to choose—peace or war. They swore unanimously that during that interval all animosity should cease on their side, after which, having entertained them in the best manner their situation in the woods afforded, they wished them a happy journey to Paramaribo.

Upon this occasion, one of the Rebel officers represented to Mr. Sober and to Mr. Abercrombie what a pity it was that the Europeans, who pretend to be a civilized nation, should be so much the occasion of their own ruin by their inhuman cruelties towards their slaves.

> We desire you (continued this Negro) to tell your Governor and your Court that in case they want to raise no new gangs of Rebels, they ought to take care that the planters keep a more watchful eye over their own property and not so often trust them to the hands of a parcel of drunken managers and overseers, who by wrongfully whipping the Negroes, debauching their wives and children, neglecting the sick, etc., are the ruin of the Colony and willfully drive to the woods such quantities of stout, handsome people who by their sweat got your subsistence and without whose hands your colony must drop to nothing, and to whom at last in this pitiful manner you are glad to come and ply for friendship.

Mr. Abercrombie now begged of them to be accompanied with one or two of their principal officers to Paramaribo, where he promised they should be vastly well treated etc., but the chief, Araby, answered him with a smile that there would be sufficient time a year thereafter, once the peace was thoroughly concluded, and that then even his youngest son should be at their service to receive his education among them. And as for his subsistence and even for that of his descendants, he should take the sole care upon himself without ever giving the Christians the smallest trouble. After this, the commissioners left the Rebels and all arrived safe and sound at Paramaribo.

The year of deliberation being ended, the Governor and Court sent out two fresh commissioners to the Negro camp to bring the so much wished-for peace to a thorough conclusion. After a great deal of canvassing and ceremonies on both sides, with the presents being promised to the Negroes according to their wishes (as some nations pay tribute to the Emperor of Morocco), at last it was finally agreed on. And as a proof of their affection for the Europeans, the Negroes indiscriminately insisted that, during their remaining stay in the Rebel camp, each of the commissioners should take for his constant companion one of their handsomest young women. They also treated them with game, fish, fruit, and the best of all that the forest afforded, entertaining them without intermission with music, dancing, and cheering, besides firing one volley after another, after which they returned contented to town.

This done, the above presents were sent to the Negroes near the River Marawina by Mr. Mayer, escorted by six hundred men, soldiers and slaves, and which gentleman had nearly baffled the whole business by—contrary to his orders and from a pusillanimous principle—delivering all the presents to the Rebels without receiving the hostages in return. Fortunately, however, Araby kept his word and sent down four of his best officers as pledges to Paramaribo. By this the peace was perfectly accomplished, when a treaty of twelve or fourteen articles was signed by two white commissioners and sixteen of Araby's black captains in 1761, which ceremony took place on the Plantation Auka on the River Surinam where all the parties met—this being the spot of rendezvous appointed for the purpose, after four different embassies had been sent by the Europeans to the Negroes.

But signing this treaty alone was still not looked on as sufficient by the Rebel chief Araby and his people, who all immediately swore an oath, and insisted on the commissioners doing the same, after the manner in practice by themselves, not trusting entirely, they said, in that made use of by the Christians, which they had seen too often broken, whereas for a Negro to break his oath is absolutely without example (of this, at least, I never saw or heard of an instance during all the time that I lived in the Colony), which plainly argues that the Africans are not so entirely destitute of morality and even religion as a number of ignorant Europeans imagine, and which I hope still more clearly to demonstrate on other occasions.

The solemnity made use of on this day consisted in both parties, with a lance or penknife, letting themselves a few drops of blood from the arm into a calabash or cup with clean spring water, into which were also mixed a few particles of dry earth, and of which all present were obliged to drink a draught upon the spot, Europeans and Africans without exception, which they call drinking each other's blood. This was done after having first scattered a few drops upon the ground, when their *gadoman* or priest, with up-cast eyes and outstretched arms, took Heaven and Earth as witness, and with a most audible voice and awful manner, invoked God's curse and malediction on all such as should first break this sacred treaty made between them, from that moment henceforth to all eternity, to which the multitude answered "*Da so,*" which signifies in their language "Amen." The solemnity being ended, Araby and each captain was presented with a fine large cane and silver pommel on which were engraved the arms of the Colony (to distinguish them from other Negroes, as had already been done with the Saramaka captain, Adu, in 1749).

The above-mentioned Negroes are called Aukas [Ndjukas], after the name of the plantation where the peace articles were signed, by which name they are distinguished from the Saramakas, whom I have already described.

The Auka Negroes have indeed behaved indifferently well ever since the foregoing treaty—fortunately for the Colony of Surinam, from which they must yearly receive (as I have said, among a number of other articles) a handsome quantity of ball and gunpowder.

This same year, 1761, a peace was also a second time concluded with the Saramaka Rebels who were at present commanded by a Negro called Wii instead of their former chief, Adu, who was dead. But, unfortunately, this second peace was broken by a Rebel captain called Musinga, who had received none of the presents, and which presents had been again on their way to the chief, Wii, as they had been formerly on their way to the chief, Adu, cut off and captured by the individual and enterprising devil, Zamzam. However, with this difference: this time none of the detachment that were sent with them were murdered as on the preceding time, or even one single person hurt.

The above Captain Musinga now fought desperately against the colonists. He gave battle face to face and beat back above 150 of their best troops, which were sent out against him, killing numbers and taking away all their baggage and ammunition. However, very soon after this, when the real cause of Musinga's discontent became known, means were found and adopted to pacify this gallant warrior, by making him receive and share the presents sent out by the colonists on an equal footing with his brother heroes, when peace was a third and last time concluded in 1762 between the Saramaka Rebels and the Colony, which has providentially been kept sacred and inviolable, the same as with the Negroes of Auka, to this day.

On their arrival at Paramaribo, the hostages and chief officers of both the above-mentioned Negro cohorts were entertained at the Governor's own table, having previously paraded in state through the town, accompanied by His Excellency, and in his own private carriage.

By their capitulation to the Dutch, the above Auka and Saramaka Rebels must yearly receive, as I have mentioned, a handsome quantity of arms and ammunition from the Colony, for which those have received in return the Negroes' promises of being their faithful allies, to deliver up all deserters (for which they receive proper bounties), never to appear armed at Paramaribo above five or six at a time, and also to keep their settlements at a proper distance from the town or plantations—the Saramaka Negroes at the River Saramacca, and the Auka Negroes near the River Marawina, where one or two white men called Postholders were to reside among them as a species of envoy. Both these tribes were now supposed to be in all some three thousand people. However, only several years later their numbers were computed by those who were sent to visit their settlements to be no less than fifteen or twenty thousand people (including wives and children). They have already become overbearing and even insolent, brandishing their silver-headed canes under the noses of the inhabitants by way of derision and independence, forcing from them liquors and very often money and, if they refuse, putting them in mind how (when they were their slaves) they murdered their parents and their husbands. From what I have just mentioned, and with their numbers increasing from day to day, I must conclude that should ever the peace be once more broken, the above new allies will become the most dreadful foes that ever the Colony of Surinam will have to deal with. I would mention besides the example and encouragement these treaties give other slaves to revolt even without provocation against their masters, and obstinately fight for the same privileges. At the same time, those planters who dare so inhumanely to persecute their slaves without a cause deserve, in my opinion, no better treatment, and this, most assuredly, too often is the consequence.

◆   ◆   ◆

Having dispatched these letters to Holland, and having now had the opportunity also to see the whole process of a sugar plantation, I shall here give an accurate account of it.

The buildings usually consist of an elegant dwelling house for the planter, outhouses for the overseer and bookkeeper, besides a carpenter's lodge, kitchens, storehouses, etc., and stables if the sugar mills are worked by horses or mules—which were not required on the Hope [River] where the wheels went round by water, being saved in canals that surround the estate during the spring tides, by the means of sluices, or floodgates, and which, being let open when the water in the river is very low, the contents run out like a deluge, and set the whole work a-going.

As to the construction of a sugar mill (which is generally built at the amazing expense of from four to seven or eight thousand pounds). I cannot enter into the particular description of it, but shall only say that the large- or water wheel, which moves perpendicularly, corresponds with another large wheel that is placed in a horizontal direction, and this again with three perpendicular cylinders or rollers of cast iron that are under it, supported on a strong beam and placed so close together that, when the whole is in motion, they imbibe and crush to atoms whatever comes between them, and in which manner the sugar cane is bruised, to separate the juice or liquor from the trash.

Those mills that are worked by cattle are also made on the same construction, with this difference only, that the horses or mules answer the purpose of the horizontal wheel by dragging round a large beam, like the hand of a dial.

If the water mills can work the fastest, and are the cheapest, they must wait for the opportunity of the spring tides, whereas the cattle mills have the advantage of always being ready for use, whenever the proprietor thinks it convenient.

Adjoining the mill house is a large apartment (both being built of brick) in which are fixed by masonry the coppers or large cauldrons to boil the liquid sugar, which are usually five in number. On the opposite side are the coolers, being large square flat-bottomed wooden vessels, into which the sugar is put from the cauldrons so that it may cool before it goes into the hogsheads, which are placed next to them on strong channeled rafters that receive the molasses as it drips from the sugar and conduct it into a square cistern underneath the whole, and made for the purpose of preserving it.

Adjoining this apartment is a distillery, where the dross or scum taken from the boiling sugar is converted into a kind of rum, which I have before mentioned and is generally known by the name of kill-devil throughout the Colony.

Having thus far described the buildings (besides which all estates in Surinam keep a tent-boat and several other small craft with a covered dock to keep them dry and repair them), I shall now say something of the grounds, and the cultivation of the cane.

The sugar estates in this colony often consist of more than five or six hundred acres, the parts for cultivation being divided into squares, where the pieces of cane (about one foot long) are stuck in the ground in an oblique position but in straight lines, which is usually done in the rainy season, when the earth is well-soaked and most rich. Here the shoots that spring from the joints grow for a time of twelve or sixteen months, when they become yellow, thick like a German flute, from six to ten feet in height, and jointed, forming a very beautiful appearance, with pale green leaves like those of a leek, but longer and denticulated, which hang down when the crop begins to be ripe for cutting. During all this period, pulling up the weeds is the principal business of the slaves, to prevent the canes from being impoverished by their luxurious progress.

After this, the sugar canes are cut in pieces of three or four feet long, and (being divested of their leaves) tied in bundles or faggots, when they are next transported to the mill by water (which shows the double usefulness of the canals) and where, within the space of twenty-four hours, they ought to be bruised, to prevent the juice from fermenting and becoming sour by the great heat of the climate.

I must not forget to say that some sugar estates have more than four hundred slaves, the expense of buying whom, and erecting the buildings (the ground excepted) frequently amounts to twenty or twenty-five thousand pounds sterling.

We shall now examine the progress of the sugar cane through the mill, where it is bruised between the working cylinders or rollers (which are, as I said, three in number), through which it passes twice, viz., once it enters and once it returns, when it is changed to trash, and its pithy substance into liquid, which is conducted, as it is extracted, through a channeled beam, from the mill to the adjoining boiling house, where it is received into a species of wooden cistern.

So very dangerous is the work of those Negroes who enter the canes in the rollers, that should one of their fingers catch between them, which frequently happens by inadvertency, the whole arm is instantly shattered to atoms, if not part of the body, for which reason a hatchet is generally kept ready to chop off the limb, before the working of the mill can be stopped. The other danger is that should a Negro slave dare to taste that sugar which he produces by the sweat of his brow, he would run the hazard of paying the expense by some hundred lashes, if not by the breaking out of all his teeth. Such are the hardships, and dangers, to which the sugar-making Negroes are exposed.

From the above wooden cistern, the liquor is let into the first copper cauldron, filtering through a kind of grating to keep back the trash that may have escaped from the mill; here, having been boiled for some time and been skimmed, it is put in the next cauldron, and so forth, till it reaches the fifth or last, where it gets that thickness or consistency which is required to put it in the coolers. It is here to be observed that a few pounds of lime and alum are thrown into the cauldrons to make it work, and granulate, while the whole is well mixed, and boiled gradually stronger and stronger, as it proceeds towards the end, or the last cauldron.

Being next put in the wooden coolers, the sugar is well stirred about so that the grain or body is equally dispersed throughout the vessels where, when it becomes cold, it has the appearance of being frozen, being candied all over, with a brown glazed consistency, not unlike pieces of highly polished walnut tree.

From these coolers, it is next put in the hogsheads (which weigh, at an average, one thousand pounds each), where it then settles and where (through the crevasses and small holes made in the bottoms) it is purged of its remaining liquid contents, which are called molasses (which, as I have said, are received in an underground cistern), after which the sugar has undergone its last operations, and is fit for transportation to Europe, where it is refined, and cast into loaves, etc. I shall only further observe that the larger is the grain, the better is allowed to be the sugar. N.B. the best estates make six hundred barrels.

I will now conclude this account by once more repeating that no soil in the world is so very rich and proper for the cultivation of the sugar cane as is Surinam, or indeed all Guiana, which is in a manner never exhausted, and produces at an average three or four hogsheads of sugar per acre.

⤫ Discussion Questions ⤫

1. How does Ligon compare the working life of servants and slaves in Barbados? How does he compare these two groups in terms of their motivations and methods of resistance to their masters' authority?

2. Where in Ligon's account of Barbados do you see evidence of cultural adaptations made between the island's European and African inhabitants? How do the slaves express their African cultural heritage in their music, religion, and recreation?

3. According to Stedman, why were slaves in Surinam in a constant state of rebellion? Why did planters there find it necessary to negotiate with such rebels? Where do you see evidence in these diplomatic negotiations of cultural exchange and adaptation between Europeans and Africans? Why

do you suppose slave rebellion was far more prevalent in Stedman's Surinam than Ligon's Barbados?

4. Using Ligon and Stedman, explain the process of sugar production, from harvesting cane to export. What dangers were involved for workers in the mills? How did planters manage the production process, and how did they attempt to limit their losses?

Suggested Readings

For the origins and nature of the Caribbean plantation complex, see Philip D. Curtin, *The Rise and Fall of the Plantation Complex: Essays in Atlantic History* (Cambridge, England: Cambridge University Press, 1990), and Robin Blackburn, *The Making of New World Slavery* (London: Verso Press, 1997). Sidney Mintz's *Sweetness and Power: The Place of Sugar in Modern History* (New York: Penguin Books, 1985) places the plantation complex within a wider, transatlantic context of sugar production and consumption. For more on Richard Ligon's Barbados, see Richard S. Dunn, *Sugar and Slaves: The Rise of the Planter Class in the English West Indies, 1624–1713* (Chapel Hill, N.C: University of North Carolina Press, 1972). The operation of the Caribbean plantation complex at the time of John Stedman's sojourn in Surinam is described in Arthur L. Stinchcombe, *Sugar Island Slavery in the Age of Enlightenment: The Political Economy of the Caribbean World* (Princeton, N.J.: Princeton University Press, 1995). Jack P. Greene explores the Caribbean's impact on the colonization of North America in "Colonial South Carolina and the Caribbean Connection," in *Imperatives, Behaviors, and Identities: Essays in Early American Cultural History* (Charlottesville, Va.: University of Virginia Press, 1992), 68–86.

Slave resistance, rebellion, and maroonage have received much attention in histories of the plantation complex. For an overview, see Richard Price, *Maroon Societies: Rebel Slave Communities in the Americas* (Garden City, N.Y: Anchor Press, 1973); for a more focused look at the maroons encountered by Stedman, see Price's *The Guiana Maroons* (Baltimore: Johns Hopkins University Press, 1976). For other New World maroon communities, see Mavis C. Campbell, *The Maroons of Jamaica, 1655–1796: A History of Resistance, Collaboration, and Betrayal* (Granby, Mass.: Bergin and Garvey, 1988), and Jane Landers, *Black Society in Spanish Florida* (Urbana, Ill.: University of Illinois Press, 1999).

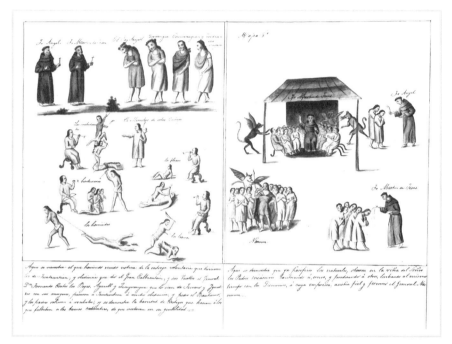

Spanish Missionaries and Indian Converts in Mexico

These images from Mexico tell the viewer much about how Spanish missionaries approached their work (see Selection 1). In the upper left, two missionaries convert the village's leading families, who bow in submission to their new spiritual overlords. The scene below them depicts the sins that the Spanish associated with unconverted Indians: indolence, superstition, murder, lasciviousness, and disobedience. The scene on the right depicts the missionaries attending to their converts so as to protect them from the evils of backsliding and paganism, represented by the winged demonic figures in the background. How does this scene of conversion compare with those presented in the opening illustrations for Chapters 3 and 10?

Source: Converting the Indians. From Pablo Beaumont, Cronica de Michoacan. (Rare Manuscript Division, New York Public Library)

The Spanish and Portuguese in the Americas

Introduction

Columbus's voyage of 1492 sparked a European competition for New World empire that lasted for over 300 years. Spain and Portugal led this scramble, and for most of the sixteenth century, the Old World's invasion of the New was shaped by these two powers. The Iberian Peninsula's position as a gateway between the Mediterranean Sea and the Atlantic Ocean helps explain this development. Spain and Portugal had strong maritime industries that enjoyed the patronage of their rulers and investment from merchants in Italian city-states such as Genoa and Venice. Also, the Iberian Peninsula had been a crossroads for peoples from Europe, North Africa, and the Near East for centuries—fertile ground for the exchange of the geographic and technical knowledge necessary to support oceanic navigation. Lastly, the Peninsula's southwestern orientation into the Atlantic gave its inhabitants a natural advantage in exploring sea routes to sub-Saharan Africa, Asia, and eventually America. For a century prior to Columbus's voyage, the Spanish and Portuguese were conquering and colonizing islands in the eastern Atlantic, and that experience provided important precedents for their forays into the Americas.

Thus, there are many good reasons to consider the Spanish and Portuguese together when studying the Atlantic World, but important differences did exist in their approaches to colonization. The Spanish organized their American enterprise on a model inherited from their centuries-long *Reconquista* of the Iberian Peninsula from Islamic Moors. Treating Native Americans in much the same way as they had the Moors and native peoples of the Canary Islands, the Spanish subjugated them militarily, planted colonists to occupy the new territory, and then incorporated the conquered people into Spanish society through a combination of forced labor and religious conversion. The Portuguese, on the other hand, modeled their invasion of America after commercial enterprises they pursued elsewhere in the world, trading with the natives and eventually transplanting the plantation complex from their eastern Atlantic colonies to Brazil.

In 1494, before the Spanish and Portuguese even comprehended the geographic extent of the Americas, they agreed in the Treaty of Tordesillas to a north-to-south boundary line through the Atlantic Ocean that would divide their overseas dominions. As subsequent voyages of exploration would discover, the bulk of the Americas fell west of this line and therefore into Spanish hands. The exception was Brazil, which jutted far enough eastward to fall under Portuguese jurisdiction, which also included West Africa and the trade routes around the Cape of Good Hope into the Indian Ocean. This artificial border had important ramifications for peoples throughout the Atlantic World. The Spanish found themselves nominal lords over a dominion populated by millions of Indians and containing untold wealth; within a generation, a lethal combination of Spanish germs and military power subdued the mighty Aztecs and Incas and turned their homelands into the center of Spain's overseas empire. The Portuguese, on the other hand, concentrated their energies as much in the East as in the West, creating a global trading empire in which Brazil played a role as an exporter of sugar and importer of African slaves (see Figure 6.1).

Spanish expansion in the Americas was motivated by the pursuit of mineral wealth. Spanish adventurers flocked to the Caribbean in the wake of Columbus looking for the source of the gold they found in jewelry worn by the natives. They joined small expeditionary forces known as *entradas*, usually organized under the leadership of a single man and financed privately by investors and participants. The most spectacular successes for such enterprises occurred in Mexico from 1519 to 1521, when Hernando Cortés conquered the Aztecs, and in Peru from 1532 to 1533, when Francisco Pizzaro conquered the Incas, but many others ended disastrously, as hostile Indians and unfamiliar terrain put an end to the fortune seekers.

After the initial wave of conquest, mining became the central economic activity of Spain's New World empire. To meet the insatiable demand for workers in Peruvian and Mexican mines, the Spanish transplanted to America the *encomienda*, a system of tribute labor they had imposed on conquered peoples in Iberia and the Canary Islands. Typically, Indian villages paid this tribute by sending individuals to work for the Spanish on a rotating basis during the course of the year. While Spanish mines demanded the most labor, Indians also worked on Spanish rural estates (*haciendas*) and in the workshops of Spanish towns. The Church helped maintain this system by converting Indians to Christianity and encouraging them to submit to Spanish authority. Indians resisted these impositions, sometimes in organized rebellions that cost many lives, but more often in less obvious ways, such as continuing to practice their native rituals and beliefs in secret or under the guise of observing Christian ceremonies.

The Spanish reliance on Indian labor led to a close association between invaders and natives that produced a sizable population of *mestizos*, the offspring of Spanish men and native women. The Spanish

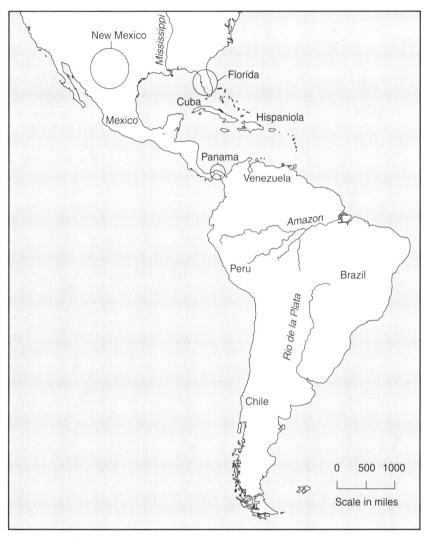

Figure 6.1   Iberian America
Spanish and Portuguese Possessions in Central and South America.
Source: Adapted from: James Lockhart and Stuart B. Schwartz, *Early Latin America: A History of Colonial Spanish America and Brazil* (Cambridge, Eng.: Cambridge University Press, 1983), 255.

also brought African slaves with them to the Americas, and a smaller population of mulattoes, free blacks, and enslaved Africans found a place in Spanish American society, chiefly as domestic servants, retainers, and urban workers. By 1700, Spanish America featured an amalgam of European, Indian, and African peoples, with a small Spanish population on top, a much larger free *mestizo* population in the middle, and bottom rungs occupied by mulattoes, Indians, and Africans living in varying degrees of submission to their Spanish rulers.

The Portuguese took a very different approach to New World colonization. With no native empires to plunder for gold and silver, Brazil seemed to offer little more than a place to cut wood and resupply ships. In keeping with their methods in Africa and Asia, the Portuguese built coastal forts in Brazil to trade with the natives and keep out European rivals, but their presence in Brazil was negligible until colonists began planting sugar there in the mid-sixteenth century. Faced with the same labor shortage as the Spanish, the Portuguese carried African slaves across the Atlantic to work their plantations, and by the seventeenth century they had created the first full-blown slave society in the Western Hemisphere. Intermarriage and sexual relations between the Portuguese and Africans in Brazil created new social categories. These groups were dominated by the offspring of Portuguese men and African women, who were known collectively as *pardos*. Like Spanish America's *mestizos*, *pardos* occupied an important place in Brazilian society, often working as producers of subsistence crops and as urban craftsmen. They represented the middling status between freedom and slavery made possible by intermarriage and cultural assimilation.

As the Atlantic economy expanded and diversified, the Spanish and Portuguese experiences in the Americas tended to converge. Mining, for example, became a central part of the economy of southern Brazil after the discovery of gold in the interior region of Minas Gerais in the 1690s. Likewise, in the late colonial period, Cuban sugar plantations became an important source of Spanish wealth. Perhaps the most significant point of convergence was the role that peoples of mixed-race descent came to play in Spanish and Portuguese colonies. The Spanish and Portuguese shared a legal tradition that encouraged the incorporation of strangers and former enemies into society by religious conversion, and in the case of slaves, by allowing them to negotiate terms of self-purchase with their owners. In Iberian America, this practice meant that a non-European's skin color or other physical features could never definitively fix his or her status in either freedom or slavery. While full equality with their European rulers was an impossibility, *mestizos*, *pardos*, Indians, and Africans could—by way of marriage, conversion, and emancipation—gain a legal and social status suspended somewhere between unconditional freedom and abject enslavement.

The readings in this chapter examine the colonization of Iberian America through the lens of encounters between the colonizers and Native Americans or Africans. In the first reading, an Indian and Spanish official offer differing perspectives on the Pueblo Revolt in New Mexico, the most famous episode of Indian resistance to Spanish rule in North America. The second selection looks at plantation society in Brazil and dissects the racial and social hierarchy there. As you read these sources, look for similarities between them that illustrate the Iberian approach to overseas expansion. How do the Spanish and Portuguese regard Africans and Native Americans? How do they create new social groups out of their encounters with them? What are the points of tension within those social orders?

SELECTION 1: Two Views of the Pueblo Revolt in New Mexico, 1680

The Spanish established their first settlements north of the Rio Grande in 1598. Throughout the seventeenth century, this province of New Mexico remained an outpost of Spanish power, with a small population of settlers and Franciscan priests centered in Santa Fe, claiming lordship over the villages of Pueblo Indians surrounding them. Under the *encomienda* system, the Spanish forced the Pueblos to labor on their *haciendas*, while Franciscan priests established missions in their villages to eradicate native spiritual beliefs and replace them with Christianity.

In 1680, after years of enduring forced labor and religious persecution under their new overlords, the Pueblos executed a carefully planned rebellion against the Spanish, killing several hundred colonists and approximately two-thirds of the missionaries. The surviving colonists fled the province, crossing the Rio Grande back into Mexico. The Spanish did not return until the 1690s, when they faced more armed resistance before finally reasserting control over the region. In the following reading, two eyewitnesses describe the Pueblo Revolt. First, an aged Indian named Don Pedro Nanboa testifies before the Spanish about the causes of the Pueblos' discontent. Second, the governor of New Mexico, Don Antonio de Otermín, describes the Indians' siege of Santa Fe and the bloody battle that followed.

*D*eclaration of one of the rebellious Christian Indians who was captured on the road. [Place of El Alamillo, September 6, 1680.]

In the place of El Alamillo, jurisdiction of El Socorro, on the 6th day of the month of September, 1680, for the prosecution of this case, and so that an Indian who was captured on the road as the camp was marching may be examined, in order to ascertain the plans, designs, and motives of the rebellious enemy, his lordship, the señor governor and captain-general, caused the said Indian to appear before him. He received the oath from him in due legal form, in the name of God, our Lord, and on a sign of the cross, under charge of which he promised to tell the truth concerning what he might know and as he

From Charles Wilson Hackett, *Revolt of the Pueblo Indians of New Mexico and Otermín's Attempted Reconquest, 1680–1682,* translated by Charmion Clair Shelby, 2 volumes (Albuquerque, N.M.: University of New Mexico Press, 1942), I:60–61, 94, 98–105.

might be questioned. Having been asked his name and of what place he is a native, his condition, and age, he said that his name is Don Pedro Nanboa, that he is a native of the pueblo of Alameda, a widower, and somewhat more than eighty years of age. Asked for what reason the Indians of this kingdom have rebelled, forsaking their obedience to his Majesty and failing in their obligation as Christians, he said that for a long time, because the Spaniards punished sorcerers and idolaters, the nations of the Teguas, Taos, Pecuríes, Pecos, and Jemez had been plotting to rebel and kill the Spaniards and the religious [missionaries], and that they had been planning constantly to carry it out, down to the present occasion. Asked what he learned, saw and heard in the juntas and parleys that the Indians have held, what they have plotted among themselves, and why the Indians have burned the church and profaned the images of the pueblo of Sandia, he said that he has not taken part in any junta, nor has he harmed any one; that what he has heard is that the Indians do not want religious or Spaniards. Because he is so old, he was in the cornfield when he learned from the Indian rebels who came from the sierra that they had killed the Spaniards of the jurisdiction and robbed all their haciendas, sacking their houses. Asked whether he knows about the Spaniards and religious who were gathered in the pueblo of La Isleta, he said that it is true that some days ago there assembled in the said pueblo of La Isleta the religious of Sandia, Jemez, and Zia, and that they set out to leave the kingdom with those of the said pueblo of La Isleta and the Spaniards—not one of whom remained—taking along their property. The Indians did not fight with them because all the men had gone with the other nations to fight at the villa and destroy the governor and captain-general and all the people who were with him. He declared that the resentment which all the Indians have in their hearts has been so strong, from the time this kingdom was discovered, because the religious and the Spaniards took away their idols and forbade their sorceries and idolatries; that they have inherited successively from their old men the things pertaining to their ancient customs; and that he has heard this resentment spoken of since he was of an age to understand. What he has said is the truth and what he knows, under the oath taken, and he signs and ratifies it, it being read and explained to him in his language through the interpretation of Captain Sebastián Montaño, who signed it with his lordship, as the said Indian does not know how, before me, the present secretary.

❖   ❖   ❖

Letter of the governor and captain-general, Don Antonio de Otermin, from New Mexico [to Fray Francisco de Ayeta], in which he gives him a full account of what has happened to him since the day the Indians surrounded him. [September 8, 1680.]

My very reverend father, Sir, and friend, most beloved Fray Francisco de Ayeta: The time has come when, with tears in my eyes and deep sorrow in my heart, I commence to give an account of the lamentable tragedy, such as has never before happened in the world, which has occurred in this miserable kingdom and holy custodia, His divine Majesty having thus permitted it because of my grievous sins. Before beginning my narration, I desire, as one obligated and grateful, to give your reverence the thanks due for the demonstrations of affection and kindness which you have given in your solicitude in ascertaining and inquiring for definite notices about both my life and those of the rest in this miserable kingdom, in the midst of persistent reports which had been circulated of the deaths of myself and the others, and for sparing neither any kind of effort nor large expenditures. For this, only Heaven can reward your reverence, though I do not doubt that his Majesty (may God keep him) will do so.

◆　　◆　　◆

On Tuesday, the 13th of the said month [August], at about nine o'clock in the morning, there came in sight of us in the suburb of Analco, in the cultivated field of the hermitage of San Miguel, and on the other side of the river from the villa, all the Indians of the Tanos and Pecos nations and the Queres of San Marcos, armed and giving war whoops. As I learned that one of the Indians who was leading them was from the villa and had gone to join them shortly before, I sent some soldiers to summon him and tell him on my behalf that he could come to see me in entire safety, so that I might ascertain from him the purpose for which they were coming. Upon receiving this message he came to where I was, and, since he was known, as I say, I asked him how it was that he had gone crazy too—being an Indian who spoke our language, was so intelligent, and had lived all his life in the villa among the Spaniards, where I had placed such confidence in him—and was now coming as a leader of the Indian rebels. He replied to me that they had elected him as their captain, and that they were carrying two banners, one white and the other red, and that the white one signified peace and the red one war. Thus if we wished to choose the white it must be upon our agreeing to leave the country, and if we chose the red, we must perish, because the rebels were numerous and we were very few; there was no alternative, inasmuch as they had killed so many religious and Spaniards.

On hearing this reply, I spoke to him very persuasively, to the effect that he and the rest of his followers were Catholic Christians, asking how they expected to live without the religious; and said that even though they had committed so many atrocities, still there was a remedy, for if they would return to obedience to his Majesty they would be pardoned; and that thus he should go back to his people and tell them in my name all that had been said to him, and persuade them to agree to it and to withdraw from where they were; and that he was to advise me of what they might reply. He came back from there after a short time, saying that his people asked that all classes of Indians who were in our power be given up to them, both those in the service of the Spaniards and those of the Mexican nation of that suburb of Analco. He demanded also that his wife and children be given up to him, and likewise that all the Apache men and women whom the Spaniards had captured in war be turned over to them, inasmuch as some Apaches who were among them were asking for them. If these things were not done they would declare war immediately, and they were unwilling to leave the place where they were because they were awaiting the Taos, Pecuríes, and Teguas nations, with whose aid they would destroy us.

Seeing his determination, and what they demanded of us, and especially the fact that it was untrue that there were any Apaches among them, because they were at war with all of them, and that these parleys were intended solely to obtain his wife and children and to gain time for the arrival of the other rebellious nations to join them and besiege us, and that during this time they were robbing and sacking what was in the said hermitage and the houses of the Mexicans, I told him (having given him all the preceding admonitions as a Christian and a Catholic) to return to his people and say to them that unless they immediately desisted from sacking the houses and dispersed, I would send to drive them away from there. Whereupon he went back, and his people received him with peals of bells and trumpets, giving loud shouts in sign of war.

With this, seeing after a short time that they not only did not cease the pillage but were advancing toward the villa with shamelessness and mockery, I ordered all the soldiers to go out and attack them until they succeeded in dislodging them from that place. Advancing for this purpose, they joined battle, killing some at the first encounter. Finding themselves repulsed, they took shelter and fortified themselves in the said hermitage and the houses of the Mexicans, from which they defended themselves a part of the day with the firearms that they had and with arrows. We having set fire to some of the houses in which they were, thus having them surrounded and at the point of perishing, there appeared on the road from Tesuque a band of the people whom they were awaiting, who were all the Teguas. Thus it was necessary to go to prevent these latter from passing on to the villa, because the casas reales [royal houses] were poorly defended; whereupon the said Tanos and Pecos fled to the mountains and the two parties joined together, sleeping that night in the sierra of the villa. Many of the rebels remained dead and wounded, and our men retired to the casas reales with one soldier killed and the maese de campo [commanding officer], Francisco Gómez, and some fourteen or fifteen soldiers wounded, to attend them and intrench and fortify ourselves as best we could.

On the morning of the following day, Wednesday, I saw the enemy come down all together from the sierra where they had slept, toward the villa. Mounting my horse, I went out with the few forces that I had to meet them, above the convent. The enemy saw me and halted, making ready to resist the attack. They took up a better position, gaining the eminence of some ravines and thick timber, and began to give war whoops, as if daring me to attack them.

I paused thus for a short time, in battle formation, and the enemy turned aside from the eminence and went nearer the sierras, to gain the one which comes down behind the house of the maese de campo, Francisco Gómez. There they took up their position, and this day passed without our having any further engagements or skirmishes than had already occurred, we taking care that they should not throw themselves upon us and burn the church and the houses of the villa.

The next day, Thursday, the enemy obliged us to take the same step as on the day before of mounting on horseback in fighting formation. There were only some light skirmishes to prevent their burning and sacking some of the houses which were at a distance from the main part of the villa. I knew well enough that these dilatory tactics were to give time for the people of the other nations who were missing to join them in order to besiege and attempt to destroy us, but the height of the places in which they were, so favorable to them and on the contrary so unfavorable to us, made it impossible for us to go and drive them out before they should all be joined together.

On the next day, Friday, the nations of the Taos, Pecuríes, Jemez, and Queres having assembled during the past night, when dawn came more than 2,500 Indians fell upon us in the villa, fortifying and intrenching themselves in all its houses and at the entrances of all the streets, and cutting off our water, which comes through the arroyo [stream] and the irrigation canal in front of the casas reales. They burned the holy temple and many houses in the villa. We had several skirmishes over possession of the water, but, seeing that it was impossible to hold even this against them, and almost all the soldiers of the post being already wounded, I endeavored to fortify myself in the casas reales and to make a defense without leaving their walls. The Indians were so dexterous and so bold that they came to set fire to the doors of the fortified tower of Nuestra Señora de las Casas Reales, and, seeing such audacity and the manifest risk that we ran of having the casas reales set on fire, I resolved to make a sally into the plaza of the said casas reales with all my available force of soldiers, without any protection, to attempt to prevent the fire which the enemy was trying to set. With this endeavor we fought the whole afternoon, and, since the enemy, as I said above, had fortified themselves and made embrasures in all houses, and had plenty of harquebuses [muskets], powder, and balls, they did us much damage. Night overtook us and God was pleased that they should desist somewhat from shooting us with harquebuses and arrows. We passed this night, like the rest, with much care and watchfulness, and suffered greatly from thirst because of the scarcity of water.

On the next day, Saturday, they began at dawn to press us harder and more closely with gunshots, arrows, and stones, saying to us that now we should not escape them, and that, besides their own numbers, they were expecting help from the Apaches whom they had already summoned. They fatigued us greatly on this day, because all was fighting, and above all we suffered from thirst, as we were already oppressed by it. At nightfall, because of the evident peril in which we found ourselves by their gaining the two stations where the cannon were mounted, which we had at the doors of the casas reales, aimed at the entrances of the streets, in order to bring them inside it was necessary to assemble all the forces that I had with me, because we realized that this was their [the Indians'] intention. Instantly all the said Indian rebels began a chant of victory and raised war whoops, burning all the houses of the villa, and they kept us in this position the entire night, which I assure your reverence was the most horrible that could be thought of or imagined, because the whole villa was a torch and everywhere were war chants and shouts. What grieved us most were the dreadful flames from the church and the scoffing and ridicule which the wretched and miserable Indian rebels made of the sacred things, intoning the alabado and the other prayers of the church with jeers.

Finding myself in this state, with the church and the villa burned, and with the few horses, sheep, goats, and cattle which we had without feed or water for so long that many had already died, and the rest were about to do so, and with such a multitude of people, most of them children and women, so that our numbers in all came to about a thousand persons, perishing with thirst—for we had nothing to drink during these two days except what had been kept in some jars and pitchers that were in the casas reales—surrounded by such a wailing of women and children, with confusion everywhere, I determined to take the resolution of going out in the morning to fight with the enemy until dying or conquering. Considering that the best strength and armor were prayers to appease the divine wrath, though on the preceding days the poor women had made them with such fervor, that night I charged them to do so increasingly, and told the father guardián and the other two religious to say mass for us at dawn, and exhort all alike to repentance for their sins and to conformance with the divine will, and to absolve us from guilt and punishment. These things being done, all of us who could mounted our horses, and the rest went on foot with their harquebuses, and some Indians who were in our service with their bows and arrows, and in the best order possible we directed our course toward the house of the maese de campo, Francisco Xavier, which was the place where (apparently) there were the most people and where they had been most active and boldest. On coming out of the entrance to the street it was seen that there was a great number of Indians. They were attacked in force, and though they resisted the first charge bravely, finally they were put to flight, many of them being overtaken and killed. Then turning at once upon those who were in the streets leading to the convent, they also were put to flight with little resistance. The houses in the direction of the house of the said maese de campo, Francisco Xavier, being still full of Indians who had taken refuge in them, and seeing that the enemy with the punishment and deaths that we had inflicted upon them in the first and second assaults were withdrawing toward the hills, giving us a little room, we laid siege to those who remained fortified in the said houses. Though they endeavored to defend themselves, and did so, seeing that they were being set afire and that they would be burned to death, those who remained alive surrendered and much was made of them. The deaths of both parties in this and the other encounters exceeded three hundred Indians.

Finding myself a little relieved by this miraculous event, although I had lost much blood from two arrow wounds which I had received in the face and from a remarkable gunshot wound in the chest on the day before, I immediately had water given to the cattle, the horses, and the people. Because we now found ourselves with very few provisions for so many people, and without hope of human aid, considering that our not having heard in so many days from the people on the lower river would be because of their all having been killed, like the others in the kingdom, or at least of their being or having been in dire straits, with the view of aiding them and joining with them into one body, so as to make the decisions most conducive to his Majesty's service, on the morning of the next day, Monday, I set out for La Isleta, where I judged the said comrades on the lower river would be. I trusted in divine providence, for I left without out a crust of bread or a grain of wheat or maize, and with no other provision for the convoy of so many people except four hundred animals and two carts belonging to private persons, and, for food, a few sheep, goats, and cows.

In this manner, and with this fine provision, besides a few small ears of maize that we found in the fields, we went as far as the pueblo of La Alameda, where we learned from an old Indian whom we found in a maizefield that the lieutenant general with all the residents of his jurisdictions had left some fourteen or fifteen days before to return to El Paso to meet the wagons. This news made me very uneasy, alike because I could not be persuaded that he would have left without having news of me as well as of all the others in the kingdom, and because I feared that from his absence there would necessarily follow the abandonment of this kingdom. On hearing this news I acted at once, sending four soldiers to overtake the said lieutenant general and the others who were following him, with orders that they were to halt wherever they should come up with them. Going in pursuit of them, they overtook them at the place of Fray Cristóbal. The lieutenant general, Alonso García, overtook me at the place of Las Nutrias, and a few days' march thereafter I encountered the maese de campo, Pedro de Leiva, with all the people under his command, who were escorting these wagons and who came to ascertain whether or not we were dead, as your reverence had charged him to do, and to find me, ahead of the supply train. I was so short of provisions and of everything else that at best I should have had a little maize for six days or so.

Thus, after God, the only succor and relief that we have rests with your reverence and in your diligence. Wherefore, and in order that your reverence may come immediately, because of the great importance to God and the king of your reverence's presence here, I am sending the said maese de campo, Pedro de Leiva, with the rest of the men whom he brought so that he may come as escort for your reverence and the wagons or mule-train in which we hope you will bring us some assistance of provisions. Because of the haste which the case demands I do not write at more length, and for the same reason I can not make a report at present concerning the above to the señor viceroy, because the *autos* [legal documents] are not verified and there has been no opportunity to conclude them. I shall leave it until your reverence's arrival here. For the rest I refer to the account which will be given to your reverence by the father secretary, Fray Buenaventura de Verganza. I am slowly overtaking the other party, which is sixteen leagues from here, with the view of joining them and discussing whether or not this miserable kingdom can be recovered. For this purpose I shall not spare any means in the service of God and of his Majesty, losing a thousand lives if I had them, as I have lost my estate and part of my health, and shedding my blood for God. May He protect me and permit me to see your reverence in this place at the head of the relief. September 8, 1680. Your servant, countryman, and friend kisses your reverence's hand.
DON ANTONIO DE OTERMÍN

SELECTION 2: A Description of Plantation Society in Portuguese Brazil

The Portuguese pioneered sugar cultivation in the New World in Pernambuco, a region in northeastern Brazil. Between 1816 and 1818, a French businessman named L. F. de Tollenare toured this region and its plantations. His report perceptively explains how access to land and labor combined with race to create a distinctive social hierarchy in Brazil. The planters who owned land, slaves, and sugar mills sat on top of this pyramid. Free whites, blacks, *pardos*, and Indians fell into subsequent levels depending upon whether they cultivated sugar or subsistence crops and whether they worked for themselves or others. Slaves were the foundation of this order, their labor absolutely necessary to the colony's economy.

I will divide the inhabitants of these regions into three classes (I am not speaking of the slaves, who are nothing but cattle). These three classes are:

1. The owners of sugar mills [*senhores de engenho*], the great landowners.
2. The *lavradores*, a type of tenant farmer.
3. The *moradores*, squatters or small cultivators.

The sugar-mill owners are those who early received land grants from the crown, by donation or transfer. These subdivided grants constitute considerable properties even today, as can be seen from the expanses of 7,000 and 10,000 acres of which I spoke earlier; the crown does not have more lands to grant; foreigners should be made aware of this.

There are some sugar-mill owners who interest themselves in the theoretical aspects of agriculture and who make some effort to improve the methods of cultivation and production. I was conscious of their existence, at least, because of the derision of which they were the object. I visited six mills and encountered few notable men.

With bare legs, clad in a shirt and drawers or a dressing gown of printed calico, the sugar-mill owner, armed with a whip and visiting the dependencies of his estate, is a king who has only animals about him: his blacks; his squatters or *moradores*, slaves whom he mistreats; and some hostile vassals who are his tenants or *lavradores*.

The great distances and lack of security on the roads do not encourage contacts with neighbors. Not even in the church are there opportunities to meet, because each mill either has its own chapel, or, what is more frequently the case, there isn't any church and no religious worship is carried on at all. The Portuguese government, which requires that a chaplain sail aboard merchant ships, would perhaps promote the progress of civilization by ordering that a priest be maintained at mills which have a certain number of blacks.

When a sugar-mill owner visits another one, the ladies do not make their appearance. I spent two days in the house of one of them, a very charming man who overwhelmed me with kindness, and I did not see his family either in the living room or at the dinner table. On a different occasion I arrived unex-

From *Children of God's Fire: A Documentary History of Black Slavery in Brazil*, edited by Robert Edgar Conrad (University Park, Penn.: Pennsylvania State University Press, 1994), 63–71.

pectedly after supper at the house of another of them, the splendor of which promised better taste; I noticed on the floor a piece of embroidery which seemed to have been tossed there suddenly. I asked for a glass of water in order to have a chance to go into the next room, but they made me wait for a long time. The lady of the house prepared a choice meal, but I did not see her. Furthermore, the same thing happened to me in a country house near Recife that belonged to a native of Lisbon.

In these houses, where the owners reside for the whole year, one does not observe anything fashioned to make them comfortable; one does not even find the avenue which among [the French] adorn both the simple property and the sumptuous chateau, neither parks, nor gardens, nor walks, nor pavillions. Living in the midst of forests, the inhabitants seem to fear shadows; or, more precisely stated, up to the edge of the forest around the mill everything is denuded and scorched to a distance of a quarter of a league. I witnessed at Salgado [a sugar plantation near the town of Cabo] the cutting down for firewood of orange groves which the previous owner had planted near the house, either for his pleasure or his profit.

Generally the residences are elevated on pillars; the cellar serves as a stable or as a dwelling place for the blacks; a long stairway provides access to the main floor, and it is on this level, or terrace, where one can enjoy the cool air. The rooms do not have ceilings; instead the timberwork of the roof is exposed and, between its extremities and the walls that hold it up, there is a free space of five inches to increase the air currents. The interior divisions are made with simple lath partitions measuring nine to ten feet in height, so that all the rooms have the roof as a common ceiling.

Luxury consists of a great variety of silverware. When a foreigner is entertained, in order to wash himself he is given splendid vessels made of this metal, of which also the coffee trays used at table, the bridles and stirrups for the horses, and knife hilts are made. Some sugar-mill owners showed me luxurious and expensive English firearms, and I also saw porcelain tea sets from England of the most beautiful type.

I ought to say a few words about meals. Supper consists of an abundant and thick soup, in which garlic abounds, or some other plant of a very pronounced and disagreeable taste which I did not recognize. The first plate is boiled meat which is not very succulent, the tastelessness of which they try to conceal with bacon, which is always a little rancid, and with manioc flour, which each serves himself with his fingers. For a second plate they serve a chicken ragout and rice with pepper. Bread is not seen, although it is much appreciated; they could manufacture it from foreign flour, which Recife is well supplied with, but it is not the custom. The black men or mulatto women (I saw many of the latter serving at table) fill the glasses with wine as soon as they are emptied, but people do not persist in drinking; liqueurs are not served with dessert.

❖   ❖   ❖

The sugar-mill owners are the only landholders. The only exceptions I know of are some chapels erected 100 or 150 years ago by the piety of the

Portuguese and endowed with 50 to 60 uncultivated acres. . . . The extension of the lands owned by the mills is therefore immense, and the capital invested in them is much less considerable than it was in the French [Caribbean] islands. Only the most important establishments have 140 to 150 blacks. One could estimate the importance of the mills by the number of slaves, if it were not for the existence of the *lavradores*.

The *lavradores* are tenants without leases. They plant cane, but do not own mills. They send the harvested cane to the mill that they are dependent upon, where it is transformed into sugar. Half of it belongs to the *lavrador* and half to the sugar-mill owner. The latter keeps the molasses, but furnishes the cases for the sugar. Each one pays his tithe separately. The *lavradores* normally possess from six to ten blacks and themselves wield the hoe. They are Brazilians of European descent, little mixed with mulattoes. I counted from two to three *lavradores* per mill.

This class is truly worthy of interest since it possesses some capital and performs some labor. Nevertheless, the law protects it less than it does the mill owners. Since they do not make contracts, once a piece of land becomes productive, the mill owner has the right to expel them without paying compensation. It should be recognized that leases of only a year are not very favorable to agriculture. The *lavrador* builds only a miserable hut, does not try to improve the soil, and makes only temporary fences, because from one year to the next he can be expelled, and then all his labor is lost. He invests his capital in slaves and cattle, which he can always take with him. . . .

❖   ❖   ❖

If I estimate an average of eight blacks for each *lavrador,* and sugar production at fifty *arrobas* [about 1,600 lbs.] per slave, which is not too much considering the vigilance and labor of the master himself, I can calculate the annual income of each *lavrador* at four hundred *arrobas* of sugar [about 12,800 pounds], which six or seven years ago was sold for about 3,000 francs. Now, this income is clear, since the *lavrador* does not buy anything at all to feed his blacks, and he lives very frugally from the manioc he plants.

Therefore, this class of capitalists, if favored by the government, is destined some day to exercise a major role in the political economy of Brazil. Consider the influence that they would have if the government would guarantee leases for nine years, and especially if an agrarian law were adopted that would obligate the present owners to make concessions, at stipulated prices, of certain parts of their uncultivated lands to anyone who might wish to buy them. Yet today everything remains exactly the opposite. I was witness to a rich mill owner's expulsion from his property of *all* the *lavradores* and squatters whom his less wealthy predecessors had allowed to establish themselves there. The number of exiles reached almost 600 persons, the property measuring two square leagues in size [about thirty square miles].

❖   ❖   ❖

The *lavradores* are quite proud to receive on a basis of equality the foreigner who comes to visit them. Under the pretext of seeking shelter, I entered the houses of several to speak with them. The women disappeared as in the homes of ladies, though I was always offered sweets. I never managed to get them to accept the little presents of cheap jewelry which I had supplied myself with for the trip. This noble pride caused me to respect the hard-working *lavradores*, a class intermediate between the haughty mill owner and the lazy, subservient, and humble squatter. The *lavrador* has a miserable house, for the reasons I have already mentioned. However, when he abandons the hoe to go to Serinhaem [a nearby town] or to church, he dresses himself up like a city man, rides a good horse, and has stirrups and spurs made of silver.

The *moradores* or squatters are small settlers to whom the sugar-mill own-ers grant permission to erect a hut in the middle of the forest and to farm a small piece of land. The rent they pay is very small, worth at the most a tenth part of their gross product, without an obligation to pay the royal tithe. Like the *lavradores*, they do not have a contract, and the master can send them away whenever he wishes. As a general rule they are mixtures of mulattoes, free blacks, and Indians, but Indians and pure blacks are rarely encountered among them. This free class comprises the true Brazilian population, an im-poverished people because they perform little labor. It would seem logical that from this class a number of salaried workers would emerge, but this does not happen. The squatter refuses work, he plants a little manioc, and lives in idle-ness. His wife has a small income because, if the manioc crop is good, she can sell a bit of it and buy some clothing. This comprises their entire expense, be-cause their furniture consists of only a few mats and clay pots. Not even a manioc scraper is found in all their houses.

The squatters live isolated, far from civil and religious authority, without comprehending, so to speak, the value of property. They replaced the Brazilian savages but have less value, since the latter at least had some political and na-tional affiliation. The squatters know only their surroundings, and look upon all outsiders practically as enemies. The sugar-mill owners court their women for their pleasure; they flatter them greatly, but from these seductions acts of vengeance as well as stabbings result. Generally speaking, this class is hated and feared. Because they pay them little or badly and often rob them, the sugar-mill owners who have the right to dismiss the squatters fear taking this dangerous step in a country that lacks police. Assassinations are common, but do not result in any pursuit whatsoever. I knew a certain mill owner who did not travel alone a quarter of a league from his house, because of the hostility and treachery of his squatters. He had incurred their wrath, and I had similar reasons to fear them when I entered their huts.

❖ ❖ ❖

I promised to make a quick survey of the black population. I am not in pos-session, however, of enough information about the laws that govern them to be able to deal with the matter adequately. Here is what I can say at the mo-ment in respect to them.

The Salgrado mill contains about 130 to 140 slaves, including those of all ages, but there is no written list of them. Deducting the children, the sick, and the people employed in domestic service and in the infirmary, there remain only about a hundred people who are fit for agricultural labor. During the four or five months that the sugar harvest lasts, the toil of the mill blacks is most violent; they alternate so as to be able to stay on their feet for eighteen hours. I said earlier that they received for food a pound of manioc flour and seven ounces of meat. Here it is distributed already cooked. There are few properties on which slaves are allowed to plant something for themselves. Passing through the forests I sometimes came upon small clearings where the blacks had come secretly to plant a little manioc. These were certainly not the lazy ones. Nevertheless, Gonçalo [a slave] told me not to speak about it to their master, because this could expose them to punishment.

Upon arrival from Africa, the blacks who have not been baptized in Angola, Mozambique, or another place where there are Portuguese governors, receive baptism upon disembarking; this is nothing but a pointless formality, because they are not given any instruction whatsover. At certain mills I saw the blacks being married by the priest, but in others they are united only by their whims or inclinations. In either case the master may sell separately the husband and the wife and the children to another buyer, regardless of how young they may be. A black baby is worth 200 francs at birth. Some masters make their slaves hear mass, but others save the cost of a chaplain, claiming that the sacrifice of the mass is a matter too grand for such people. Finally, there are mill owners who are more or less formalistic in matters of religion, and more or less able to appreciate its influence upon the conduct and habits of their slaves. It seems to me that it is in the interest of the masters to maintain family ties.

At the Salgado mill I saw only good slave quarters; everywhere, for that matter, they are of stone and lime and well roofed. Those of Salgado are ten feet wide and fifteen feet in depth, with a small interior division forming almost two rooms. It has a door which can be locked with a key, and a round opening toward the field to provide ventilation. The brick floor is two feet above the level of the adjacent ground, which makes such houses much more healthful than those of many French peasants. Each black is supposed to have his own private room, but love and friendship generally prevent them from living alone.

A mat, a clay cup or a gourd, sometimes a few claypots, and some tatters and rags make up the furnishings of the home of a black couple. All have permission to light a fire in their rooms and they take advantage of it. Their food is furnished to them already prepared, so that they have no need to cook. However, the fire is a distraction for them and serves for preparing fish or other food which they manage to acquire, lawfully or not. I observed that they were very careful to lock their doors and that when they were barred inside their houses they opened them with great reluctance. Although I was rather friendly with them in Salgado, I had some difficulty in satisfying my curiosity regarding the interior of their huts. I also saw some of the latter that were made of mud and covered with cocoa leaves.

❖   ❖   ❖

The black women generally have a flexible and elegant figure, the shoulders and arms very well formed. Many are seen who could qualify as pretty women if their necks were longer, giving more freedom to their heads. Their breasts are firm and fleshy, and they seem to understand their value, proving themselves very wise by concealing them, since this, in fact, is the way they commit terrible sins. It is unusual to see a black woman, even seventeen or eighteen years of age, whose neck has retained the shape which we prize so much and which European art imitates more or less badly. Nevertheless, they are not without a certain ability to hide its flaccidness [goiter?] with a piece of blue or red cloth. They tie these under their armpits, arrange the draping nicely over their waists and thighs, and make a large knot over the bosom, which hides the deformity I have just mentioned. The shoulders remain naked and the knees nearly uncovered, the scantiness of the cloth, which is made even tinier because of the part reserved for creating the knot, betraying all the body's movements, and I must say that they are all attractive and very graceful. . . . Their legs are normal, but their feet are damaged by hard work and the lack of footwear. They habitually have their heads uncovered, though some are given round hats which are not very becoming to them. They are happy when they can adorn themselves with a necklace or some bits of jewelry. Many of them, lacking such ornaments, attach a feather or a small round stick of wood to their ears. A tobacco pipe a foot long is usually thrust through the knotted cloth over the breast, and there it figures majestically like the dagger belonging to a leading lady of the theater.

This is the portrait of the black women who fix themselves up a bit. One sees others in a state of abandonment which is much less picturesque, dressed in a tattered shirt and an old petticoat which leaves the part beneath the breasts uncovered. Always, however, when they wrap their bodies or heads with a piece of cloth, the result is quite agreeable.

◆   ◆   ◆

The men have a better appearance when they are naked than the women, because of the flabbiness of the breasts that disfigures the latter. They are less robust than our porters, but the habit of going about without clothing makes their movements less wooden. What they possess that is better are their arched chests and their sinewy thighs. It is rare to see gray and wrinkled persons among them. Their black, shiny-smooth skin, destitute of hair, allows one to observe the entire play of their very active muscles. The arms and especially the legs are usually weak, but I saw some blacks with Apollo-like physiques.

Those coming from Africa have their shoulders, arms, and chests covered with symmetrical marks, which seem to be made with a hot iron, and the women also display these marks. For clothing the men are given a shirt and some breeches, but these garments evidently make them uncomfortable, and few preserve them, particularly the shirts. Most of the time they are satisfied with tying a rope around their loins from which hangs, both in front and behind, a small piece of cloth with which they try to hide that which modesty does not permit them to display.

The children also get clothing, but they make quick work of it so that they can go about naked. When they reach fourteen or fifteen years of age they are beaten with switches to make them more careful. At that time some are seen wearing their shirts hung over one shoulder in the fashion of Roman patricians, and, seen thus, they are reminiscent of Greek statues.

The blacks employed in domestic service, or close to their masters, dress with less elegance and more in the European manner. They take care of their breeches and shirts and sometimes even possess a waistcoat. Gonçalo had an embroidered shirt, and when he wore his lace hat and small trinkets which I had given him his pride was greater than that of any dandy; but when we went out hunting, his greatest pleasure was to leave at both his necessary and unnecessary items of clothing.

⚞ Discussion Questions ⚟

1. What reasons does Don Pedro Nanboa give to explain the Pueblos' revolt against the Spanish? What evidence can you find in the account of Don Antonio de Otermín to support or contradict that explanation?

2. What was the basis of Spanish power in New Mexico? What weaknesses did the Pueblo Revolt expose in the Spanish colonial order? How can you use these accounts of the Pueblo Revolt to assess the impact of Spanish colonization on Native American lives?

3. How does race figure into Tollenare's description of colonial Brazil's social and economic order? White planters and African slaves occupy the opposite sides of this social spectrum, but how are other social groups defined and positioned between them? How does the type of work a person does in this society help define his or her place in the social order?

4. Religion and labor were key factors in shaping the hierarchy of colonial societies in Iberian America. Compare and contrast how these readings describe the spiritual condition of non-Europeans; what motives did the Spanish and Portuguese have for converting the Indians and Africans who worked for them?

Suggested Readings

For works that consider the colonization of Iberian America in a transatlantic context, see J. H. Elliott, *Spain and Its World, 1500–1700: Selected Essays* (New Haven, Conn.: Yale University Press, 1989), and A. J. R. Russell-Wood, *The Portuguese Empire, 1415–1808: A World on the Move* (1992; Baltimore: The Johns Hopkins University Press, 1998). The best overview of Iberian America that treats both the Spanish and Portuguese is James Lockhart and Stuart B. Schwartz, *Early Latin America: A History of Colonial Spanish America and Brazil* (Cambridge, England: Cambridge University Press, 1983).

Useful studies of how intermarriage between Europeans, Africans, and Native Americans shaped Spanish America's social order include Ramón A. Gutiérrez, *When Jesus Came, the Corn Mothers Went Away: Marriage, Sexu-*

ality, and Power in New Mexico, 1500–1846 (Stanford, Calif.: Stanford University Press, 1991), and R. Douglas Cope, *The Limits of Racial Domination: Plebian Society in Colonial Mexico City, 1660–1720* (Madison, Wisc.: University of Wisconsin Press, 1994). A classic study of miscegenation in Brazil and its effects on the slave system and social order there is Carl N. Degler, *Neither Black nor White: Slavery and Race Relations in Brazil and the United States* (Madison, Wisc.: University of Wisconsin Press, 1971).

The Spanish encounter with Native Americans is described in Nancy M. Farriss, *Maya Society Under Colonial Rule: The Collective Enterprise of Survival* (Princeton N.J.: Princeton University Press, 1984), and Inga Clendinnen, *Ambivalent Conquests: Maya and Spaniard in Yucatan, 1517–1570* (Cambridge, England: Cambridge University Press, 1987). For further discussion of the Spanish kingdom of New Mexico and the Pueblo Revolt, see David J. Weber, *The Spanish Frontier in North America* (New Haven, Conn.: Yale University Press, 1992), and Andrew L. Knaut, *The Pueblo Revolt of 1680: Conquest and Resistance in Seventeenth-Century New Mexico* (Norman, Okla.: University of Oklahoma Press, 1995).

CHAPTER 7

Cityscape of New Amsterdam in 1655

New Amsterdam was renowned for its multiethnic character and commercial orientation (see Selection 1). It played a central role in shipping furs from the interior of North
America to Europe and was part of the Dutch trading network in the Atlantic World.
The tall, single-posted wooden structure in the foreground is a crane for loading and
unloading ships; the smaller wooden structure to the left of the crane is the gallows,
where authorities in Atlantic seaports typically hanged criminals and pirates as a warning to sailors and laborers working the docks. What architectural elements in this
cityscape indicate New Amsterdam's Dutch origins?

Source: Courtesy of the New York State Library, Manuscripts and Special Collections

The Dutch, French, and English in North America

Introduction

Europeans colonized North America at a much slower pace than South America or the Caribbean, but not because they were unaware of it. The problem was that they could find none of the gold and silver enriching the Spanish *conquistadors* in Mexico and Peru. For more than a century after Columbus, European encounters with North America were motivated not so much by a desire to exploit the continent as to get around it. Merchants and mapmakers imagined a Northwest Passage that would carry ships into the Pacific and westward to Japan and China. Such dreams did not die easily, even as they claimed the lives and fortunes of those who pursued them.

The first Europeans to draw a profit from North America were fishing crews that set up seasonal camps in Nova Scotia and Newfoundland to catch and dry the cod that swam offshore in the Grand Banks. These expeditions occasionally included contact with the native inhabitants of the region, in which the visitors exchanged manufactured goods such as cloth, kettles, and liquor for the pelts of furbearing animals. In the Southeast, the Chesapeake Bay region attracted pirates seeking a refuge from which they could launch raids against the Spanish treasure fleets in the Caribbean.

Fish, furs, and a place to hide: hardly as enticing as gold and silver. Yet the Dutch, French, and English gradually warmed to the idea of colonizing North America and in doing so, integrated it into the Atlantic World. These powers pioneered the use of joint-stock companies, which worked much like modern corporations, raising money by selling shares to investors and splitting any profits between them. Indian relations figured prominently in the success or failure of these ventures, and the Dutch, French, and English competed fiercely with each other for the native alliances that would ensure a profitable fur trade. From the start, their colonies developed close economic ties to the plantation complex in the Caribbean, opening a conduit for trade and migration from that region by which African slavery gained footholds in North America.

In describing North American colonization, it is helpful to call to mind the different models followed by the Spanish and Portuguese (see Chapter 6). While there were distinctive elements to the Dutch, French, and English endeavors, each also represented a variation on practices first pursued by the Iberian powers. The Dutch regarded North America in much the same way as the Portuguese did Brazil, as one outpost in a global trading network. Indeed, the Dutch entered the race for empire in the late sixteenth century on the heels of the Portuguese, successfully challenging their monopoly on trade with India and the Spice Islands of Southeast Asia, and then briefly controlling Portuguese possessions in Africa and Brazil in the 1630s and 1640s.

During this period of rapid overseas expansion, Amsterdam merchants formed the West India Company to oversee their commercial interests in the New World. This joint-stock venture established the colony of New Netherland in North America. The Dutch claimed a broad expanse of territory between the Delaware and Connecticut Rivers, but the heart of New Netherland was the Hudson River Valley. At the northern end, 150 miles into the continent's interior, traders at Fort Orange (modern Albany) collected furs from the Indians. They shipped them downriver to New Amsterdam (modern New York City), a seaport that attracted a diverse group of merchants and mariners. When French missionary Isaac Jogues (see Chapter 3, pp. 45–50) visited the city in 1643, he noted that its inhabitants spoke 18 different languages and professed six different faiths. Dutch ships sailing between Africa, Brazil, the Caribbean, and New Netherland carried much of seventeenth-century North America's international trade, including the first African slaves brought to the continent. The West India Company tried to recruit settlers for New Netherland, but as long as the fur trade dominated the colony's economy, its population remained small and transient. Squeezed by more populous colonies to the north and south, New Netherland capitulated to the English in 1664, who renamed it New York. Many Dutch mercantile families chose to remain there under English rule, and they continued to influence the cultural and economic development of this region well into the eighteenth century.

The French colonization of North America curiously blended Spanish and Portuguese precedents. As with the Spanish, missionary work among Native Americans was a central prop of French colonial power. Religious orders dedicated solely to this task made converts in Indian villages along the St. Lawrence and Great Lakes waterways; when they achieved a critical mass, they resettled the Christian Indians in *reserves* closer to French settlements (see Chapter 3), where they formed a bulwark against the French colonists' native and European enemies. Unlike the Spanish, the French did not forcibly convert natives nor did they demand tributary labor from them. Instead, their missionary work went hand in hand with the extension of their trade. Following tactics reminiscent of the Portuguese in West Africa, French missionaries converted natives while traders intermarried with them, creating a cooperative relationship by which the newcomers extracted a valuable commodity from the continent's interior, in this case furs rather than slaves.

The French empire in North America consisted primarily of allied Indian villages, inland forts, and the canoes that ferried people and goods between them. French colonists known as *habitants* worked farms in the St. Lawrence River Valley and the eastern Canadian province known as Acadia (modern Nova Scotia). French traders, soldiers, and missionaries followed the Great Lakes westward and built forts at portages between these waterways, such as Niagara, Detroit, and Michilimackinac. By the early eighteenth century, the French had navigated the Mississippi and established posts in the Illinois country and Louisiana. Yet, for all their skillful navigation of the continent's interior, the French never achieved a stable rate of population growth in North America. The Crown encouraged and sometimes even compelled emigration to Canada, but most would-be settlers found the French sugar colonies in the Caribbean more enticing. When France and Britain went to war in 1754 for control of North America, French influence extended over far more territory, but their colonial population of 80,000 was dwarfed by the one million inhabitants of the British colonies. The French found the defense of their North American dominions untenable, and in 1763 they ceded Canada to Britain and Louisiana to Spain.

As has already been hinted at, the great advantage the English enjoyed over their imperial rivals in North America was the rapid growth of their colonial population. This would suggest that the English followed the example of the Spanish, conquering native peoples and planting settlers in their place. Early English incursions into the Chesapeake Bay did resemble Spanish *entradas*: Small expeditions of privately financed adventurers searched for gold and silver and dealt harshly with any natives who resisted them. But unlike the Spanish, the English were reluctant to intermarry with Indians, and no equivalent of Spanish America's *mestizo* population emerged in the English colonies. Instead, English migration to North America in the seventeenth century was marked by more balanced sex ratios between male and female colonists than anywhere else in the Atlantic World. The religious groups that populated New England (Puritans) and New Jersey and Pennsylvania (Quakers) tended to migrate as families, and in the temperate climate of those northern colonies, they enjoyed lower mortality rates and higher birth rates than colonists in the tropics. In the Chesapeake Bay region, early English emigration had a more skewed sex ratio, roughly six males to every female, but one that was still considerably more balanced than in Spanish America (10:1) or Brazil (20:1).

African slaves made up another significant portion of British North America's colonial population. While every English colony recognized and sanctioned the institution of slavery, only those south of Pennsylvania developed into slave societies on the model of the plantation complex. In the Chesapeake, slaves cultivated tobacco and accounted for 40 percent of the colonial population. In South Carolina, a colony that was initially settled by planters and slaves from Barbados, slaves accounted for 60 percent of the population, making it the only colony in North America with a black majority. Like their European counterparts, Africans living in North America generally found a healthier climate than in other regions of the New World, and they achieved a positive rate of reproduction by the mid-eighteenth century, a demographic feat unmatched in any other Atlantic zone of colonization at that time.

North America's most striking difference with the other zones of New World colonization was its failure to develop an interracial population similar to Spanish America's *mestizos* or Brazil's *pardos*. Only the French exhibited anything like the Iberian penchant for incorporating strangers into their colonial society by intermarriage, and sexual unions between French traders and Indian women produced a significant *métis* population in western Canada. The English, on the other hand, avoided such practices. In their plantation colonies, they prohibited marriage between blacks and whites, and the English colonial social order afforded little room or opportunity to people of multiracial heritage. Whereas the meeting of Africans, Indians, and Europeans in Iberian America created new interracial groups and social orders, the same encounter in North America had by 1750 produced a population sharply divided into racial categories of black, red, and white.

The readings in this chapter describe the colonization of North America from the Dutch, French, and English perspectives. In the first selection, a Dutch traveler in the late seventeenth century comments on the ethnic diversity of New Amsterdam/New York City and its inhabitants' relations with the local Indians. In the second, a French military officer during the 1750s compares the Christian Indians and non-Christian Indians of New France. In the third, an inhabitant of Philadelphia discusses English colonial population growth and what he sees as the future of Indians, Africans, and Europeans in North America. As you read these sources, compare them to each other and what you learned about the Spanish and Portuguese in the previous chapter. How did the Dutch, French, and English experiences parallel and diverge from each other? What factors best explain the very different ways in which Africans, Indians, and Europeans interacted with each other in North America and South America?

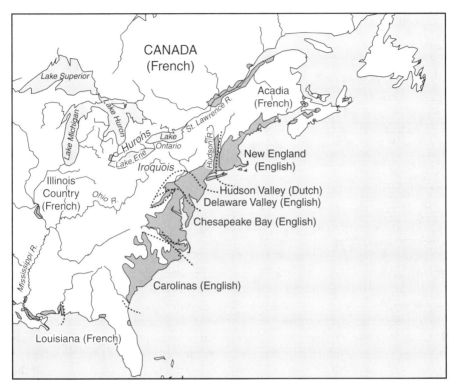

Figure 7.1   The Dutch, French, and English in North America
Dutch, French, and English zones of colonization in North America.
Source: Adapted from: D. W. Meinig, *The Shaping of America: A Geographical Perspective on
500 Years of History. Volume 1: Atlantic America, 1492–1800* (New Haven: Yale University Press,
1986), 245.

SELECTION 1: **A Dutch Traveler in New Netherland/
New York, 1679–1680**

Jasper Danckaerts was a native of the Netherlands who belonged to a Protestant
sect known as the Labadists. From 1679 to 1680, he traveled to North America
with a fellow believer to investigate moving their church across the Atlantic
(they eventually settled in Maryland). Although the Dutch had ceded New
Netherland to the English in the 1660s, the society Danckaerts encountered in
the Hudson Valley was still predominantly Dutch in character, and he quickly
felt at home. The diary he kept during his American sojourn provides an interesting look at New Netherland's population as it moved from Dutch to English
rule. In the passages that follow, Danckaerts describes his visit to Staten Island
and his negative impressions of the Dutch fur trade (see Figure 7.1).

11th, Wednesday. We embarked early this morning in his boat and rowed over to Staten Island, where we arrived about eight o'clock. He [a ferry-man] left us there, and we went on our way. This island is about thirty-two miles long and four broad. Its sides are very irregular, with projecting points and indented bays, and creeks running deep into the country. It lies for the most part east and west, and is somewhat triangular. The most prominent point is to the west. On the east side is the narrow passage which they call the channel, by which it is separated from the high point of Long Island. On the south is the great bay which is inclosed by Nayaq, Conijnen Island, Rentse-laer's Hook, Nevesinck, etc. On the west is the Raritans. On the north or northwest is New Garnisee [Jersey], from which it is separated by a large creek or arm of the river, called Kil van Kol. The eastern part is high and steep, and has few inhabitants. It is the usual place where ships, ready for sea, stop to take in water, while the captain and passengers are engaged in making their own arrangements and writing letters previous to their departure. The whole south side is a large plain, with much salt meadow or marsh, and several creeks. The west point is flat, and on or around it is a large creek with much marsh; but to the north of this creek it is high and hilly, and beyond that it begins to be more level, but not so low as on the other side, and is well populated. On the northwest it is well provided with creeks and marshes, and the land is generally better than on the south side, although there is a good parcel of land in the middle of the latter. As regards the middle or most hilly part of the island, it is uninhabited, although the soil is better than the land around it; but, in consequence of its being away from the water, and lying so high, no one will live there, the creeks and rivers being so serviceable to them in enabling them to go to the city, and for fishing and catching oysters, and for being near the salt meadows. The woods are used for pasturing horses and cattle, for being an island, none of them can get off. Each person has marks upon his own by which he can find them when he wants them. When the population of the country shall increase, these places will be taken up. Game of all kinds is plenty, and twenty-five and thirty deer are sometimes seen in a herd. A boy who came into a house where we were, told us he had shot ten the last winter himself, and more than forty in his life, and in the same manner other game. We tasted here the best grapes. There are now about a hundred families on the island, of which the English constitute the least portion, and the Dutch and French divide between them about equally the greater portion. They have neither church nor minister, and live rather far from each other, and inconveniently to meet together. The English are less disposed to religion, and inquire little after it, but in case there were a minister, would contribute to his sup-

---

From *Journal of Jasper Danckaerts, 1679–1680*, edited by Bartlett Burleigh James and J. Franklin Jameson (New York: C. Scribner's Sons, 1913), 69–70, 76–80.

port. The French and Dutch are very desirous and eager for one, for they spoke of it wherever we went, and said, in the event of not obtaining Domine Tessemaker, they would send, or had sent, to France for another. The French are good Reformed churchmen, and some of them are Walloons [Protestants from modern Belgium]. The Dutch are also from different quarters.

◆   ◆   ◆

16th, Monday. I was occupied to-day in copying my journal. In the morning there came an Indian to our house, a man about eighty years of age, whom our people called Jasper, who lived at Ahakinsack or at Ackinon [Hackensack]. Concerning this Indian our old people related that when they lived on Long Island, it was once a very dear time; no provisions could be obtained, and they suffered great want, so that they were reduced to the last extremity; that God the Lord then raised up this Indian, who went out fishing daily in order to bring fish to them every day when he caught a good mess, which he always did. If, when he came to the house, he found it alone, and they were out working in the fields, he did not fail, but opened the door, laid the fish on the floor, and proceeded on his way. For this reason these people possess great affection for him and have given him the name of Jasper, and also my *nitap,* that is, my great friend. He never comes to the Manhatans without visiting them and eating with them, as he now did, as among his old friends. We asked him why he had done so much kindness to these people. "I have always been inclined," he answered, "from my youth up to do good, especially to good people known to me. I took the fish to them because Maneto [the spirit] said to me, you must take fish to these people, whispering ever in my ear 'You must take fish to them.' I had to do it, or Maneto would have killed me." Our old woman telling us he sometimes got drunk, we said to him he should not do so any more, that the Great Sakemacker [God] who is above, was offended at such conduct and would kill him. "No," said he, laughing as if that were a mistake of ours, "it is Maneto who kills those who do evil, and leaves those who do good at peace." "That is only," we replied, "because Maneto is the slave and executioner of the Great Sakemacker above;" and we then asked him if he believed there was such a great and good *sakemacker* there? "Undoubtedly," he said, "but he remains above, and does not trouble himself with the earth or earthly things, because he does nothing except what is good; but Maneto, who also is a *sakemacker,* is here below, and governs all, and punishes and torments those men who do evil and drink themselves drunk." Hereupon we inquired of him why he did so then. "Yes," he said, "I had rather not, but my heart is so inclined that it causes me to do it, although I know it is wrong. The Christians taught it to us, and give us or sell us the drink, and drink themselves drunk." We said to him: "Listen! if we came to live near you, you would never see us drunk, nor would we give or sell you or your people any rum." "That," he replied, "would be good." We told him he must not make such a difference between himself and a Christian, because one was white and the other red, and one wore clothes and the other went almost naked, or one was called a Christian and the other an

Indian, that this great and good Sakemacker was the father of us all, and had made us all, and that all who did not do good would be killed by Maneto whether they were called Christians or Indians; but that all who should do good would go to this good *sakemacker* above. "Yes," said he, "we do not know or speak to this *sakemacker*, but Maneto we know and speak to, but you people, who can read and write, know and converse with this *sakemacker.*"

We asked him, where he believed he came from? He answered from his father. "And where did your father come from?" we said, "and your grandfather and great-grandfather, and so on to the first of the race?" He was silent for a little while, either as if unable to climb up at once so high with his thoughts, or to express them without help, and then took a piece of coal out of the fire where he sat, and began to write upon the floor. He first drew a circle, a little oval, to which he made four paws or feet, a head and a tail. "This," said he, "is a tortoise, lying in the water around it," and he moved his hand round the figure, continuing, "This was or is all water, and so at first was the world or the earth, when the tortoise gradually raised its round back up high, and the water ran off of it, and thus the earth became dry." He then took a little straw and placed it on end in the middle of the figure, and proceeded, "The earth was now dry, and there grew a tree in the middle of the earth, and the root of this tree sent forth a sprout beside it and there grew upon it a man, who was the first male. This man was then alone, and would have remained alone; but the tree bent over until its top touched the earth, and there shot therein another root, from which came forth another sprout, and there grew upon it the woman, and from these two are all men produced." We gave him four fish-hooks with which he was much pleased, and immediately calculated how much in money he had obtained. "I have got twenty-four stivers' worth," he said. He then inquired our names, which we gave him, and wished to know why he asked for them? "Well," he replied, "because you are good people and are true *nitaps;* and in case you should come into the woods and fall into the hands of the Indians, and they should wish to kill or harm you, if I know or hear of it I might help you, for they will do you no injury when they know me." For he was the brother of a *sakemacker.* We told him that we did not give them to him on that account, but only from regard because he was a good person, although the good will or thankfulness which he wished to show thereby was good. "Well," he said, "that is good, that is good," with which, after eating something, he departed.

But at noon he returned with a young Indian, both of them so drunk they could not speak, and having a calabash [bowl] of liquor with them. We chided him, but to no purpose, for he could neither use his reason nor speak so as to be understood. The young Indian with him was a *sackemacker's* son, and was bold. He wanted to have a piece of meat that was on the table, and on which we all had to make our dinner, when we told him it was not for him. "Yes," said he, "I see it is so;" nevertheless, and although we offered him something else to eat, he was evilly disposed and dissatisfied, and would take nothing except the piece of meat alone; but that was not given to him. Whereupon Jasper told him he must be quiet, that the old people and we were all his *nitaps*, and by degrees quieted him, they sitting together by the fire and drinking their rum. They left afterwards for Long Island.

17th, Tuesday. Nothing transpired to-day.

18th, Wednesday. In the afternoon Jasper, the Indian, came back again, and proceeded confidently to our room in the rear of the house, but sober and in his senses. He told us how he had been with his nephew, the *sackemacker's* son, to Long Island, among the other Indians; and that he had given away, not only his fish-hooks, but also his shoes and stockings. We found fault with him at first for having become so drunk, contrary to his promise, and when he well knew it was wrong. To which he said he had to buy some nails for an Englishman who lived near him, from another Englishman here, who had sold and given him the rum.

I must here remark, in passing, that the people in this city, who are almost all traders in small articles, whenever they see an Indian enter the house, who they know has any money, they immediately set about getting hold of him, giving him rum to drink, whereby he is soon caught and becomes half a fool. If he should then buy any thing, he is doubly cheated, in the wares, and in the price. He is then urged to buy more drink, which they now make half water, and if he cannot drink it, they drink it themselves. They do not rest until they have cajoled him out of all his money, or most of it; and if that cannot be done in one day, they keep him, and let him lodge and sleep there, but in some out of the way place, down on the ground, guarding their merchandise and other property in the meantime, and always managing it so that the poor creature does not go away before he has given them all they want. And these miserable Christians are so much the more eager in this respect, because no money circulates among themselves, and they pay each other in wares, in which they are constantly cheating and defrauding each other. Although it is forbidden to sell the drink to the Indians, yet every one does it, and so much the more earnestly, and with so much greater and burning avarice, that it is done in secret. To this extent and further, reaches the damnable and insatiable covetousness of most of those who here call themselves Christians. Truly, our hearts grieved when we heard of these things, which call so grievously upon the Supreme Judge for vengeance. He will not always let His name be so profaned and exposed to reproach and execration.

SELECTION 2: A French Military Officer Describes the Indians of Canada, 1757

Louis Antoine de Bougainville was an officer who served in the French army during the Seven Years' War (also known as the French and Indian War), the climatic struggle in the long Anglo-French rivalry for dominion in North America.

As an aide-de-camp to the famous general the Marquis de Montcalm, Bougainville traveled extensively in Canada and witnessed first hand the symbiotic relationship between Indians and colonists that was the hallmark of French colonization there. At the end of the war, Bougainville returned to Europe and joined an exploratory voyage to the South Pacific. During the American Revolution, he visited America again, this time as a French naval officer.

As his globetrotting would indicate, Bougainville was a man of considerable curiosity, and his journal from the Seven Years' War is full of insights about the strengths and weaknesses of the French regime in North America. In the passages that follow, he describes Montcalm's recruitment of Indian allies for his 1757 campaign against the British in New York. During Montcalm's frequent diplomatic councils with the Indians, Bougainville learned to distinguish between the "domesticated Indians" who lived in French missionary villages and those Indians from the "Far West" (i.e., western Great Lakes region) who were considerably more autonomous.

July 9: The Marquis de Montcalm left today with MM. de Rigaud, St. Luc, de Longueil, Junior, and Abbé Piquet to go and sing the war song at the Lake and at Sault St. Louis. We have first been to the Lac Des Deux Montagnes, which is twelve or thirteen leagues from Montreal and is formed by the Ottawa River. North of this lake is an Indian village. Indians of three different nations live there, Nipissings, Algonkins, and Iroquois. They have three separate groups of houses, although all united in the same village. They have a common church, which is attractive and properly ornamented. Two Sulpician missionaries are in charge, one for the Nipissings and the Algonkins, the other for the Iroquois.

The Indians go to pray in the church three times a day, each in his own tongue, and they attend with exemplary devotion. They serve as choir boys and chanters. The men sit on one side and the women on the other, and the choir formed by the latter is very melodious.

The cabins are well enough built but very filthy. There is a special council house for each nation and a large one, which must be three hundred feet long, for the general councils of the three nations.

Upon our arrival we were saluted by a triple discharge of two swivels and of musketry from Indians lined up on the river bank, the missionaries at their head. They led us to the church and from there to the parsonage, where the principal chiefs came to compliment the Marquis de Montcalm. In the after-

From *Adventure in the Wilderness: The American Journals of Louis Antoine de Bougainville, 1765–1760*, translated and edited by Edward P. Hamilton (1964; Norman, Okla.: University of Oklahoma Press, 1990), 122–125, 146–148, 150.

noon they held a council in which the Marquis de Montcalm told the Indians that he had come to see them and to give them through this visit marks of his friendship and esteem. Then he revealed to them the project planned against Fort George [Fort William Henry in New York], the union of all the Indians in order to co-operate in its execution, and the hope that the Marquis de Vaudreuil had that they, his children, and children of the true Faith, would help him with all their strength to destroy the common enemy. He ended by saying that he would give them three oxen for a feast and that he planned to sing the war song with them in the great council house. The Indians thanked the Marquis de Montcalm for his visit, assured him that they would follow his wishes and that in the evening they would tell him the number of warriors who would march with him.

We then visited the chiefs in their cabins. In the course of this we saw a Nipissing Indian, dishonored in the eyes of his brothers and of the Canadians because he wore breeches, covered his head, ate, dressed, and slept like a Frenchman. He goes neither to the hunt nor to war. He keeps a shop in his house filled especially with contraband goods, and he has a very lucrative business. The Indians scorn him, but do not reproach him or treat him badly. For in this place of complete liberty, *Trahit sua quemque voluptas.* ["His own liking leads each on."] This man reminds me of that thought that it is trade which most of all civilizes man.

In the evening we went to the council house, the Indians were sitting there on the floor, ranged by tribes. In the middle were hung at intervals pots filled with meat destined for the war feast. A few candles lighted up this place which seemed like a witches' cavern. Kisensik spoke first. After the ordinary compliments he asked the Marquis de Montcalm for permission to give his advice on war when the occasion offered. He then outlined his tribe's requests and the number of warriors it would furnish. The chiefs of the other two nations then spoke on the same subjects. After the Marquis de Montcalm had replied to their proposals, Aoussik, seizing a bullock's head by the horns and stalking around with it, sang his war song. The other chiefs of the three nations followed him with the same ceremony, and I sang it in the name of M. de Montcalm and was much applauded. My song was nothing else but these words: "Trample the English underfoot" cadenced to the movement of Indian cries. They then presented the Marquis de Montcalm with the first morsel, and the war feast having started, we withdrew.

The next day, the tenth, we went to Sault St. Louis. Two canoes, each with ten naked Indians, the finest men of all the villages, painted for war in red and blue, adorned with bracelets of silver and of wampum, came before us on the river a quarter league from the Sault. They brought to the Marquis de Montcalm a letter from Father la Neuville, a Jesuit, who heads this mission, in which he advised him of the ceremony about to be observed. The two canoe loads, in truth a charming sight, held the attention of all the Europeans. On the river bank we found the missionary, who received the Marquis de Montcalm upon his stepping ashore, made a short speech and led him to the church between two rows of Indians who saluted him, the chiefs with their spears and the rest with a triple discharge from their guns. They sang the *Te Deum* [a Latin hymn] in the Iroquois tongue, after which the Marquis de Montcalm was led to the council chamber, where the chiefs joined him. The same propositions, the same answers, the same ceremonies as at the Lac Des Deux Montagnes, and moreover, that of covering, in the name of the Marquis de Vaudreuil, two dead Iroquois chiefs, and of presenting me to the nation as a candidate for adoption. Three oxen given for the war feast, which went off just like that of last night. The Iroquois adopted me during this feast and gave me the name of "Garionatsigoa," which means "Great Angry Sky." Behold me then, an Iroquois war chief! My clan is that of the Turtle, first for eloquence in council, but second for war, that of the Bear being first. They exhibited me to all the nation, gave me the first morsel of the war feast, and I sang my war song, in part with their first war chief. The others dedicated theirs to me.

I paid calls on all my clan and gave the wherewithall for feasts in all the cabins. As for the rest of it, the village at the Sault is attractive, laid out in regular form with a parade ground which divides it and serves as a riding field, for they have many horses and exercise them continually. The church is pretty and well decorated. The Indians have, as do those at the Lake, fields cultivated by their women, fowl and cattle, all individually owned. They sell, buy, and trade just like Frenchmen.

❖   ❖   ❖

July 27: Today the Marquis de Montcalm went to camp at the Portage, where his presence was necessary to speed the arrangements for the colony troops, the brigading of the militia, the necessary distributions, and the assignment of bateaux [flat-bottomed boats for carrying supplies], etc.

A grand council was held to reunite and bind together by a belt of six thousand beads the 40 nations who are here. The chiefs and orators of these nations composed the council.

Kisensik, famous Nipissing chief, opened it. "My brothers," he said to the nations of the Far West, "we domesticated Indians thank you for having come to help us defend our lands against the English who wish to usurp them. Our cause is good and the Master of Life favors it. Can you doubt it, my brothers, after the fine deed you have just accomplished. We admired it, we pay you our compliments. It covers you with glory, and Lake St. Sacrement [Lake George], stained red with the blood of Englishmen, will forever attest this exploit. Let me say that it also covers us with glory, we, your brothers, and we are proud of it. Our joy should be still greater than thine, my Father," said he, addressing the Marquis de Montcalm, "thou who hast passed over the great ocean, not for thine own interest, for it is not thy cause that thou hast come to defend, it is that of the great King who said: 'Go, cross the great ocean and go and defend my children.' He will reunite you, my brothers, and bind you together with the most solemn of ties. Accept this sacred bond with joy and let nothing ever break it."

This harangue was translated by the various interpreters and received with applause.

The Marquis de Montcalm then said to them, "My children, I am delighted to see you all reunited for the good work. So long as your union lasts the English will never be able to resist you. I cannot speak better to you than your brother, Kisensik, who has just spoken. The great King has without doubt sent me to protect and defend you, but he has above all charged me to see that you are made happy and invincible by establishing among you this friendship, this unity, this joining together to carry on the good work, which should exist among brothers, children of the same father, of the great Ononthio [French governor of Canada]. I give you this belt as a sacred pledge of his word, symbol of good understanding and strength through the conjunction of the different beads which compose it. I bind you all together so that nothing can separate you before the defeat of the English and the destruction of Fort George."

This speech was then reported by the different interpreters and the belt thrown into the midst of the assembly.

It [the belt] was picked up by the orators of the different nations, who exhorted them to accept it, and Pennahouel, on presenting it to those of the Far West, said to them, "Behold a circle is drawn around you by the great Ononthio which none of us can leave. So long as we remain within its embrace the Master of Life will be our guide, will inspire us as to what we shall do and will favor all our enterprises. If some nation quits before the time, the Master of Life is not accountable for the evils that could hit them, but its misfortune will be its own and will not fall upon the nations who here promised an indissoluble union and complete obedience to their father's will." Once the orators had spoken in raising up the belt they put it down again in the midst of the assembly. The belt, following the custom of the nations, belongs to that one which has the greatest number of warriors in the army. It was without question granted to the Iroquois, who were and who almost always are the most numerous, and whose former victories over almost all of the nations of North America have given them a superior standing, which they continue to hold. They took the belt and their orator, addressing himself to the nations of the Far West, told them that, charmed by seeing their brothers reunited with them, and recognizing the help that they had just brought them for the defense of their lands, they begged them to accept this belt, pledge of their union, and to take it into their villages where it would be an eternal symbol of their friendship, of their common success, a witness which would keep in front of their eyes the happy results accomplished in this campaign, and would remind them to maintain forever this bond, the source of power of their warriors.

The Nipissing orator arose to tell the Iroquois: "My brothers, we are most thankful for this mark of respect you have shown to our brothers from the West. It was also our intention, and you have only anticipated us." One must note this procedure of the Nipissing. Its objective was to make the Iroquois realize that the Nipissings were the friends of all the Indians, and not to allow them to prescribe the right of precedence which their seniority gave them.

Pennahouel, in the name of the western Indians, thanked the Iroquois and accepted the belt. The different nations held a council that night to determine which one of them should keep it.

❖   ❖   ❖

July 28: The Indians have turned in the sticks showing the number of men they expect to go on foot. The Nipissings wished to keep their people out of this division, claiming that it was needlessly tiring; they did not succeed.

The Miamis, to the number of eight, left without telling anyone. A Potawatomi chief told the Marquis de Montcalm of it and offered to try to bring them back. He was given a belt and strings [of wampum] to help him succeed.

An English corpse came floating by the Indians' camp. They crowded around it with loud cries, drank its blood, and put its pieces in the kettle. However, it was only the western Indians who committed these cruelties. Our domesticated ones took no part in it; they spent all day in confession.

SELECTION 3: Benjamin Franklin Calculates the Population of British North America

Benjamin Franklin had recently retired from his printing business when he wrote this famous essay, in which he tried to explain the causes of the rapid population growth in England's North American colonies. As an inhabitant of Philadelphia, Franklin was well positioned to observe the eighteenth-century influx of immigrants to the mid-Atlantic colonies, and his remarks on colonial marriage patterns and birth rates indicate his awareness of the unique environmental and demographic factors that shaped English colonization in North America. The most significant part of Franklin's argument, however, was the criticism it levied at the traditional European approach to colonization, including its reliance on African slave labor and restrictions on colonial economic development. Franklin offered instead a vision of empire in which prolific English farmers would create a captive market for England's manufactured goods. His remarks about Germans, Africans, and Indians and the roles they would play in the future of North America also reflect the English reluctance to incorporate strangers into their colonial social order via intermarriage and religious conversion.

Europe is generally full settled with Husbandmen, Manufacturers, etc. and therefore cannot now much increase in People: America is chiefly occupied by Indians, who subsist mostly by Hunting. But as the Hunter, of all Men, requires the greatest Quantity of Land from whence to draw his Subsistence, (the Husbandman subsisting on much less, the Gardner on still less, and the Manufacturer requiring least of all), The Europeans found America as fully settled as it well could be by Hunters; yet these having large Tracks, were easily prevail'd on to part with Portions of Territory to the new Comers, who did not much interfere with the Natives in Hunting, and furnish'd them with many Things they wanted.

Land being thus plenty in America, and so cheap as that a labouring Man, that understands Husbandry, can in a short Time save Money enough to purchase a Piece of new Land sufficient for a Plantation, whereon he may subsist a Family; such are not afraid to marry; for if they even look far enough forward to consider how their Children when grown up are to be provided for, they see that more Land is to be had at Rates equally easy, all Circumstances considered.

Hence Marriages in America are more general, and more generally early, than in Europe. And if it is reckoned there, that there is but one Marriage per Annum [year] among 100 Persons, perhaps we may here reckon two; and if in Europe they have but 4 Births to a Marriage (many of their Marriages being late) we may here reckon 8, of which if one half grow up, and our Marriages are made, reckoning one with another at 20 Years of Age, our People must at least be doubled every 20 Years.

But notwithstanding this Increase, so vast is the Territory of North-America, that it will require many Ages to settle it fully; and till it is fully settled, Labour will never be cheap here, where no Man continues long a Labourer for others, but gets a Plantation of his own, no Man continues long a Journeyman to a Trade, but goes among those new Settlers, and sets up for himself, etc. Hence Labour is no cheaper now, in Pennsylvania, than it was 30 Years ago, tho' so many Thousand labouring People have been imported.

The Danger therefore of these Colonies interfering with their Mother Country in Trades that depend on Labour, Manufactures, etc. is too remote to require the Attention of Great-Britain.

But in Proportion to the Increase of the Colonies, a vast Demand is growing for British Manufactures, a glorious Market wholly in the Power of Britain, in which Foreigners cannot interfere, which will increase in a short Time even beyond her Power of supplying, tho' her whole Trade should be to her Colonies: Therefore Britain should not too much restrain Manufactures in

---

From Benjamin Franklin, "Observations Concerning the Increase of Mankind," in William Clark, *Observations on the late and present Conduct of the French with regard to their Encroachments on the British Colonies in North America . . . to which is added . . . Observations concerning the Increase of Mankind* (Boston: S. Kneeland, 1755), 2–15.

her Colonies. A wise and good Mother will not do it. To distress, is to weaken, and weakening the Children, weakens the whole Family.

Besides if the Manufactures of Britain (by Reason of the American Demands) should rise too high in Price, Foreigners who can sell cheaper will drive her Merchants out of Foreign Markets; Foreign Manufactures will thereby be encouraged and increased, and consequently foreign Nations, perhaps her Rivals in Power, grow more populous and more powerful; while her own Colonies, kept too low, are unable to assist her, or add to her Strength.

'Tis an ill-grounded Opinion that by the Labour of Slaves, America may possibly vie in Cheapness of Manufactures with Britain. The Labour of Slaves can never be so cheap here as the Labour of working Men is in Britain. Any one may compute it. Interest of Money is in the Colonies from 6 to 10 per Cent. Slaves one with another cost £30 Sterling per Head. Reckon then the Interest of the first Purchase of a Slave, the Insurance or Risque on his Life, his Cloathing and Diet, Expences in his Sickness and Loss of Time, Loss by his Neglect of Business (Neglect is natural to the Man who is not to be benefited by his own Care or Diligence), Expence of a Driver to keep him at Work, and his Pilfering from Time to Time, almost every Slave being *by Nature* a Thief, and compare the whole Amount with the Wages of a Manufacturer of Iron or Wool in England, you will see that Labour is much cheaper there than it ever can be by Negroes here. Why then will Americans purchase Slaves? Because Slaves may be kept as long as a Man pleases, or has Occasion for their Labour; while hired Men are continually leaving their Master (often in the midst of his Business,) and setting up for themselves.

As the Increase of People depends on the Encouragement of Marriages, the following Things must diminish a Nation, viz. 1. The being conquered; for the Conquerors will engross as many Offices, and exact as much Tribute or Profit on the Labour of the conquered, as will maintain them in their new Establishment, and this diminishing the Subsistence of the Natives discourages their Marriages, and so gradually diminishes them, while the Foreigners increase. 2. Loss of Territory. Thus the Britons being driven into Wales, and crowded together in a barren Country insufficient to support such great Numbers, diminished 'till the People bore a Proportion to the Produce, while the Saxons increas'd on their abandoned Lands; 'till the Island became full of English. And were the English now driven into Wales by some foreign Nation, there would in a few Years be no more Englishmen in Britain, than there are now People in Wales. 3. Loss of Trade. Manufactures exported, draw Subsistence from Foreign Countries for Numbers; who are thereby enabled to marry and raise Families. If the Nation be deprived of any Branch of Trade, and no new Employment is found for the People occupy'd in that Branch, it will also be soon deprived of so many People. 4. Loss of Food. Suppose a Nation has a Fishery, which not only employs great Numbers, but makes the Food and Subsistence of the People cheaper; If another Nation becomes Master of the Seas, and prevents the Fishery, the People will diminish in Proportion as the Loss of Employ, and Dearness of Provision, makes it more difficult to subsist a Family. 5. Bad Government and insecure Property. People not only leave such a Country, and settling Abroad incorporate with other Nations, lose their native Language, and become Foreigners; but the Industry of those that remain being discourag'd, the Quantity of Subsistence in the Country is lessen'd, and the Support of a Family becomes more difficult. So heavy Taxes tend to diminish a People. 6. The Introduction of Slaves. The Negroes brought into the English Sugar Islands, have greatly diminish'd the Whites there; the Poor are by this Means depriv'd of Employment, while a few Families acquire vast Estates; which they spend on Foreign Luxuries, and educating their Children in the Habit of those Luxuries; the same Income is needed for the Support of one that might have maintain'd 100. The Whites who have Slaves, not labouring, are enfeebled, and therefore not so generally prolific; the Slaves being work'd too hard, and ill fed, their Constitutions are broken, and the Deaths among them are more than the Births; so that a continual Supply is needed from Africa. The Northern Colonies having few Slaves increase in Whites. Slaves also pejorate the Families that use them; the white Children become proud, disgusted with Labour, and being educated in Idleness, are rendered unfit to get a Living by Industry.

Hence the Prince that acquires new Territory, if he finds it vacant, or removes the Natives to give his own People Room; the Legislator that makes effectual Laws for promoting of Trade, increasing Employment, improving Land by more or better Tillage; providing more Food by Fisheries; securing Property, etc. and the Man that invents new Trades, Arts or Manufactures, or new Improvements in Husbandry, may be properly called *Fathers* of their Nation, as they are the Cause of the Generation of Multitudes, by the Encouragement they afford to Marriage.

As to Privileges granted to the married, (such as the *Justrium Liberorum* [special liberties granted to mothers of three or more children] among the Romans), they may hasten the filling of a Country that has been thinned by War or Pestilence, or that has otherwise vacant Territory; but cannot increase a People beyond the Means provided for their Subsistence.

Foreign Luxuries and needless Manufactures imported and used in a Nation, do, by the same Reasoning, increase the People of the Nation that furnishes them, and diminish the People of the Nation that uses them. Laws therefore that prevent such Importations, and on the contrary promote the Exportation of Manufactures to be consumed in Foreign Countries, may be called (with Respect to the People that make them) *generative Laws,* as by increasing Subsistence they encourage Marriage. Such Laws likewise strengthen a Country, doubly, by increasing its own People and diminishing its Neighbours.

Some European Nations prudently refuse to consume the Manufactures of East-India. They should likewise forbid them to their Colonies; for the Gain to the Merchant, is not to be compar'd with the Loss by this Means of People to the Nation.

Home Luxury in the Great, increases the Nation's Manufacturers employ'd by it, who are many, and only tends to diminish the Families that indulge in it, who are few. The greater the common fashionable Expence of any Rank of People, the more cautious they are of Marriage. Therefore Luxury should never be suffer'd to become common.

The great Increase of Offspring in particular Families, is not always owing to greater Fecundity of Nature, but sometimes to Examples of Industry in the Heads, and industrious Education; by which the Children are enabled to provide better for themselves, and their marrying early, is encouraged from the Prospect of good Subsistence.

If there be a Sect therefore, in our Nation, that regard Frugality and Industry as religious Duties, and educate their Children therein, more than others commonly do; such Sect must consequently increase more by natural Generation, than any other Sect in Britain.

The Importation of Foreigners into a Country that has as many Inhabitants as the present Employments and Provisions for Subsistence will bear; will be in the End no Increase of People; unless the New Comers have more Industry and Frugality than the Natives, and then they will provide more Subsistence, and increase in the Country; but they will gradually eat the Natives out. Nor is it necessary to bring in Foreigners to fill up any occasional Vacancy in a Country; for such Vacancy . . . will soon be filled by natural Generation. Who can now find the Vacancy made in Sweden, France or other Warlike Nations, by the Plague of Heroism 40 Years ago; in France, by the Expulsion of the Protestants; in England, by the Settlement of her Colonies; or in Guinea, by 100 Years Exportation of Slaves, that has blacken'd half America? The thinness of Inhabitants in Spain is owing to National Pride and Idleness, and other Causes, rather than to the Expulsion of the Moors, or to the making of new Settlements.

There is in short, no Bound to the prolific Nature of Plants or Animals, but what is made by their crowding and interfering with each others Means of Subsistence. Was the Face of the Earth vacant of other Plants, it might be gradually sowed and overspread with one Kind only; as, for Instance, with Fennel; and were it empty of other Inhabitants, it might in a few Ages be replenish'd from one Nation only; as, for Instance, with Englishmen. Thus there are suppos'd to be now upwards of One Million English Souls in North-America, (tho' 'tis thought scarce 80,000 have been brought over Sea) and yet perhaps there is not one the fewer in Britain, but rather many more, on Account of the Employment the Colonies afford to Manufacturers at Home. This Million doubling, suppose but once in 25 Years, will in another Century be more than the People of England, and the greatest Number of Englishmen will be on this Side the Water. What an Accession of Power to the British Empire by Sea as well as Land! What Increase of Trade and Navigation! What Numbers of Ships and Seamen! We have been here but little more than 100 Years, and yet the Force of our Privateers in the late War, united, was greater, both in Men and Guns, than that of the whole British Navy in Queen Elizabeth's Time. How important an Affair then to Britain, is the present Treaty for settling the Bounds between her

Colonies and the French, and how careful should she be to secure Room enough, since on the Room depends so much the Increase of her People?

In fine, A Nation well regulated is like a Polypus; take away a Limb, its Place is soon supply'd; cut it in two, and each deficient Part shall speedily grow out of the Part remaining. Thus if you have Room and Subsistence enough, as you may by dividing, make ten Polypes out of one, you may of one make ten Nations, equally populous and powerful; or rather, increase a Nation ten fold in Numbers and Strength.

And since Detachments of English from Britain sent to America, will have their Places at Home so soon supply'd and increase so largely here; why should the Palatine Boors [Germans] be suffered to swarm into our Settlements, and by herding together establish their Language and Manners to the Exclusion of ours? Why should Pennsylvania, founded by the English, become a Colony of *Aliens,* who will shortly be so numerous as to Germanize us instead of our Anglifying them, and will never adopt our Language or Customs, any more than they can acquire our Complexion.

Which leads me to add one Remark: That the Number of purely white People in the World is proportionably very small. All Africa is black or tawny. Asia chiefly tawny. America (exculsive of the new Comers) wholly so. And in Europe, the Spaniards, Italians, French, Russians and Swedes, are generally of what we call a swarthy Complexion; as are the Germans also, the Saxons only excepted, who with the English, make the principal Body of White People on the Face of the Earth. I could wish their Numbers were increased. And while we are, as I may call it, *Scouring* our Planet, by clearing America of Woods, and so making this Side of our Globe reflect a brighter Light to the Eyes of Inhabitants in Mars or Venus, why should we in the Sight of Superior Beings, darken its People? why increase the Sons of Africa, by Planting them in America, where we have so fair an Opportunity, by excluding all Blacks and Tawneys, of increasing the lovely White and Red? But perhaps I am partial to the Complexion of my Country, for such Kind of Partiality is natural to Mankind.

∼ Discussion Questions ∼

1. What evidence does Danckaerts present of ethnic and religious diversity on Staten Island? Describe the tone of his encounter with the old Indian: What effects does Danckaerts think the Dutch fur trade has had on the Indians' welfare?

2. How does Bougainville compare those Indians who live under the supervision of missionaries with those from the western Great Lakes? What evidence do you find in this source of the ways in which the French and Indians influenced and altered each other's way of conducting diplomacy and warfare? How does it illustrate the linkage between trade, religion, and war in the French colonial endeavor?

3. To what causes does Franklin attribute the rapid population growth in British North America, and how does he think the British should adapt their colonial policy to take advantage of it? How might Franklin's argument be used to justify seizing land from its native owners, and why is he opposed to expanding slavery in North America?

4. All of these sources comment in one way or another on the colonizers' interaction with the native inhabitants of North America. What assumptions and prejudices about Indians did the Dutch, French, and English share? What other factors (e.g., geography, climate, economy) might explain the different course that the European-Indian encounter took in their respective zones of colonization?

Suggested Readings

Historians have typically taken a regional approach to studying the colonization of North America, but the rising interest in the Atlantic World has led to several studies that compare this process across ethnic, national, and geographic borders. For a comprehensive account that includes Spanish Florida and New Mexico as well as the French, Dutch, and English experiences addressed in this chapter, see D. W. Meinig, *The Shaping of America: A Geographical Perspective on 500 Years of History Volume I: Atlantic America, 1492–1800* (New Haven, Conn.: Yale University Press, 1986). Gary B. Nash's *Red, White, and Black: The Peoples of Early North America*, 4th edition (Upper Saddle River, N.J.: Prentice-Hall, 2000) provides admirable coverage of the various ethnic and racial groups involved in North American colonization. Ian K. Steele's *Warpaths: Invasions of North America* (New York: Oxford University Press, 1994) compares and contrasts the Dutch, French, English, and Spanish experiences in warfare against each other and Native Americans. Daniel K. Richter looks at the Dutch, French, and English colonization of the Northeast from the Native American perspective in *Ordeal of the Longhouse: The Peoples of the Iroquois League in the Era of European Colonization* (Chapel Hill, N.C.: University of North Carolina Press, 1992). The Anglo-French rivalry for dominion over the interior of the continent is described in Eric Hinderaker, *Elusive Empires: Constructing Colonialism in the Ohio Valley, 1673–1800* (Cambridge, England: Cambridge University Press, 1997).

The founding and operation of New Netherland is placed in an Atlantic context by Oliver A. Rink in *Holland on the Hudson: An Economic and Social History of Dutch New York* (Ithaca, N.Y.: Cornell University Press, 1986). A good study of the multiethnic society encountered by Jasper Danckaerts in New Netherland/New York is Joyce D. Goodfriend, *Before the Melting Pot: Society and Culture in Colonial New York City, 1664–1730* (Princeton, N.J.: Princeton University Press, 1992). For overviews of French colonization in North America, see W. J. Eccles, *France in America* (New York: Harper & Row, Publishers, 1972), and Allan Greer, *The People of New France* (Toronto:

University of Toronto Press, 1997). Denys Delâge puts the Canadian fur trade and French-Indian relations into an Atlantic context in *Bitter Feast: Amerindians and Europeans in Northeastern North America*, translated by Jane Brierley (Vancouver: UBC Press, 1993). Works on English colonization noteworthy for their Atlantic context include Jack P. Greene, *Pursuits of Happiness: The Social Development of Early Modern British Colonies and the Formation of American Culture* (Chapel Hill, N.C.: University of North Carolina Press, 1988) and David Hackett Fischer, *Albion's Seed: Four British Folkways in America* (New York: Oxford University Press, 1989).

A Seventeenth-Century Buccaneer

Pirate crews often included escaped servants and slaves who lived in maroon communities scattered throughout the Caribbean (see Selection 1). These multiethnic and multiracial communities survived through a combination of cutting wood and hunting feral pigs and cattle, the meat and hides of which they sold to plantations and passing ships. The name "buccaneer" has its root in "boucan," meaning to roast or dry meat over an open fire, as is illustrated here in the bottom left inset. How does this image contradict the popular image of Caribbean pirates?

Source: Alexander Exquemelin, *Histoire des Advanturiers*, Paris: (Courtesy of the James Ford Bell Library, University of Minnesota)

The Wooden World: Maritime Labor and Piracy

Introduction

Dr. Samuel Johnson, the great eighteenth-century English writer, once said of maritime work, "no man will be a sailor who has contrivance enough to get himself into jail; for being in a ship is being in jail only with the chance of being drowned. . . . A man in jail has more room, better food, and commonly better company." Johnson's opinion of a sailor's life is indicative of the contempt in which the upper classes typically held those men who earned their livings on the high seas. A wealthy London gentleman such as Johnson may have regarded the sailors crowding his city's wharves and taverns as little better than common criminals, but he could not have enjoyed his high style of living without them, for it was their labor that brought the fruits of overseas commerce—silks, china, tobacco, coffee, tea, sugar—to his door.

The Atlantic empires described in the previous two chapters were bound together by ships and the crews that sailed them. Mercantilism, an economic theory that shaped the colonial policy of all European powers in the Atlantic World, calculated a nation's wealth in terms of its international trade; nations grew rich by exporting more than they imported and by monopolizing their colonies' commerce with the rest of the world. Ships and seamen were national assets in this equation. Empire was something intangible—a claim to dominion over a foreign place or people—until maritime laborers made it profitable by loading, transporting, and unloading their cargoes.

Contemporaries referred to shipboard life as the "wooden world," and the men who inhabited it experienced extremes of personal autonomy and subordination. At a time when the vast majority of people labored on a specific plot of land to which they were tied by leases and local custom for a lifetime, sailors were remarkably mobile. They worked according to contracts that bound them to a ship's master only for the duration of a voyage. They could range among continents in their search for employment and easily abandon one captain for another by jumping ship. Time spent at sea freed them from the

149

supervision of traditional social authorities at home, such as family and church. Of course, a sailor's life could be equally circumscribed on both land and sea. Onboard ship, he lived in close quarters with his shipmates and under the absolute authority of his captain. Discipline was swift and violent, including floggings, beatings, and confinement. At home, a sailor lacked political representation and social status. He typically lived among the other propertyless urban poor and shared their substandard housing, sanitation, and diets. A sailor's geographic mobility should not be confused with social mobility. Regardless of the city or nation, maritime workers in the Atlantic World occupied one of the lowest rungs on the social ladder.

The risks of a seafaring life encouraged sailors to develop particular attitudes and values that were expressed in their appearance, habits, and politics. Contemporaries recognized sailors by their body and dress. Exposure to the elements, shipboard accidents, and diseases associated with tropical climates weathered sailors' faces and disfigured their bodies. Tattoos visually set them apart from other urban laborers, and often featured nautical images such as anchors and mermaids to denote pride of profession. Sailors wore distinctive clothing as well: canvas jackets and tarred pants (to insulate them from wind and water), which earned them the nickname "Jack Tar" in the English-speaking world. The stereotype of the sailor as a rootless, godless, and drunken ruffian was a product of the fatalism and liberality that seafaring encouraged. Well aware of the high mortality rates involved in their work, sailors preferred to part with their money rather than save it. Their spendthrift ways included generous support of other sailors and their kin whenever the death or injury of a shipmate called for charity. While locked out of the traditional channels of political power, sailors were by no means apolitical. Like the rest of the working poor, they practiced their politics "out-of-doors" by rioting against authorities who violated their notions of customary rights and social justice. In particular, sailors targeted press gangs that forced men into service aboard naval vessels, notorious for their low pay and harsh discipline. Anti-impressment riots were some of the most violent episodes of civil unrest in the Atlantic World, and the issue remained a politically charged one for seafarers into the nineteenth century.

Another distinctive element of maritime labor in the Atlantic World was its multiethnic and multiracial quality. Ship crews were a composite of Europeans, Africans, and Americans and mirrored the international nature of the profession. Portuguese pilots could be found on vessels from all nations; African and African-American sailors helped European ships navigate coastal waters on both sides of the Atlantic; Native Americans participated in northern New England's whalefishery. Sailors also engaged in and in some cases were the offspring of interracial sexual relations. Diego el Mulato was born a slave of European-African parents in Havana, but achieved notoriety as the leader of Dutch pirates in the seventeenth-century Caribbean. For some maritime slaves, such as Olaudah Equiano (see Chapter 8, pp. 67–76), petty trading from port to port enabled them to purchase their freedom. Other slaves found seafaring a welcome break from the monotony of work on land. Free blacks were drawn to maritime work for the relative independence it provided from white authority and the links it offered to other African-American communities. While black sailors earned less than their white counterparts and still faced racism on the high seas, they nonetheless helped shape an African-American consciousness by founding churches and mutual aid societies in their seaport communities and by transmitting anti-slavery ideology throughout the Atlantic World.

By its very nature, international seafaring encouraged the erosion of established identities and the creation of new ones. Nowhere was this tendency more evident than in the experience of pirates. Piracy came to the New World on the heels of Columbus. French, Dutch, and English privateers, adventurers licensed by their governments to seize enemy ships during wartime, hunted their fortunes by attacking the Spanish treasure fleets that carried American gold and silver to Europe. Favorite pirate haunts included Tortuga, a French-controlled island just east of the passage between Cuba and Hispaniola, and the Bahamas, from which pirates preyed upon ships navigating the straits between Florida and Cuba. In addition to hijacking Spanish silver, pirates plundered coastal cities and engaged in contraband slave trading.

The complexion of Atlantic piracy changed as the nationalist privateers of the early colonial period gave way to seafaring adventurers of no fixed political allegiance. In the seventeenth century, communities of *buccaneers* developed in the Caribbean; made up of runaway slaves, Native Americans, and European sailors and servants who had deserted their masters, they lived autonomously by cutting wood, hunting feral pigs and cattle, and exporting meat and hides to the sugar islands. By 1700, with British naval power commanding much of the Atlantic, a new breed of pirates known as freebooters emerged, sailing under no particular flag and attacking ships and seaboard settlements indiscriminately. In the last great wave of Atlantic piracy, about 5,000 such freebooters preyed on transoceanic trade between 1716 and 1726. As the British Navy pursued them, freebooters fanned out into the Carolinas of North America, Sierra Leone in West Africa, and even Madagascar in the Indian Ocean. Approximately 500 of them were executed in colonial and British ports, their bodies left to rot in the gallows as testimony to the new rule of law on the high seas.

The readings in this chapter offer three different perspectives on seafaring in the Atlantic World. In the first selection, a former Dutch servant who went to sea in the Caribbean explains the nature of piracy there. In the second, an African slave relates the story of a thirteen-year adventure spanning the Atlantic that began when he shipped out of New England for a voyage to Jamaica. In the third, a New York woman who joined her husband on a whaling voyage in the 1840s comments on the physical and spiritual condition of sailors at sea. As you read these sources, consider what they have to say about the attractions and risks of a seafaring life in the Atlantic World. What drew sailors to this employment? What deprivations did these authors endure as a result of their voyages? Where do you see evidence in their narratives of particular cultural values or identities rooted in their experiences at sea?

SELECTION 1:   A Dutch Pirate in the Seventeenth-Century Caribbean

Alexander Olivier Exquemelin was a native of the Netherlands who came to the Caribbean in the 1660s as an indentured servant of the French West India Company. Upon gaining his freedom, he went to sea as a buccaneer. Exquemelin told the tale of his exploits in a book first published in the Netherlands; an English translation appeared in 1684 with the author's name anglicized as John Esquemeling. *The Buccaneers of America* is an important eyewitness account of Caribbean piracy. While it is filled with lurid accounts of pillage and torture, it also includes details on the "nuts and bolts" of how this profession operated. In the passages that follow, Exquemelin describes his transition from servitude to piracy on the French island of Tortuga, the recruitment and organization of a pirate crew, and economic and sexual relations between pirates and Indian women.

The Governors of this island [Tortuga] did always behave themselves as proprietors and absolute lords thereof until the year 1664; at which time the West India Company of France took possession thereof, and sent thither for their Governor Monsieur Ogeron. These planted the colony for themselves, by the means of their factors [agents] and servants, thinking to drive some considerable trade thence with the Spaniards, even as the Hollanders do from Curaçoa [a Dutch sugar colony]. But this design did not answer their expectation. For with other nations they could drive no trade, by reason they could not establish any secure commerce from the beginning with their own. Forasmuch as at the first institution of this Company in France, they made an agreement with the pirates, hunters, and planters, first possessors of Tortuga, that these should buy all their necessaries from the said Company, taking them upon trust. And, although this agreement was put in execution, yet the factors of the Company soon after found that

From John Esquemeling, *The Buccaneers of America*, edited by William Stallybrass, second edition (London: William Crooke, 1684), 20–22, 59–61, 233–234.

they could not recover either moneys or returns from those people. Insomuch as they were constrained to bring some armed men into the island, in behalf of the Company, for to get in some of their payments. But neither this endeavour nor any other could prevail towards settling the secure trade with those of the island. And hereupon the Company recalled their factors, giving them orders to sell all that was their own in the said plantation, both the servants belonging to the Company (which were sold, some for 20, others for 30, pieces-of-eight [Spanish coins]), as also all other merchandizes and properties which they had there. With this resolution all their designs fell to the ground.

In this occasion I was also sold, as being a servant under the said Company, in whose service I came out of France. But my fortune was very bad, for I fell into the hands of the most cruel tyrant and perfidious man that ever was born of woman, who was then Governor, or rather Lieutenant-General, of that island. This man treated me with all the hard usages imaginable, yea, with that of hunger, with which I thought to have perished inevitably. Withal he was willing to let me buy my freedom and liberty, but not under the rate of 300 pieces-of-eight, I not being master of one, at that time, in the whole world. At last through the manifold miseries I endured, as also affliction of mind, I was thrown into a dangerous fit of sickness. This misfortune, being added to the rest of my calamities, was the cause of my happiness. For my wicked master, seeing my condition, began to fear lest he should lose his moneys with my life. Hereupon he sold me the second time to a surgeon for the price of 70 pieces-of-eight. Being in the hands of this second master, I began soon after to recover my health through the good usage I had received from him, as being much more humane and civil than that of my first patron. He gave me both clothes and very good food, and after that I had served him but one year he offered me my liberty, with only this condition, that I should pay him 100 pieces-of-eight when I was in a capacity of wealth so to do. Which kind proposal of his I could not choose but accept with infinite joy and gratitude of mind.

Being now at liberty, though like unto Adam when he was first created by the hands of his Maker—that is, naked and destitute of all human necessaries, nor knowing how to get my living—I determined to enter into the wicked order of the Pirates, or Robbers at Sea. Into this Society I was received with common consent both of the superior and vulgar sort, and among them I continued until the year 1672. Having assisted them in all their designs and attempts, and served them in many notable exploits, of which hereafter I shall give the reader a true account, I returned to my own native country.

◆   ◆   ◆

Before the Pirates go out to sea, they give notice unto everyone that goes upon the voyage, of the day on which they ought precisely to embark, intimating also unto them their obligation of bringing each man in particular so many pounds of powder and bullets as they think necessary for that expedition. Being all come on board, they join together in council, concerning what place they ought first to go unto wherein to get provisions—especially of flesh, seeing they scarce eat anything else. And of this the most common sort among them is pork. The next food is tortoises, which they use to salt a little. Sometimes they resolve to rob such or such hog-yards, wherein the Spaniards often have a thousand head of swine together. They come unto these places in the dark of the night, and, having beset the keeper's lodge, they force him to rise and give them as many heads as they desire, threatening withal to kill him in case he disobeys their commands or makes any noise. Yea, these menaces are oftentimes put in execution, without giving any quarter unto the miserable swinekeepers or any other person that endeavours to hinder their robberies.

Having gotten provisions of flesh sufficient for their voyage, they return unto their ship. Here their allowance, twice a day to every one, is as much as he can eat, without either weight or measure. Neither does the steward of the vessel give any greater proportion of flesh, or anything else, unto the Captain than unto the meanest mariner. The ship being well victualled, they call another council, to deliberate towards what place they shall go to seek their desperate fortunes. In this council, likewise, they agree upon certain articles, which are put in writing, by way of bond or obligation, which every one is bound to observe, and all of them, or the chiefest, do set their hands unto. Herein they specify, and set down very distinctly, what sums of money each particular person ought to have for that voyage, the fund of all the payments being the common stock of what is gotten by the whole expedition; for otherwise it is the same law, among these people as with other Pirates: *No prey, no pay*. In the first place, therefore, they mention how much the Captain ought to have for his ship. Next the salary of the carpenter, or shipwright, who careened, mended, and rigged the vessel. This commonly amounts unto 100 or 150 pieces-of-eight; being, according to the agreement, more or less. Afterwards for provisions and victualling they draw out of the same common stock about 200 pieces-of-eight. Also a competent salary for the surgeon and his chest of medicaments, which usually is rated at 200 or 250 pieces-of-eight. Lastly, they stipulate in writing what recompense or reward each one ought to have that is either wounded or maimed in his body, suffering the loss of any limb, by that voyage. Thus they order for the loss of a right arm 600 pieces-of-eight, or 6 slaves; for the loss of a left arm 500 pieces-of-eight, or 5 slaves; for a right leg 500 pieces-of-eight, or 5 slaves; for a left leg 400 pieces-of-eight, or 4 slaves; for an eye 100 pieces-of-eight, or one slave; for a finger of the hand the same reward as for the eye. All which sums of money, as I have said before, are taken out of the capital sum or common stock of what is gotten by their piracy. For a very exact and equal dividend is made of the remainder among them all. Yet herein they have also regard unto qualities and places. Thus the Captain, or chief Commander, is allotted five or six portions to what the ordinary seamen have; the Master's Mate only two; and other Officers proportionable to their employment. After whom they draw equal parts from the highest even to the lowest mariner, the boys not being omitted. For even these draw half a share, by reason that, when they happen to take a better vessel than their own, it is the duty of the boys to set fire unto the ship or boat wherein they are, and then retire unto the prize which they have taken.

They observe among themselves very good orders. For in the prizes they take, it is severely prohibited unto every one to usurp anything in particular unto themselves. Hence all they take is equally divided, according to what has been said before. Yea, they make a solemn oath to each other not to abscond, or conceal the least thing they find amongst the prey. If afterwards any one is found unfaithful, and has contravened the said oath, immediately he is separated and turned out of the society. Among themselves they are very civil and charitable to each other. Insomuch that, if any wants what another has, with great liberality they give it one to another. As soon as these Pirates have taken any prize of ship or boat, the first thing they endeavour is to set on shore the prisoners, detaining only some few for their own help and service, unto whom also they give their liberty after the space of two or three years. They put in very frequently for refreshment at one island or another, but more especially into those which lie on the Southern side of the isle of Cuba. Here they careen their vessels, and in the meanwhile some of them go to hunt, others to cruize upon the seas in canoes, seeking their fortune. Many times they take the poor fishermen of tortoises, and, carrying them to their habitations, they make them work so long as the Pirates are pleased.

◆   ◆   ◆

The custom of this island is such that, when any Pirates arrive there, every one has the liberty to buy for himself an Indian woman, at the price of a knife or any old axe, wood-bill, or hatchet. By this contract the woman is obliged to remain in the custody of the Pirate all the time he stays there. She serves him in the meanwhile, and brings him victuals of all sorts that the country affords. The Pirate, moreover, has liberty to go when he pleases, either to hunt, or fish, or about any other divertisements of his pleasure; but withal is not to commit any hostility, or depredation upon the inhabitants, seeing the Indians bring him in all that he stands in need of, or that he desires.

Through the frequent converse and familiarity these Indians have with the Pirates, they sometimes use to go to sea with them, and remain among them for whole years, without returning home. Whence it comes that many of them can speak English and French, and some of the Pirates their Indian language. They are very dexterous at darting with the javelin, whereby they are very useful to the Pirates towards the victualling their ships, by the fishery of tortoises, and *manitas*, a sort of fish so called by the Spaniards. For one of these Indians is alone sufficient to victual a vessel of an hundred persons. We had among our crew two Pirates who could speak very well the Indian language.

SELECTION 2: An African's Seafaring Odyssey in the Atlantic World

Slaves sometimes went to sea as wage-earning sailors, their masters allowing them to do so in return for a cut of their pay. Such employment provided slaves with the opportunity to escape temporarily their usual work, to visit other African communities in the Atlantic World, and perhaps even to earn the money necessary to buy their freedom. Briton Hammon shipped out of Massachusetts in December 1747 for Jamaica, but his winter sojourn to the

Caribbean turned into a thirteen-year odyssey of shipwreck, captivity, imprisonment, and redemption. His remarkable story, which was North America's first published slave narrative, is certainly singular for its circumstances, but it opens an important window onto the lives of African seafarers and the constant risks they shared with their white counterparts, from exposure to the elements to the depredations of pirates and foreign enemies.

O n Monday, 25th Day of *December,* 1747, with the leave of my Master, I went from *Marshfield,* with an Intention to go a Voyage to Sea, and the next Day, the 26th, got to *Plymouth,* where I immediately ship'd myself on board of a Sloop, Capt. *John Howland,* Master, bound to *Jamaica* and the *Bay.*—We sailed from *Plymouth* in a short Time, and after a pleasant Passage of about 30 Days, arrived at *Jamaica;* we was detain'd at *Jamaica* only 5 Days, from whence we sailed for the *Bay,* where we arrived safe in 10 Days. We loaded our Vessel with Logwood, and sailed from the *Bay* the 25th Day of *May* following, and the 15th Day of *June,* we were cast away on *Cape-Florida,* about 5 Leagues from the Shore; being now destitute of every Help, we knew not what to do or what Course to take in this our sad Condition:—The Captain was advised, intreated, and beg'd on, by every Person on board, to heave over but only 20 Ton of the *Wood,* and we should get clear, which if he had done, might have sav'd his Vessel and Cargo, and not only so, but his own Life, as well as the Lives of the Mate and Nine Hands, as I shall presently relate.

After being upon this Reef two Days, the Captain order'd the Boat to be hoisted out, and then ask'd who were willing to tarry on board? The whole Crew was for going on Shore at this Time, but as the Boat would not carry 12 Persons at once, and to prevent any Uneasiness, the Captain, a Passenger, and one Hand tarry'd on board, while the Mate, with Seven Hands besides myself, were order'd to go on Shore in the Boat, which as soon as we had reached, one half were to be Landed, and the other four to return to the Sloop, to fetch the Captain and the others on Shore. The Captain order'd us to take with us our Arms, Ammunition, Provisions and Necessaries for Cooking, as also a Sail to make a Tent of, to shelter us from the Weather; after having left the Sloop we stood towards the Shore, and being within Two Leagues of the same, we espy'd a Number of Canoes, which we at first took to be Rocks, but soon found our Mistake, for we perceiv'd they moved towards us; we presently saw an English Colour hoisted in one of the Canoes, at the Sight of which we were not a little rejoiced, but on our advancing yet nearer, we found them, to our very great Surprize, to be *Indians* of which there were Sixty; being now so near

From Briton Hammon, *A Narrative of the Uncommon Sufferings and Surprizing Deliverance of Briton Hammon, A Negro Man, Servant to General Winslow, of Marshfield, New England, Who Returned to Boston, after having been Absent almost Thirteen Years* (Boston: Green and Russell, 1760), 3–13.

them we could not possibly make our Escape; they soon came up with and boarded us, took away all our Arms Ammunition, and Provision. The whole Number of Canoes (being about Twenty,) then made for the Sloop, except Two which they left to guard us, who order'd us to follow on with them; the Eighteen which made for the Sloop, went so much faster than we that they got on board above Three Hours before we came along side, and had kill'd Captain *Howland*, the Passenger and the other hand; we came to the Larboard side of the Sloop, and they order'd us round to the Starboard, and as we were passing round the Bow, we saw the whole Number of *Indians*, advancing forward and loading their Guns, upon which the Mate said, "*my Lads we are all dead Men*," and before we had got round, they discharged their Small Arms upon us, and kill'd Three of our hands, viz. *Reuben Young* of *Cape-Cod*, Mate; *Joseph Little* and *Lemuel Doty* of *Plymouth*, upon which I immediately jump'd overboard, chusing rather to be drowned, than to be kill'd by those barbarous and inhuman Savages. In three or four Minutes after, I heard another Volley which dispatched the other five, viz. *John Nowland*, and *Nathaniel Rich*, both belonging to *Plymouth*, and *Elkanah Collymore*, and *James Webb*, Strangers, and *Moses Newmock*, Molatto. As soon as they had kill'd the whole of the People, one of the Canoes padled after me, and soon came up with me, hawled me into the Canoe, and beat me most terribly with a Cutlass, after that they ty'd me down, then this Canoe stood for the Sloop again and as soon as she came along side, the *Indians* on board the Sloop betook themselves to their Canoes, then set the Vessel on Fire, making a prodigious shouting and hallowing like so many Devils. As soon as the Vessel was burnt down to the Water's edge, the *Indians* stood for the Shore, together with our Boat, on board of which they put 5 hands. After we came to the Shore, they led me to their Hutts, where I expected nothing but immediate Death, and as they spoke broken English, were often telling me, while coming from the Sloop to the Shore, that they intended to roast me alive. But the Providence of God order'd it otherways, for He appeared for my Help, *in this Mount of Difficulty*, and they were better to me then my Fears, and soon unbound me, but set a Guard over me every Night. They kept me with them about five Weeks, during which Time they us'd me pretty well, and gave me boil'd Corn, which was what they often eat themselves. The Way I made my Escape from these Villains was this; A Spanish Schooner arriving there from *St. Augustine* [in Florida], the Master of which, whose Name was *Romond*, asked the *Indians* to let me go on board his Vessel, which they granted, and the Captain knowing me very well, weigh'd Anchor and carry'd me off to the *Havanna*, and after being there four Days the *Indians* came after me, and insisted on having me again, as I was their Prisoner;—They made Application to the Governor, and demanded me again from him; in answer to which the Governor told them, that as they had put the whole Crew to Death, they should not have me again, and so paid them Ten Dollars for me, adding, that he would not have them kill any Person hereafter, but take as many of them as they could, of those that should be cast away, and bring them to him, for which he would pay them Ten Dollars a-head. At the *Havanna* I lived with the Governor in the Castle about a Twelve-month, where I was walking thro' the Street, I met with a Press-Gang who immediately prest me, and put me into Goal, and with a Number of others I was confin'd till next Morning, when we were all brought out, and ask'd who would go on board the King's Ships, four of which having been lately built, were bound to *Old-Spain,* and on my refusing to serve on board, they put me in a close Dungeon, where I was confin'd *Four Years and seven months;* during which Time I often made application to the Governor, by Persons who came to see the Prisoners, but they never acquainted him with it, nor did he know all this Time what became of me, which was the means of my being confin'd there so long. But kind Providence so order'd it, that after I had been in this Place so long as the Time mention'd above the Captain of a Merchantman, belonging to *Boston,* having sprung a Leak was obliged to put into the *Havanna* to refit, and while he was at Dinner at *Mrs. Betty Howard's,* she told the Captain of my deplorable Condition, and said she would be glad, if he could by some means or other relieve me; The Captain told *Mrs. Howard* he would use his best Endeavours for my Relief and Enlargement.

Accordingly, after Dinner, came to the-Prison, and ask'd the Keeper if he might see me; upon his Request I was brought out of the Dungeon, and after the Captain had Interrogated me, told me, he would intercede with the Governor for my Relief out of that miserable Place, which he did, and the next Day the Governor sent an Order to release me; I lived with the Governor about a Year after I was delivered from the Dungeon, in which Time I endeavour'd three Times to make my Escape, the last of which proved effectual; the first Time I got on board of Captain *Marsh,* an *English* Twenty Gun Ship, with a Number of others, and lay on board conceal'd that Night; and the next Day the Ship being under sail, I thought myself safe, and so made my Appearance upon Deck, but as soon as we were discovered the Captain ordered the Boat out, and sent us all on Shore—I intreated the Captain to let me, in particular, carry on board, begging, and crying to him, to commiserate my unhappy Condition, and added, that I had been confin'd almost five Years in a close Dungeon, but the Captain would not hearken to any Intreaties, for fear of having the Governor's Displeasure, and so I was obliged to go on Shore.

After being on Shore another Twelvemonth, I endeavour'd to make my Escape the second Time, by trying to get on board of a Sloop bound to *Jamaica,* and as I was going from the City to the Sloop, was unhappily taken by the Guard, and ordered back to the Castle, and there confined.—However, in a short Time I was set at Liberty, and order'd with a Number of others to carry the *Bishop* from the Castle, thro' the Country, to confirm the old People, baptize Children, etc. for which he receives large Sums of Money.— I was employ'd in this Service about Seven Months, during which Time I lived very well, and then returned to the Castle again, where I had my Liberty to walk about the City, and do Work for my self;—The *Beaver,* an *English* Man of War then lay in the Harbour, and having been informed by some of the Ship's Crew that she was to sail in a few Days, I had nothing now to do, but to seek an Opportunity how I should make my Escape.

Accordingly one Sunday Night the Lieutenant of the Ship with a Number of the Barge Crew were in a Tavern, and *Mrs. Howard* who had before been a Friend to me, interceded with the Lieutenant to carry me on board: the Lieutenant said he would with all his Heart, and immediately I went on board in the Barge. The next Day the *Spaniards* came along side the *Beaver*, and demanded me again, with a Number of others who had made their Escape from them, and got on board the Ship, but just before I did; but the Captain, who was a true *Englishman*, refus'd them, and said he could not answer it, to deliver up any *Englishmen* under *English* Colours.—In a few Days we set Sail for *Jamaica*, where we arrived safe, after a short and pleasant Passage.

After being at *Jamaica* a short Time we sail'd for *London*, as convoy to a Fleet of Merchantmen, who all arrived safe in the *Downs*, I was turned over to another Ship, the *Arcenceil*, and there remained about a Month. From this Ship I went on board the *Sandwich* of 90 Guns; on board the *Sandwich*, I tarry'd 6 Weeks, and then was order'd on board the *Hercules*, Capt. *John Porter*, a 74 Gun Ship, we sail'd on a Cruize, and met with a *French* 84 Gun Ship, and had a very smart Engagement, in which about 70 of our Hands were Kill'd and Wounded, the Captain lost his Leg in the Engagement, and I was Wounded in the Head by a small Shot. We should have taken this Ship, if they had not cut away the most of our Rigging; however, in about three Hours after, a 64 Gun Ship, came up with and took her.—I was discharged from the *Hercules* the 12th Day of *May* 1759 (having been on board of that Ship 3 Months) on account of my being disabled in the Arm, and render'd incapable of Service, after being honourably paid the Wages due to me. I was put into the *Greenwich* Hospital where I stay'd and soon recovered.—I then ship'd myself a Cook on board Captain *Martyn*, an arm'd Ship in the King's Service. I was on board this Ship almost Two Months, and after being paid my Wages, was discharg'd in the Month of *October*. —After my discharge from Captain *Martyn*, I was taken sick in *London* of a Fever, and was confin'd about 6 Weeks, where I expended all my Money, and left in very poor Circumstances; and unhappy for me I knew nothing of my *good Master's* being in *London* at this my very difficult Time. After I got well of my sickness, I ship'd myself on board of a large Ship bound to *Guinea*, [West Africa] and being in a publick House one Evening, I overheard a Number of Persons talking about Rigging a Vessel bound to *New-England*, I ask'd them to what Part of *New-England* this Vessel was bound? they told me, to *Boston*; and having ask'd them who was Commander? they told me, Capt. *Watt*; in a few Minutes after this the Mate of the Ship came in, and I ask'd him if Captain *Watt* did not want a Cook, who told me he did, and that the Captain would be in, in a few Minutes; and in about half an Hour the Captain came in, and then I ship'd myself at once, after begging off from the Ship bound to *Guinea*; I work'd on board Captain *Watt's* Ship almost Three Months, before she sail'd, and one Day being at Work in the Hold, I overheard some Persons on board mention the Name of *Winslow*, at the Name of which I was very inquisitive, and having ask'd what *Winslow* they were talking about? They told me it was *General Winslow*; and that he was one of the Passengers, I ask'd them what *General Winslow*? For I never knew *my good Master*, by that Title before; but after enquiring more particularly I found it must be *Master*, and in a few Days Time the Truth was joyfully verify'd by a happy Sight of his Person, which so overcome me, that I could not speak to him for some Time—*My good Master* was exceeding glad to see me, telling me that I was like one arose from the Dead, for he thought I had been Dead a great many Years, having heard nothing of me for almost Thirteen Years.

SELECTION 3: A Woman's Perception of Life on a Whaling Ship

Within the maritime world, a clear division of labor separated men and women. Men went to sea while women stayed behind to maintain family, home, and community in port towns and cities. Only rarely did women accompany male partners who worked on overseas voyages, and rarer still is the woman who left behind a written account of the experience. At the peak of the North American whalefishery in the mid-nineteenth century, some women did join their husbands at sea. They tended to be ship captains' wives who chose to endure the rigors of a whaling expedition rather than the long-term absence of their spouses, whose work often took them away from home for a year or two at a time.

Martha Smith Brewer Brown joined her husband Captain Edwin Peter Brown on a whaling voyage out of Long Island, New York in 1847. The Browns circumnavigated the globe, hunting whales primarily in the Pacific and Arctic Oceans. Martha kept a journal while at sea, in which she recorded her impressions of life and work aboard ship. A pious woman, she expressed concern for the state of the sailors' souls and described how shipboard life ran counter to good Christian habits and morals. Through her eyes we see in sharp relief the contrast between the values of seafarers and landed society.

MONDAY 10 [DECEMBER 1847]   *[in margin: "John died"]*

This morning about 7 we were called in the stereage to witness the departure of an immortal soul. He died very suden. The Capt. went in imediately and he gasped but once. He never strugled, nor groned nor to appearance mooved a musle. He said last evening he felt that he must die, felt prepared, and was willing to go this morning. At 6 he told Steward he thought he could stand it to get to New Holland [Australia]—he did not have his reason all the time. A short time before he died the boy said [he] heard him singing and laughing. He is Portugee and could not understand him. We think he might have been happy, but we do not know. It is not probile he knew he was dying. He never left a message for his friends although the Capt. often asked him if he had not something he wished to say to them. I heardly think he

---

From *She Went A-Whaling: The Journal of Martha Smith Brewer Brown from Orient, Long Island, New York, Around the World on the Whaling Ship Lucy Ann, 1847–1849,* transcribed and edited by Anne MacKay (Orient, N.Y.: Oysterponds Historical Society, 1993), 47–52.

would have given us the names of his parents or friends of his own accord. He was young, only 15. I hope he has gone to a brighter and happyer world, but that we can not know. We will leave him in the hands of a just God who doeth all things well. He was buried this afternoon at 4 oclock. It was a sollemn sight to see his body launched into the deep. I think nearly every one wept. Oh that they may lay it to heart and realized their turn will soon come. They are far from being what we would wish them to be. They have looked rather thoughtfull today and I pray the impressions may not be banished as soon as his body is out of our sight. Poor boy, I cannot realize he is gone. Poor in the world estimate, but if he had sincerely repented of his sins and was truly a child of grace, how much richer far than we who remain behind. Whether he felt any dred of being buried in the sea or not, I do not know. He did not say any thing about it, and we did not mention the subject to him, but it matters not where the body is if the soul is prepared for heaven, prepared to meet its God.

THURSDAY 13   *[in margin: "ate porpossis"]*

Today I have the unspeakable pleasure of seeing a whale brought along side. The second mate struck him. I was on deck most of the time they were off, notwithstanding it was somewhat rainy. It was past 7 when they came on board, and after getting dinner it was to late to cut him in. Like wise it was blowing pretty strong so we were obliged to lay by him all night. It [is] quite encourageing to think we have got one of the thirty of forty we have got to get, ere we can anticipate returning home. It looks like a long day I can assure you to look ahead to the time when this ship shall be full of oil and we homeward bound.

FRIDAY 14

Morning rather unpleasent but commenced cutting in about 10 AM. And of cours the Capt. worked hard. Evry time the ship roaled, the whail went nearly all under water, but they succeeded in getting him in at 9 pm. Weather quite good. Got supper, cleared up, but have not commenced boiling yet.

SATURDAY 15

Called the Capt. between 5 and 6. Lowered for whale—no success. Commenced boiling before breakfast but have not made very grate headway. Will be under the necesity of boiling tomorrow, Sunday, but I do not see how whaleman can in evry way keep the Sabbath. They can truly not go off in the boats and take them, but if they have one alongside or in the bluber room, it appears necessary they should take care of it.

MONDAY 17

Today hands imployed brakeing out the fore peek and stowing down 42 barrels of oil. Merely a nest egg. Hope they will have the good luck to get the nest full soon and set the sails for home. Finished boiling this morning about day light. It has been very pleasent all day. I have been making my blue dress after supper. They caught two nice large porposses—now for a feast on fresh meet agane. By the bye it goes well.

WEDNESDAY 19

Another pleasent day and I have improved it washing. Had a good time. Got my cloths dry before night, but lost one apron overboard—the first time I have had the bad luck to loos anything. Got through little, afternoon. Had fried parters [potatoes?] as turnovers for dinner.

JANUARY 23, 1848,   *Indian Ocian, Ship Lucy Ann*

To day has been a lovely day, a good breeze and a compleet day for whaleing. The Capt., I think, has been quite anxous to see whale. The first time he has been to the masthead [on] Sunday, but he who know all things saw best not to tempt them. And here I will add we have not seen a whale on Sunday since we have been out. How kind is Almighty God to withhold temptation when there is not strenght of mind sufficient to resist it. I fear and tremble evry week that we shall see them but it is my earnest prayer that God will be gracious and tempt us no further than we are able to bare.

The 23 of Jan was my dear Father's bearth day. If he was living to day he would be 68 years old. But as our heavenly Father saw fit 8 years ago to remove him from this world of trouble, sorow and pain, of which he always had his share, to one we trust of perfect bliss, happyness. He can never more come to us, but we can go to him. Then let us strive to meet him in heaven, dear brothers and sisters, for that is our privalage.

MONDAY 31

Nothing in particular to day. Strong brizes from the west. In the morning at 2 am raised Vandieman's land [Tasmania], but at so grate a distance it appeared like a cloud. Nothing was visable and of course we were not much interested. I think I should be nearly intoxicated with delight if I could once more get ashore where I could feel at home, and go as I was a mind to—for instance on Long Island. But let me get ashore any where, I anticipate I should enjoy it some.

TUESDAY, FEB 1ST   *[in margin: "man flogged"]*

Ship Lucy Ann Between New Holland & New Zealand Feb 1848

Today has been quite pleasant, and it is very acceptable to think that we may now have some good weather, for it has been nothing but a succession of gales and bad weather since we left the cape of Good Hope. But if it is not one thing is another. Sunday morn when the Capt. first got up, he went on deck and caught to [two] of the foremast hands fighting, in direct oposition to the rules and regulation of the ship. He sent one out on the bowsprit and the other to the mizenmast and kept them there untill 10 oc [o'clock] without their breakfast. It was their watch below. This morning, or before noon, he appeared at the fore castle—lo and behold there were four gambling for tobacco. Two managed to get rid of their cards so that he could not know certainly they were playing, but the others said they were. Seaman he sent out on the bowsprit agane, for he was the one sent there for fiting [fighting], and Rider to the mizenmast head. Kept them there all the forenoon, their watch below agane. In the afternoon he called them of [off] aft, read to them apiece on the results of gambling and lectured them full a half hour, threw their cards overboard. Agane, at 8 bels in the evening Baldwin, one of the boatsteerers, came with a complaint that Seaman had been calling him a horred name—the third offence three days a runing. The Capt.'s patienes was clear gone—he went on deck and gave him 5 or 6 lashes with the end of the topgalent bowlin [rope used to tie a sail]. Then for the first time I learned he had floged a man several weeks before. What will come next I do not know. You who live on land do not know half the trials a sea Capt. is subject to. If you do not like a man's conduct you can pay him and let him go, or you can flee to the law. But here there is no such thing. Of course there must be some rules and regulation on board ship. When a man is made acquainted with them in the first of it, what can he expect but abide the conciquences if he does not abide by the rules. So Mother, you see I have very little influence so far.

FRIDAY 11

This morning at daylight raised two Ships, one of them cutting in. At 8 PM raised three Kings [island off of New Zealand] steered for them. About 2 PM sent two boats ashore to see if any-thing was to be got in the way of provision. The third mate soon returned with the chief, said there was plenty of potatoes and that was what we wanted. He came abord to make the bargain with the Capt. but more expressly to get some Rum. They could not land that side of the Island we was, but this kanacker [a Polynesian man] came down the rocks some way. The Capt. made a trade with him, sent them back. But by this the current was runing so strong and the wind ahead, the second boat could not get around, and was obliged to land the Chief where they took him. So the third mate walked across the land to the other boat, or the landing place, to have Mr. Sisen take the potatoes. But mean time he had come around, thinking the Capt. had not sent him back. When they got on board nothing had been seen of the other boat, and of course we imagined the boat had swamped and all were drowned. But alass [at last] they come and brought 10 little pon fish. This ends our tour of the three Kings.

SATURDAY EVE FEBRUARY 12

And so we are spared to enjoy the privalages of another Saturday night, and if we cannot meet with our friends at the temperance meeting nor in social prayer, we know that our Savior is present to hear our feeble petiton if offered in faith. What a blessed privalage. I think at times what could we do here without the Bible and the family alter [altar]. I long to live nearer to God and enjoy more of that love. It is our privalage to do. I have to mourn daily my coldness of heart, ant [and it] appears the more I strive the more I see my imperfection—and short comeings. Today has been very pleasent. Very little wind, some of the time almost a calm. It is warm and I spend most of my time on deck. The Capt. is aloft a grate deal of the time and it is lonely below. I have just come from the deck where we have been jumping the rope for exersize—The Capt., my self, and the mates—nice sport.

SUNDAY 13

This has been a lovely day. A pretty little brieze with three studen sails out, and we have been moving at a midling rate. But with all this pleasentness we could not enjoy the privalage of hearing the sound of the church going bell, nor of assembling ourselves together without it in the house of God, to hear dispensed the words of truth and life. And if we were like many or most of our crew, would not read a word for ourselvs. Methinks our condition would be a deplorable one. What better are they than the poor heathen, especially hear at sea? They have appeared very well so far on the Sabath, they make but little noise. But what they do in the fore castle I can not say. The Capt. has not had to reprimand them once, I believe. I have proposed reading to them. Some of them say they would like to hear good reading. I desire to put it of [off] no longer than next Sabath if it is pleasent. The Capt. thinks he cannot take up his cross for he says he has no one to help him, which is very true. But I trust the Lord will help him, then surely he will be helped. The mate tries not to believe in anything, but still he has a heart, and I trust one that is susceptible of right and wrong, and a Wife that is a professer of religeon. And I hope he will ere long join her heart and hand in her heavenward journey.

≈ Discussion Questions ≈

1. According to Exquemelin, how did pirates organize their voyages? How did they determine their leadership and rates of pay? Does he present any evidence of a particular ethic or set of values that bound pirates together? Why would piracy appeal to sailors used to working in merchant or naval ships?

2. Briefly trace the course of Hammon's odyssey: what setbacks—both natural and man-made—did he encounter? To what degree do you think other sailors shared in the risks he faced at sea? Conversely, to what degree can his misfortunes be attributed to his status as an enslaved African?

3. Both Exquemelin and Hammon came to seafaring from a condition of servitude. Why do you think seafaring appealed to slaves and servants? How do you suppose their experience as sailors reshaped their sense of identity or their relationship with others?

4. What elements of shipboard work, leisure, and discipline does Martha Brown find contrary to Christian habits and morals? How do you think the crew responded to her concern for their spiritual and physical welfare? What do her impressions of shipboard life tell you about gender roles in the maritime world?

Suggested Readings

Marcus Rediker's *Between the Devil and the Deep Blue Sea: Merchant Seamen, Pirates, and the Anglo-American World, 1700–1750* (Cambridge, England: Cambridge University Press, 1987) offers an engaging account of the working life of British seamen in the eighteenth century. Rediker and Peter Linebaugh link sailors to the wider experience of laboring peoples in the Atlantic World in *The Many-Headed Hydra: Sailors, Slaves, Commoners, and the Hidden History of the Revolutionary Atlantic* (Boston: Beacon Press, 2000). For enslaved and free African American sailors, see W. Jeffrey Bolster, *Black Jacks: African American Seamen in the Age of Sail* (Cambridge, Massachusetts: Harvard University Press, 1997), and for a study of sailors' politics, see Jesse Lemisch, *Jack Tar vs. John Bull: The Role of New York's Seamen in Precipitating the Revolution* (New York: Garland Publishing, 1997). Simon P. Newman analyzes the unique physical appearance of sailors, especially their tattoos, in "Reading the Bodies of Early American Seafarers," *William and Mary Quarterly*, third series, 55 (1998): 59–82.

Kris Lane provides a comprehensive account of Atlantic World piracy in *Pillaging the Empire: Piracy in the Americas, 1500–1750* (Armonk, N. Y.: M. E. Sharpe, 1998). For a look at the contest in the Caribbean from the Spanish perspective, see Carla Rahn Phillips, *Six Galleons for the King of Spain: Imperial Defense in the Early Seventeenth Century* (Baltimore: Johns Hopkins University Press, 1992). The life of one of the more infamous freebooters is used to illustrate the fate of pirates in general in Robert C. Ritchie, *Captain Kidd and the War Against the Pirates* (Cambridge, Mass.: Harvard University Press, 1986).

Two studies of the seaport communities that were home to seafarers and their families are Daniel Vickers, *Farmers and Fishermen: Two Centuries of Work in Essex County, Massachusetts, 1630–1850* (Chapel Hill N. C.: University of North Carolina Press, 1994), and Lisa Norling, *Captain Ahab Had a Wife: New England Women and the Whalefishery, 1720–1870* (Chapel Hill N. C.: University of North Carolina Press, 2000). Works that explore Atlantic seafaring through the lenses of gender and sexuality include B. R. Burg, *Sodomy and the Perception of Evil: English Sea Rovers in the Seventeenth Century Caribbean* (New York: New York University Press, 1983); *Iron Men, Wooden Women: Gender and Seafaring, 1700–1920*, edited by Margaret Creighton and Lisa Norling (Baltimore: Johns Hopkins University Press, 1996); and Joan Druett, *Petticoat Whalers: Whaling Wives at Sea, 1820–1920* (Hanover, N. H.: University Press of New England, 2001).

Cuſtom-Houſe, Philadelphia, Entred inwards.
Ship Amity, William Murray, from Jamaica.
Ship Boneta, Thomas Read, from London.
Entred Outwards.
Brig. Philadelphia Hope, George Spafford, to Weſt-Indies.
Sloop Surinam, Henry Norwood, to Barbadoes
Cleared Out.
Sloop Adventure, Robert Rawle, for Surinam.
Ship Samuel and Ann, Thomas Glentworth, to Madera.
Brigt. Clementina, Joſeph Arthur, to Antigua.
Brigt. Henrietta, Samuel Farra, for Madera.
Ship Cupid, Stephen Pugh, for Gibraltar.
Ship Three Batchelors, William Spafford, for Barbadoes.
Ship Mary, Robert Sanders, for Iſle of Man.
Buried in the ſeveral Burying-Grounds ſince the 4th Inſtant.
Church --------------- 2. ⎫ ⎧Baptiſts ------------------- o.
Quakers ----------- 1. ⎬ ⎨   ⎧Whites ------ o.
Presbyterians ------ o. ⎭ ⎩Strangers, ⎨Blacks ------- o.

A D V E R T I S E M E N T S.
JUſt Imported in the Ship *Boneta*, Capt.
Thomas Reed, Maſter, from *London*, (lying near the
Market Wharff) a Parcel of very likely Servant Men and
Boys, of ſundry Trades, as well as Husbandmen: To be
ſold by *Edward Horne* and *William Rawle*, very Reaſona-
ble, (as alſo good *Newcaſtle* Coal) for Caſh, Flower or
Bread.

Advertisement for Servants for Sale from a Colonial Newspaper
The vast majority of European migrants to eighteenth-century North America arrived
in some form of indentured servitude. Newly arrived servants were sold in seaport
markets, and the wording of this newspaper advertisement follows closely that used in
similar ads for slaves. What words or phrases in this advertisement suggest that these
servants were regarded as cargo rather than passengers on the ships that carried them?
What evidence do you see that some of these servants came from the middle rather
than bottom rungs of the social order?
Source: The Library Company of Philadelphia

The Atlantic Highway: European Migrations

Introduction

For thousands of years of human history, the Atlantic Ocean was a barrier, the edge of the known world for peoples living on both sides of it. Columbus changed all that with his voyage of 1492, turning the Atlantic into a highway connecting two previously isolated worlds. All sorts of goods passed back and forth across this highway, and of course, people did too. By far, the largest component of this human exchange was the 10 million Africans who crossed the ocean in the Atlantic Slave Trade (see Chapter 4, pp. 64–83). The colonization of the Americas set Europeans in motion as well, and about 1.4 million of them crossed the Atlantic between 1500 and 1800.

This human tide ebbed and flowed from region to region depending upon a variety of circumstances, and many of these people stayed only temporarily in the Western Hemisphere. When we label them as *immigrants* (meaning *coming to*), we romanticize them as brave souls who bid farewell to friends and families, never looked back, and made new lives for themselves in a strange land. But the Atlantic Ocean was a highway with eastbound as well as westbound lanes. Emigrants (meaning *coming from*) left Europe for the Americas but could and occasionally did return home. Even if they settled permanently in the new land, they maintained contact with family, neighbors, and business partners in the Old World by sending letters and messengers back along the same routes they had traveled. If we were to observe this movement from a midpoint in the Atlantic, it would not resemble a group of individuals scrambling over some natural barrier separating east from west. Rather, we would see people constantly moving back and forth, creating networks of communication and exchange that bound the continents closer together in a web of interdependence.

The European states that built empires in the New World tried as much as possible to regulate this transatlantic movement. On the one hand, they wanted to populate their overseas dominions with loyal subjects who could defend the territory from hostile natives, rebellious slaves, or foreign enemies. In the race for empire, whichever state populated a territory first had the surest claim to it. On the other hand, governments wanted to control who went overseas. Some states, such as Spain and France, did not want religious nonconformists in their colonies. Others, such as England and the Netherlands, were more tolerant of religious differences, but tried to recruit settlers for specific economic purposes. All European states wanted to keep track of who was going, so that emigrants would not leave without paying debts or taxes owed at home, and many policymakers believed that too much emigration would hurt a nation by draining it of its most important resource: people.

The state's attempt to supervise migration from above was countered by the initiative of emigrants from below. Historians often use a "push-pull" model to describe the motives for human migration: Certain conditions push people out of their homeland while others pull them toward a new destination. Emigrants in early modern Europe responded to a variety of pushes and pulls that the state could not, or in some cases did not wish, to control. For example, the conversion of farmland into pasturage in Britain between 1500 and 1850 uprooted thousands of rural workers; the state abetted this displacement by allowing landlords to enclose lands previously used in common by rural villagers. Families dispossessed by this change fed the stream of British emigration to the New World. Explosive population growth in Europe also contributed to the pool of emigrants, as did the religious wars of the Protestant Reformation. In the Rhine River Valley, aristocrats strengthened laws designed to tie peasants to the land, but when famine and warfare made life there unbearable, the inhabitants ignored such restrictions and sought passage to Eastern Europe or North America. When a state tried to take advantage of such a push by directing emigrants to certain destinations or purposes, its efforts could easily go awry. In 1710, England's Queen Anne sponsored the emigration of 3,000 Germans to New York, where she expected them to work in the pine forests of the Hudson Valley making naval stores. Once in America, the Germans abandoned their overseers and settled their own farming communities on a remote frontier, collectively thumbing their noses at the colonial governor who tried to stop them. Thus could the best-laid plans fall apart when emigrants slipped the grasp of state officials.

Most Europeans who came to the Americas prior to 1800 did so in some form of bondage, typically indentured servitude. In exchange for signing a contract, or indenture, promising their labor to a master for a fixed number of years, emigrants secured transatlantic passage and the necessaries of life while they served their time. English servants typically agreed to terms of service lasting four to five years. French *engagés* served three years, but the Crown later halved that term in an effort to increase white emigration to its sugar colonies. German-speaking redemptioners, who often traveled as families, negotiated the length of their service based upon the balance they owed for their passage once they landed in America. Those who had their debt paid or "redeemed" by relatives or friends walked off the ship free people; those not so fortunate sold themselves or family members into servitude to make up the difference.

Soldiers, sailors, and convicts also arrived in America in a form of servitude. Men who enlisted in the army or navy faced long terms of service that exposed them to disease, bodily danger, and brutal discipline. It is no wonder that many deserted when in America to look for more comfortable circumstances elsewhere. Potential emigrants from Spain, for example, had to go through a licensing process designed to weed out non-Catholics, debtors, and criminals. Many Spaniards circumvented this system by enlisting in the convoys that guarded the Atlantic treasure fleets and then jumping ship in America. In the first half of the seventeenth century, this tactic accounted for 50 percent of Spanish emigration to the New World. The British Transportation Act of 1718 gave convicted felons the choice between servitude in America or the noose at home. During the eighteenth century, this policy brought an estimated 50,000 English, Irish, and Scots to North America, accounting for about 25 percent of the emigration from the British Isles to America in that period. Orphans, vagrants, and other socially marginal folk faced similar types of state-sanctioned emigration throughout the colonial era.

Servitude and military service were occupations that attracted young, single, male emigrants from urban seaports. Another component of the Atlantic migration consisted of people from rural communities who maintained contact with families and friends back home after the Atlantic crossing, thereby creating private networks that publicized and sponsored emigration from one region to another. Rather than reflecting a breakdown of traditional community and kinship ties, this type of emigration, in which religious ties figured prominently, transplanted local identities and values in a wholesale fashion from one side of the ocean to the other. English Puritans and Quakers migrated to New England and Pennsylvania respectively, forming their American communities in ways that imitated distinctive regional patterns back home. French-speaking Protestants known as Huguenots were barred from French colonies, but they found an open door in British North America, where they named settlements such as New Rochelle and New Paltz after their European hometowns. German-speaking sects such as the Mennonites, Moravians, and Dunkers came to Pennsylvania because freedom from a state-sponsored church allowed them to recreate their spiritual and social communities with little interference. Many of the Jews expelled from Portugal in the early sixteenth century moved to Brazil. From there, some were drawn to the religiously tolerant Dutch colonies in the Caribbean and New Netherland, creating a network of Jewish communities that spanned the Americas.

The long-term trend in Atlantic migration was away from state control and in favor of individual initiative. Most state-supervised efforts to encourage or limit emigration to certain groups or regions crumbled in the face of the New World's insatiable demand for human labor and the Old World's surplus of population. The Atlantic highway beckoned the disenfranchised, the desperate, and the ambitious, who paid much less attention to national borders and identities than government officials would have liked. In the eighteenth and nineteenth centuries, the tide of European emigration swelled with peoples such as Germans, Scots-Irish (descendants of Scottish colonizers of Northern Ireland), and Scandinavians whose home states had no American empires of their own. Their migration further eroded the state's power to tie people to the land and helped shape the modern notion of a universal human right to freedom of movement across national borders.

The readings in this chapter focus on Atlantic migrations in the eighteenth century. They offer a look at emigration from German, French, and Scottish perspectives and express a range of emotions about it. It is important to remember that the vast majority of emigrants in this era did not leave texts describing their experiences. Literacy rates were low, and those emigrants who went as servants were the least likely to write about it. Thus, each of the sources presented below has its own bias, evident in the tone and style of the piece. As you read them, compare and contrast these biases: Does one source ring truer than the others? Is it possible to derive an accurate composite of the emigration experience from these sources?

SELECTION 1: A German Warns His Countrymen About the Perils of Migration

Gottlieb Mittelberger was an organist and teacher who joined the tide of emigration from the Rhine River Valley to Pennsylvania in the eighteenth century. When he made his voyage in 1750, Germans were pouring into Pennsylvania in such numbers that Benjamin Franklin complained they threatened to "Germanize us instead of our Anglifying them" (see p. 145). Despite his freedom from servitude and ability to settle among other Germans, Mittelberger did not like Pennsylvania, and in 1754 he returned to the family he had left at home. Two years later he published an account of his American sojourn to serve as a warning to other potential emigrants. His harshest criticism fell upon the *newlanders*, or recruitment agents, who used exaggerated stories of New World wealth to lure gullible souls into servitude. In his effort to expose the newlanders, Mittelberger provided a heart-wrenching account of the transatlantic crossing and the sale of servants once they landed in Philadelphia.

This journey lasts from the beginning of May until the end of October, that is, a whole six months, and involves such hardships that it is really impossible for any description to do justice to them. The reason for this is that the Rhine boats must pass by thirty-six different customs houses between Heilbronn and Holland. At each of these all the ships must be examined, and these examinations take place at the convenience of the customs officials. Meanwhile, the ships with the people in them are held up for a long time. This involves a great deal of expense for the passengers; and it also means that the trip down the Rhine alone takes from four to six weeks.

When the ships with their passengers arrive in Holland they are there held up once again for from five to six weeks. Because everything is very expensive in Holland the poor people must spend nearly all they own during this period. In addition various sad accidents are likely to occur here. I have, for instance, seen with my own eyes two of the children of a man trying to board ship near Rotterdam meet sudden death by drowning.

In Rotterdam, and to some extent also in Amsterdam, the people are packed into the big boats as closely as herring, so to speak. The bedstead of one person is hardly two feet across and six feet long, since many of the boats carry from four to six hundred passengers, not counting the immense amount of equipment, tools, provisions, barrels of fresh water, and other things that also occupy a great deal of space.

Because of contrary winds it sometimes takes the boats from two to four weeks to make the trip from Holland to Cowes [in England]. But, given favorable winds, that voyage can be completed in eight days or less. On arrival everything is examined once more and customs duties paid. It can happen that ships have to ride at anchor there from eight to fourteen days, or until they have taken on full cargoes. During this time everyone has to spend his last remaining money and to consume the provisions that he meant to save for the ocean voyage, so that most people must suffer tremendous hunger and want at sea where they really feel the greatest need. Many thus already begin their sufferings on the voyage between Holland and England.

When the ships have weighed anchor for the last time, usually off Cowes in Old England, then both the long sea voyage and misery begin in earnest. For from there the ships often take eight, nine, ten, or twelve weeks sailing to Philadelphia, if the wind is unfavorable. But even given the most favorable winds, the voyage takes seven weeks.

During the journey the ship is full of pitiful signs of distress—smells, fumes, horrors, vomiting, various kinds of sea sickness, fever, dysentery, headaches, heat, constipation, boils, scurvy, cancer, mouth-rot, and similar afflictions, all of them caused by the age and the highly-salted state of the food, especially of the meat, as well as by the very bad and filthy water, which brings about the miserable destruction and death of many. Add to all that shortage of food, hunger, thirst, frost, heat, dampness, fear, misery, vexation, and lamentation

From Gottlieb Mittelberger, *Journey to Pennsylvania*, edited and translated by Oscar Handlin and John Clive (Cambridge, Mass.: The Belknap Press of Harvard University Press, 1960), 11–19.

as well as other troubles. Thus, for example, there are so many lice, especially on the sick people, that they have to be scraped off the bodies. All this misery reaches its climax when in addition to everything else one must also suffer through two to three days and nights of storm, with everyone convinced that the ship with all aboard is bound to sink. In such misery all the people on board pray and cry pitifully together.

In the course of such a storm the sea begins to surge and rage so that the waves often seem to rise up like high mountains, sometimes sweeping over the ship; and one thinks that he is going to sink along with the ship. All the while the ship, tossed by storm and waves, moves constantly from one side to the other, so that nobody aboard can either walk, sit, or lie down and the tightly packed people on their cots, the sick as well as the healthy, are thrown every which way. One can easily imagine that these hardships necessarily affect many people so severely that they cannot survive them.

I myself was afflicted by severe illness at sea, and know very well how I felt. These people in their misery are many times very much in want of solace, and I often entertained and comforted them with singing, praying, and encouragement. Also, when possible, and when wind and waves permitted it, I held daily prayer meetings with them on deck, and, since we had no ordained clergyman on board, was forced to administer baptism to five children. I also held services, including a sermon, every Sunday, and when the dead were buried at sea, commended them and our souls to the mercy of God.

Among those who are in good health impatience sometimes grows so great and bitter that one person begins to curse the other, or himself and the day of his birth, and people sometimes come close to murdering one another. Misery and malice are readily associated, so that people begin to cheat and steal from one another. And then one always blames the other for having undertaken the voyage. Often the children cry out against their parents, husbands against wives and wives against husbands, brothers against their sisters, friends and acquaintances against one another.

But most of all they cry out against the thieves of human beings! Many groan and exclaim: "Oh! If only I were back at home, even lying in my pigsty!" Or they call out: "Ah, dear God, if I only once again had a piece of good bread or a good fresh drop of water." Many people whimper, sigh, and cry out pitifully for home. Most of them become homesick at the thought that many hundreds of people must necessarily perish, die, and be thrown into the ocean in such misery. And this in turn makes their families, or those who were responsible for their undertaking the journey, oftentimes fall almost into despair—so that it soon becomes practically impossible to rouse them from their depression. In a word, groaning, crying, and lamentation go on aboard day and night; so that even the hearts of the most hardened, hearing all this, begin to bleed.

One can scarcely conceive what happens at sea to women in childbirth and to their innocent offspring. Very few escape with their lives; and mother and child, as soon as they have died, are thrown into the water. On board our ship, on a day on which we had a great storm, a woman about to give birth and unable to deliver under the circumstances, was pushed through one of the portholes into the sea because her corpse was far back in the stern and could not be brought forward to the deck.

Children between the ages of one and seven seldom survive the sea voyage; and parents must often watch their offspring suffer miserably, die, and be thrown into the ocean, from want, hunger, thirst, and the like. I myself, alas, saw such a pitiful fate overtake thirty-two children on board our vessel, all of whom were finally thrown into the sea. Their parents grieve all the more, since their children do not find repose in the earth, but are devoured by the predatory fish of the ocean. It is also worth noting that children who have not had either measles or smallpox usually get them on board the ship and for the most part perish as a result.

On one of these voyages a father often becomes infected by his wife and children, or a mother by her small children, or even both parents by their children, or sometimes whole families one by the other, so that many times numerous corpses lie on the cots next to those who are still alive, especially when contagious diseases rage on board.

Many other accidents also occur on these ships, especially falls in which people become totally crippled and can never be completely made whole again. Many also tumble into the sea.

It is not surprising that many passengers fall ill, because in addition to all the other troubles and miseries, warm food is served only three times a week, and at that is very bad, very small in quantity, and so dirty as to be hardly palatable at all. And the water distributed in these ships is often very black, thick with dirt, and full of worms. Even when very thirsty, one is almost unable to drink it without loathing. It is certainly true that at sea one would often spend a great deal of money just for one good piece of bread, or one good drink of water—not even to speak of a good glass of wine—if one could only obtain them. I have, alas, had to experience that myself. For toward the end of the voyage we had to eat the ship's biscuit, which had already been spoiled for a long time, even though in no single piece was there more than the size of a thaler [a coin] that was not full of red worms and spiders nests. True, great hunger and thirst teach one to eat and drink everything—but many must forfeit their lives in the process. It is impossible to drink sea water, since it is salty and bitter as gall. If this were not the case, one could undertake such an ocean voyage with far less expense and without so many hardships.

When at last after the long and difficult voyage the ships finally approach land, when one gets to see the headlands for the sight of which the people on board had longed so passionately, then everyone crawls from below to the deck, in order to look at the land from afar. And people cry for joy, pray, and sing praises and thanks to God. The glimpse of land revives the passengers, especially those who are half-dead of illness. Their spirits, however weak they had become, leap up, triumph, and rejoice within them. Such people are now willing to bear all ills patiently, if only they can disembark soon and step on land. But, alas, alas!

When the ships finally arrive in Philadelphia after the long voyage only those are let off who can pay their sea freight or can give good security. The others, who lack the money to pay, have to remain on board until they are purchased and until their purchasers can thus pry them loose from the ship. In this whole process the sick are the worst off, for the healthy are preferred and are more readily paid for. The miserable people who are ill must often still remain at sea and in sight of the city for another two or three weeks—which in many cases means death. Yet many of them, were they able to pay their debts and to leave the ships at once, might escape with their lives.

◆   ◆   ◆

This is how the commerce in human beings on board ship takes place. Every day Englishmen, Dutchmen, and High Germans come from Philadelphia and other places, some of them very far away, sometime twenty or thirty or forty hours' journey, and go on board the newly arrived vessel that has brought people from Europe and offers them for sale. From among the healthy they pick out those suitable for the purposes for which they require them. Then they negotiate with them as to the length of the period for which they will go into service in order to pay off their passage, the whole amount of which they generally still owe. When an agreement has been reached, adult persons by written contract bind themselves to serve for three, four, five, or six years, according to their health and age. The very young, between the ages of ten and fifteen, have to serve until they are twenty-one, however.

Many parents in order to pay their fares in this way and get off the ship must barter and sell their children as if they were cattle. Since the fathers and mothers often do not know where or to what masters their children are to be sent, it frequently happens that after leaving the vessel, parents and children do not see each other for years on end, or even for the rest of their lives.

People who arrive without the funds to pay their way and who have children under the age of five, cannot settle their debts by selling them. They must give away these children for nothing to be brought up by strangers; and in return these children must stay in service until they are twenty-one years old. Children between five and ten who owe half-fare, that is, thirty florins, must also go into service in return until they are twenty-one years old, and can neither set free their parents nor take their debts upon themselves. On the other hand, the sale of children older than ten can help to settle a part of their parents' passage charges.

A wife must be responsible for her sick husband and a husband for his sick wife, and pay his or her fare respectively, and must thus serve five to six years not only for herself or himself, but also for the spouse, as the case may be. If both should be ill on arrival, then such persons are brought directly from the ship into a hospital, but not until it is clear that no purchaser for them is to be found. As soon as they have recovered, they must serve to pay off their fare, unless they have the means immediately to discharge the debt.

It often happens that whole families—husband, wife, and children—being sold to different purchasers, become separated, especially when they cannot pay any part of the passage money. When either the husband or the wife has died at sea, having come more than halfway, then the surviving spouse must pay not only his or her fare, but must also pay for or serve out the fare of the deceased.

When both parents have died at sea, having come more than halfway, then their children, especially when they are still young and have nothing to pawn or cannot pay, must be responsible for their own fares as well as those of their parents, and must serve until they are twenty-one years old. Once free of service, they receive a suit of clothing as a parting gift, and if it has been so stipulated the men get a horse and the women a cow.

SELECTION 2: A French Account of a Passage to Canada

"Jolicoeur" Charles Bonin, or J. C. B. as he identified himself in his narrative, was a well-educated 18-year-old when he set out from his home in Paris in 1751 to seek work with an uncle in the port city of La Rochelle. His uncle's death forced him to reconsider his options, and he decided to head for Canada, where he enlisted in the army and served in the Seven Years' War. Like many French emigrants to America, Bonin was young, single, and transient; at no time did he seem to consider his move permanent, and he returned to France in 1761. He wrote his narrative many years later, in a style that combines an old soldier's war stories with history and travelogue. In the passages that follow, he provides a colorful account of his transatlantic passage, as well as explanations for his decisions to emigrate and enlist in the army.

Year 1751:—I left Paris on the 15th of March to go to La Rochelle, with my father's permission. I was then eighteen years old. While I was walking along the road, I came upon a detachment of one hundred and twenty recruits led by an officer. He was taking them to the Isle of Rhée, the place of their departure. This officer hailed me, and questioned me about the purpose of my trip, my affairs and financial resources. I replied that I was going, with my father's permission, to join my uncle who was captain of the posts at La Rochelle, and had been awaiting me for six months. As for my financial resources, they were not large but sufficient for me until my arrival. Then my uncle would put me in the way of earning more. After this reply, the officer proposed that I travel with him to my destination, where he was going to stay, but on condition that I take care of his things on the way. To this I consented willingly. By my behavior I gained his confidence, and was lodged and fed with him.

When we arrived at La Rochelle, I thanked him and took leave of him in order to go and join my uncle. But when I arrived at his place, I was indeed surprised to learn that the latter had been buried a week before. Because of this misfortune, together with the smallness of my resources for returning to Paris, I decided to find the officer I had just left, and tell him what had happened. This man offered to take me with him to the Isle of Rhée, where he hoped to get me a job from the governor of the citadel. I accepted his offer.

From *Travels in New France by J. C. B.*, edited by Sylvester K. Stevens, Donald H. Kent, and Emma Edith Woods (Harrisburg, Penn.: Pennsylvania Historical Commission, 1941), 1–5, 10, 15–17.

The next day, April 2nd, we crossed in two small sailboats to the Isle of Rhée. As soon as we arrived, I followed the officer, who led his recruits to the citadel and turned them over to the governor. He recommended me so highly that I was at once employed in his office. The pay was small; but in my position I dared not hesitate.

When I had worked about twelve months, I was tormented with a desire to travel. I sought information about the best country to live in; about Louisiana and Canada, the only places to which recruits were then taken from the Isle of Rhée. The sailors told me that Canada was more healthy, although its climate was colder. I decided to take their advice, and to take advantage of the first sailing, which was not far off. This I did despite the offers made by the governor, which I refused, expecting that the voyage would be more profitable. The orders had come to have a number of select recruits embark for the colonies of Louisiana and Canada. The first sailing was to Louisiana, and included two hundred men. Some of these had been companions of mine on the road. The second sailing was not delayed, and I took advantage of it.

The 12th of June, I left the Isle of Rhée, five leagues from La Rochelle, in one of two small boats which took three hundred recruits down the Charente River, which is two leagues from Rochefort. There a vessel was waiting to take us to Canada. This vessel was called the *Chariot Royal*. It was a frigate used as a transport, and although pierced for thirty-six cannon, it carried only eight. It was commanded by a naval captain named Salabéry.

The 27th of the same month of June, we set sail by a good wind from the northeast, which in two days carried us from the coast of France, setting our course to the west-northwest.

The 31st, the wind became so contrary that we had to use the bowline and tack about for several days. The sea was so rough that we experienced a bad tempest which made us put on the spencer [a low sail]. On this occasion I paid tribute to the sea with a sickness which lasted as long as the bad weather, nearly five days. All this time I could not eat. At last the wind went down, and the sea became calm. I then recovered my appetite, but, the wind falling completely, the ship stood still, and we were becalmed for two days.

July 15th, a light easterly breeze came up and helped us on our way, but not for long. For, two days later, another storm struck and made us keep on the spencer four more days. In spite of myself, I renewed the tribute to the sea that I had thought paid in full. A rough sea has a disagreeable effect on my stomach.

At last the wind began to shift, the sea became placid, and we could continue our journey, but for only twenty-four hours. A contrary wind then became so strong that we had to tack for three days. After that, the wind shifted to the south, and we went on our way to the Jacquet Bank, some distance from the Grand Banks of Newfoundland. There, a contrary wind forced us to luff for several days. Then a fierce tempest, also from the west, drove us back about eighty leagues. In these circumstances the rudder line happened to break, and the compass was put out of order. Repairs were quickly made, and four days later we could continue on our way.

August 15th, the wind was again contrary, and we had about three weeks of continual tacking.

The 14th of September, we arrived at the Grand Banks of Newfoundland, in eighty fathoms of water. Immediately the sailors cried, "Long live the King." This is a custom among the sailors when they find bottom.

The Banks of Newfoundland are nine hundred leagues west of France. They are thought to be one hundred and fifty leagues long by about ninety wide, and from fifteen to eighty fathoms deep. They are really a mountain under water. We had much to suffer on these banks from rain and contrary winds, which held us up for several days in spite of all our efforts. This is the most disagreeable and most uncomfortable place in the ocean. The sun seldom appears, and the air is filled with a cold dense fog.

The nearest land is Cape Rouge, which stretches for thirty-five leagues from east to west, and is part of the island of Newfoundland, which will be described later.

The wind had just fallen when we arrived on the Grand Banks, and since there was a beautiful calm, the sailors wanted to catch some codfish. But as it was late, they put off the party until the next day, provided the weather was favorable. Unfortunately, there was a heavy rain during the night, along with thunder and lightning. The whole sky seemed to be cracking open. There was one crash of thunder after another, and the lightning alone threw momentarily the light of day into the darkness. The thunderbolts fell near the vessel with a racket like cannon-fire. We were all terrified. During the hour and a half that the storm continued we seemed to be in the trenches. I was ready at any moment to become food for the codfish on which we had planned to feast the next day.

After two hours of worry and anxiety, between life and death, the light of day appeared; the thunder and lightning stopped; the wind ceased; and the sea became calm. The sailors repaired the damaged rigging, and we were then able, about noon, to catch some fish. In three days' fishing we took enough cod to feed us for several days.

❖   ❖   ❖

As the weather continued calm, the crew amused themselves with a baptismal ceremony that the sailors practice on those who cross the banks for the first time. For this ceremony, they disguise and old sailor with a large fur cap, a pair of high boots, a white wig on his head, a helmet, and a large white false beard. The sailor thus costumed descends from the main-topmast where he dressed. With the aid of cords and pulleys he slides to the foot of the foremast, where the other sailors receive and conduct him to the foot of the mainmast. Near this they hold the new member to a seat on the edge of a tub filled with water. There Father Terreneuve [Newfoundland] makes the new member swear to keep the secret from those who have not yet passed this latitude, with a promise never to touch the wife of another sailor. This he must promise at once. If the new member has not taken the precaution of buying drinks, he is immediately tipped into the water by the two men holding him. He then emerges to change his clothes. During this time Father Terreneuve goes away, takes off his costume, and reappears, so that the man who was ducked will not recognize him. This is the end of the ceremony, which is quite disagreeable in cold weather, and is only a game played by the sailors to get money.

❖   ❖   ❖

On the fourth [of November], taking advantage of the tide, we rounded a point of land on our left, which extended somewhat above Orleans Island and to the north. This is called Point Lévis. Then only can the city of Quebec be seen, opposite the channel by the island, and about a league to the west. We entered the roadstead and anchored at four o'clock in the afternoon, after a difficult voyage of nearly five months. As it was too late to land, we waited until the next day.

On the morning of the fifth we landed. The recruits were taken to the barracks, and I was given lodgings with a wholesale merchant named Samson, who lived in the lower town. I was very well lodged. I remained five days with this honest merchant, who treated me with kindness. In this time I roamed the city and its surroundings, getting from my host any information that I desired.

❖   ❖   ❖

In five days, I had visited the most interesting places. I was then forced to give up my life of needy idleness. I therefore determined to take up the military profession, which, though seeming severe, would nevertheless relieve me at once from my difficulties.

This decision was compelled by circumstances. I felt an inclination for a more lucrative occupation. But I made up my mind and of my own free will left the merchant with whom I had been boarding, going at once to the artillery commander to enlist in that company, because, after making inquiries, that branch of the service seemed more to my liking. They were paid sixteen to eighteen francs a month.

When I informed this officer of my wish to enlist, he said I was unfit and not tall enough to enter the artillery service. Fortunately for me, three women were there, who were willing to take an interest in my welfare, because of my well-bred air. After he had asked me various questions, which I answered frankly to the best of my ability, the officer decided to enlist me as a gunner, at the request of these ladies. They thanked him, and to show their satisfaction, proceeded to give me the nickname of "Jolicoeur [sweet-heart]." A louis of provincial paper money accompanied it, which one of them gave me. I accepted it very willingly, for I was penniless. At the same time I received the commander's orders to be present at the review by the Governor General, which was to be held the next day, November the 12th, on the Place d'Armes. The recruits were to be incorporated into the various companies of troops garrisoned in the city and not yet formed in regiments, because they were reckoned free companies of the marine. I was present at the review. All the troops were under arms in three lines, which included eighteen companies. The recruits opposite were unarmed and formed two lines.

The governor, accompanied by the staff officer, arrived about noon. When they had assigned me my place at the end of the two artillery companies, which perform the duties of grenadiers, the inspection began. When the commander spoke of me to the governor, he looked me over. That was all, as far as I was concerned. He went on to the other companies and finally to the recruits. There, each captain, according to his age, beginning with the gunners, took the number of men assigned to him. The commander of the gunners chose ten without counting me, and the other captains did the same. When the selection of men was finished, each company retired with its recruits. I was one of five taken into the second company, which was lodged over the Gate St. Jean. The next day we were given our clothing and equipment.

As usual during a review, a great many persons, even the most distinguished people of the city, were attracted by curiosity. I saw there with pleasure my three patronesses, who made much of me and gave me eighteen francs in silver. Their generosity was a happy omen for me. When I joined the company, I gave the eighteen francs I had just received to pay my initiation fee, as was the usual custom. It secured me friends in the usual soldier way, but I valued them only as far as they could serve my interest, and without making a habit of frequenting taverns with them.

They gave me as a bedfellow (for they slept double) a Parisian with a handsome and pleasing face, who had the vices of gambling and drink. He was also quarrelsome and ill-natured, often drawing his sword without the slightest provocation. In time, however, I began to acquire so much influence over him, that I subdued his fits of passion by my very presence. In the morning he was good-natured and amiable, especially toward women, whom he studied to deceive. He was extremely fond of dancing, at which he was an expert. He gave me a liking for it, by taking me with him to balls and teaching me its principles. At the end of three months I became, under his supervision, almost as proficient in that art, which helped at least for a time to turn him from his vices. Later, when I neglected him somewhat, he took up his old habits. He took advantage of my kindness to him by wearing my clothes and helping himself to my money, to a point where I was often unable to go out. This conduct cooled my friendship, and I decided to break with him.

During the month of December, a merchant offered me a place in his store to keep books and learn his business. I took it without hesitation because I had vowed, viewing the uncertainty of the future, that I would learn everything possible that I might need to use. I knew that a man who has but one aim might find himself embarrassed if that should fail him. I then began work with the merchant, who, finding me full of zeal for his interests, became my friend. I pleased him so much that he worked for my discharge from the army. This benevolent act encouraged me to show him my great gratitude, which I did with all my heart. He took all the steps he thought necessary for my discharge, but they were fruitless. I was told, indirectly, that this good man intended to take me into his business as soon as he had procured my discharge, and to give me the store, and his only daughter in marriage. She was a beautiful, well-educated young girl. On this occasion fortune was unkind, and I regretted then that I had enlisted.

SELECTION 3: Two Scottish Opinions on the Emigration Experience

In the fifteen years prior to the American Revolution, a new tide of emigration spilled out of the British Isles and into North America. A considerable number of these emigrants came from Scotland, seeking cheap lands and settling on a backcountry frontier that stretched from New York to Georgia. Promotional and support networks made up of kin and neighbors sprung up on both sides of the Atlantic to sustain this migration, and correspondence between Scotland and America provided the primary channel for exchanging information. Alexander Thomson was a farmer from near Glasgow who moved his large family to the Pennsylvania frontier in 1771. He prospered quickly on his own land and had the letter that follows published back home to inform others of the opportunity waiting for them in America.

Baikia Harvey, a 16-year-old indentured servant from the Orkney Islands, had a much different experience. He arrived in Georgia on the eve of the American Revolution and quickly found himself embroiled in guerilla warfare between patriots and loyalists. His letter to his godfather conveys a sense of the terror that his new surroundings caused him. He was killed in battle in 1779 while serving in a patriot unit attacking a British post.

Corkerhill [Thomson's farm, near Shippensburg]
in Pensilvania, August 16th, 1773.

Dear Sir,

I know well that after the promises I made you, you could not have thought that so much time would pass, before you had any letter from me. Indeed I did not forget my promise, but after I had got an agreeable settlement to myself, I was desirous to have some particular knowledge of this country, before I should undertake to write any account of it to you.

In July 1771, I and my wife and twelve of our children went aboard the Friendship in the harbour of Greenock: It was after the middle of that month when we set sail for North-America, and happily we arrived at the city Boston on the tenth of September, all in perfect health.

I believe that some of my neighbours and acquaintance thought it strange, that one of my age should forsake his native country: but I thought I had but too much reason to do as I have done: as I was blessed with a numerous family, (and I have had another child since I left Scotland) I was very desirous to provide for them: All my sons who were able to work were brought up to the business of farming, and it was by their labour that I was assisted to gain any money I have: I therefore endeavoured to have one or two of the eldest of my sons settled in farms at home; and with that view I employed myself for the space of five years, in looking out for such farms as might answer my purpose. I travelled through the country for twenty miles round the place where I lived;

From *Discoveries of America: Personal Accounts of British Emigrants to North America During the Revolutionary Era*, edited by Barbara De Wolfe (Cambridge, England: Cambridge University Press, 1997), 110–115, 121, 211–212.

but tho' I found plenty of vacant farms, I told you before, and I declare it again on the word of an honest man, that I could see no farm for which the laird [landlord] did not ask more than double the rent it was worth; so that if I had meddled with any of them I say well that my sons would never be able to pay the rent, and that in three or four years I would not have had one shilling to rub upon another.

After I had spent so much time and labour to no purpose, I confess that at length I conceived a sort of distaste for the lairds: I imagined that as they knew I had a little money, they wanted to get it from me as fast as they could; and in truth some of my neighbours observed a change in my temper, and alledged that I was turned so obstinate that I would not stay in the country, even though some laird should offer me a farm or two on reasonable terms: and I dare not say they were altogether in the wrong.

As I was going to America not for merchandizing but as a farmer; several of my acquaintance and well-wishers told me that I would save both time and money by landing at New York or Philadelphia, but I had a great curiosity to see Boston, especially as I understood that some of my father's friends had settled there long ago, and some from Paisley very lately. However I stayed at Boston but a few days; for I made all the haste I could to wait on Dr. Witherspoon [a fellow Scot and President of Princeton College] at Princeton in West-Jersey, and when I had gone there, I was sorry to hear that he had gone away a day or two before, to convoy some of his pupils home to their parents who lived in Virginia; but I had the good luck to come up with him in the city of Philadelphia. I delivered to him the letters I had from Scotland, and he received me very kindly: When he understood my errand he was very earnest to assist me to get a right farm. He advised me to take patience, and that I should not be hasty in making a bargain. But that as he was upon a journey, I should wait at Princeton till his return, when he would do all he could to get me settled in a comfortable manner: He also advised me to rent a farm for some time, but as I had so great a family with me, I was desirous to have a house of my own as soon as I could conveniently get it: and I also thought it would be better for me to improve land that was my own than any rented farm; and as I had heard so much said about the goodness of land upon the Ohio, both at home and since I had come here, I would fain have settled there at first, but as I could not conveniently do so, I bargained for the plantation on which I now live, before Dr. Witherspoon returned from Virginia; and if it had not been for the reason I have told you, I would have conducted myself entirely by his advice. But I have much cause to rejoice and none to repent that I made this purchase.

◆   ◆   ◆

It was in April 1772, that I settled on this plantation: It is situated at the distance of 150 miles from Philadelphia, and it is just as far from Fort-pit [modern Pittsburgh]; it lies in a large and beautiful valley which runs thro' all Pensylvania, Maryland, and Virginia it consists of about 430 acres, and there was a house of two stories high, and office-houses upon it: The house is built of square blocks of wood nocked or indented into one another; it is well plaistered, so that it is warm enough, and I have six convenient rooms in it.

My plantation which I have called Corkerhill, after the name of the farm where my father lived and died, and where I lived so long; My plantation consists wholly of limestone-land, and in general limestone-land is reckoned the best in this country. There is plenty of limestone for manure in every field, and it doth not cost much labour or expence to come at it; and it can be burned with the wood which we grub out when we clear the ground. Our greatest labour is to cut the wood into small pieces when we are to burn the lime.

Dear Sir, I do assure you I am well pleased with the country, and with my situation in it. I bless God that I came here, and I heartily thank every man who encouraged me and helped me to get the better of that fear which a man is under when he is to venture over so wide a sea, and indeed when, excepting my eldest son, I was to carry along with me all that was dear to me in the word, I could not but be anxious about them; but I was determined in my mind, and providence hath been very favourable to us. We are all at present in good health; and blessed be God, we have always been so since we came into this country. They say here, that the air and climate of Pensilvania agrees better with European constitutions, than even the air of Europe itself, and I am inclined to think that this is true, from that constant health which my family have enjoyed.

◆　◆　◆

We who are country people used always to think it a great matter, that the gentlemen in Scotland had orchards, we thought this a fine thing; but here, almost every farmer hath a good orchard, and indeed squashes, pimpkins [sic], gourds, cucumbers, melons, and all other garden-stuff grow in the open fields: But unluckily through the slothfulness of my predecessor, there was no orchard on the plantation when I came to it; To supply this defect, I have already planted two hundred fruit trees, and I was pleased to see that one of the trees had three apples upon it this year, though it was not planted till march last.

Dear Sir, I have said so much about my industry and labour upon the plantation, but I have said it on purpose, because I know that a vile and false report hath been published at home, that it is only lazy persons who come over here. Now you know well, and I need not tell you that the very contrary is true; the lazy are motionless, and like snails abide on the spot where they are, till they either starve, or are compelled by hunger to go a begging: whereas the industrious strive to maintain themselves by their labour without being troublesome to any body, and many of them finding it difficult to live by their labour at home, they are so far from being lazy, that they have activity and spirit to venture over to America: but I pity many of your poor people who are indeed very lazy; and it is impossible but they must be lazy, because they have found by long experience that by all their labour they can make no profit to themselves.

◆　◆　◆

Dear Sir, notwithstanding my promise, I am yet very unfit to write you a description of the country; and indeed it is needless, as you know so much and so well about it already: but for the sake of my promise, and for your satisfaction, I will tell you the truth about it as far as I can, and I shall begin with the climate.

Till I came into this country I did not, I could not imagine the climate was so fine and so healthy: The air is sweet and clear, and we find an agreeable smell; one would think that the sky is much farther distant from us than it seems to be at home. The south-west-wind rules the summer seasons, and the north-west the winter. The winters which are very agreeable continue from December till March; and we have no such black foul weather as at home, but a fine pure sky and bright heavens; no storms as at home, but fine small breezes; no winds to shake or rains to rot the corn.

Sir, I cannot express the beauty of the summer season, it is so fine, so pleasing, and healthy. While I and my sons are clearing ground, and go for a while to walk, or rest ourselves in the forest among the tall oaks on a summer day, the sight of the heavens and the smell of the air give me a pleasure which I cannot tell you how great it is. When we sit down to rest, the breezes of the south-west wind, and the whispering noise it makes on the top of the trees, together with the fine smell of the plants and flowers pleases us so exceedingly, that we are almost enchanted and unwilling to part with such a pleasure. If my dear countrymen knew the beauty and healthiness of the climate, they would not be so afraid to come to North-America. There are a good number of old people just about where I live, some sixty, some seventy, and some eighty years of age. I thought it right to tell you all this, because I know that much pains have been taken to spread abroad a bad opinion of the country and climate, as if it were unhealthy: I will not say why this hath been done, but I suspect it hath taken its rise from some designing men among you, who though they saw many people in great straits, and many next door to starving, have for some views of their own, endeavoured to terrify them from coming here.

In truth, I am sorry to hear of the great distress of farmers and tradesmen in your country. You mention this in your letter, but I have heard much more from some folks I lately met with when I was at Philadelphia; and so far as I understand, the weavers and other tradesmen, as also many farmers are in a far worse condition than they were when I came away in the year 1771, for it seems the tradesmen cannot get employment, and the meal continues to be as dear as it was. If the tradesmen and farmers would come here, they would soon find themselves in a better condition; and there is plenty of room for them all, yea for all the people that are in the three kingdoms. And this is the best poor man's country in the world, for the price of provisions is cheap, and the price of labour is dear; and there are many people in Pensilvania and the neighbouring provinces, who had to work here to pay their freight, who have good plantations and are in wealthy circumstances: But this country is chiefly profitable to those farmers who bring along with them one, two, or three hundred pounds; such farmers can afford to eat good pork, beef, or mutton, as often as those who have one, two, or three hundred pounds of yearly rent in Scotland; that is to say, if they have some tolerable skill in farming, and live upon the land they take up here; and I believe there are no farmers in the world who live on so coarse and so poor food as do the generality of farmers in poor Scotland.

❖   ❖   ❖

I had almost forgot to tell you, That when I was at Philadelphia, I saw some Scotch newspapers in which a great deal was said about the death of emigrants by sea and their wretched state after they have come to the American towns. As I have said already, I never heard of any ill happening to emigrants by sea, and if they suffer any harm here, it will be rather from the hospitality than from the cruelty of this people; no doubt those who are forced to indent must be in a state of dependance till they have served out their time, and I pity their case. But as I have told you, I know several people here who served to pay their freight, who have now good plantations. However, our opinion here is, That both your farmers and tradesmen should come away before they grow so poor that they will have nothing to bring with them, or even to pay their freight. . . .

I am, . . .

Alexander Thomson

❖   ❖   ❖

Dear Godfather

I am very sorry that I did not take your Advise and stay at home with you as I have found to my sad Experence that I ought not to have slighting your Advise Mr Gordon us'd me vere good to me but Mr Brown us'd me vere ill and I Runaway from them & wint to the Armey that was mar[c]hing up to the Back parts of South Carolina against a sett of people they call Torrys in this Country and when I cam back I went to One Mr LeRoy Hammond a Merchant in So. Carolina & he Bought my time which I am vere glad of for he & his Lady uses me vere will & gives me Cloaths & I Ride with my Master & Loves them Both You'l Please to send me all the Money you can Colect that is my Due by the first safe oppertunity that I may be enabled to Buy my time & Put myself to some Tradesman to Learn his calling for a Tradsman has good Wages in this Country I beg that none of my Relation[s] may come to this Country Except they are able to pay their passage thir Selves and then they may come as soon as they like this is a good poor mans Country when a man once getts into a way of Liveing but our Country people knows Nothing when they come hear the Americans are Smart Industours hardy people & fears Nothing our people is only Like the New Negros that comes out of the ships at first whin they come amongst them[.] I am Just Returnd from the Back parts Where I seed Eight Thousand Men in Arms all with Riffel'd Barrill Guns which they can kill the Bigness of a Dollar Betwixt Two & three hundreds yards Distance the Little Boys not Bigger then my self has all their Guns & marshes with their Fathers & all thir Cry is Liberty or Death Dear Godfather tell all my Country people not to come hear for the Americans will Kill them Like Deer in the Woods & they will never see them they can lie on their Backs & Load & fire & every time they Draw sight at any thing they are sure to kill or Criple & they Run in the Woods Like Horses I seed the Liberty Boys take Between Two & three hundred Torrys & one Liberty man would take & Drive four or five before him Just as the Shepards do the sheep in our

Country & they have taken all their Arms from them and putt the Headmen in Gail [jail]—so that they will never be able to make head against them any more—Pray Remember me to my Dear freind Mr. James Riddoh Mrs. Gordon Madam Allin Madam Young My Uncle & Aunt & all their Femily & in perticular Mr. John Gordon—I am Dear Godfather Your Most Obident and Huml. Godson

    Snowhill Near Augusta in Georgia   Baikia Harvey
    Decemr. 30th 1775
    P.S. Please to write me the first Oppertunity to the Care of Mr. John Houston in Savannah Georgia Province etc.

⤳ Discussion Questions ⤳

1. According to Gottlieb Mittelberger and Charles Bonin, what were some of the perils faced by emigrants during the transatlantic passage? How do you think those perils compared to those faced by slaves coming from Africa in the Middle Passage (see Chapter 4, pp. 73–76)? Why do you think the tone of Bonin's account of the voyage differs so much from Mittelberger's?

2. According to Alexander Thomson, what were the keys to succeeding in America? Why does he describe Pennsylvania as "the best poor man's country in the world"? On what grounds do you think Mittelberger would take issue with him?

3. Both Bonin and Baikia Harvey ended up in military service after they emigrated to America. Why do you think this occupation attracted recent emigrants?

4. How do these emigrant-authors describe the circumstances that pushed them out of their original homes? What pulled them to their particular destinations in America? How do you think their social position in Europe affected the conditions of their emigration and their reactions to America? Taking into consideration these differences in backgrounds and circumstances, should you make generalizations about the migration experience from these sources?

Suggested Readings

Human migration has become one of the most important unifying themes in Atlantic World history, enabling scholars to compare and contrast the experiences of different peoples, nations, and regions at different times during the colonization of the Americas. Two useful overviews are *Europeans on the Move: Studies on European Migration, 1500–1800*, edited by Nicholas Canny (Oxford: Clarendon Press, 1994), and *"To Make America": European Emigration in the Early Modern Period*, edited by Ida Altman and James Horn

(Berkeley: University of California Press, 1991). Noteworthy for their comparative approach are Marianne S. Wokeck, *Trade in Strangers: The Beginnings of Mass Migration to North America* (University Park, Penn: The Pennsylvania State University Press, 1999), which analyzes eighteenth-century German and Irish emigration to Pennsylvania, and Alan L. Karras, *Sojourners in the Sun: Scottish Migrants in Jamaica and the Chesapeake, 1740–1800* (Ithaca, N.Y.: Cornell University Press, 1992), which compares the Scottish experiences in North America and the Caribbean.

Several important studies focus on emigration from the British Isles to North America. For the seventeenth century, see Alison Games, *Migration and the Origins of the English Atlantic World* (Cambridge, Mass.: Harvard University Press, 1999). For the eighteenth century, see Bernard Bailyn, *Voyagers to the West: A Passage in the Peopling of America on the Eve of the Revolution* (New York: Random House, 1986). David Hackett Fischer explores how the successive waves of emigration from the British Isles shaped the cultural geography of the United States in *Albion's Seed: Four British Folkways in America* (New York: Oxford University Press, 1989). A. Roger Ekirch discusses British convict migration to North America in *Bound for America: The Transportation of British Convicts to the Colonies, 1718–1775* (New York: Oxford University Press, 1987). Migrations and their effect on American attitudes about naturalization and citizenship are discussed in Marilyn C. Baseler, *"Asylum for Mankind": America, 1607–1800* (Ithaca, N.Y.: Cornell University Press, 1998).

For eighteenth-century German migration, see Aaron Spencer Fogleman, *Hopeful Journeys: German Immigration, Settlement, and Political Culture in Colonial America, 1717–1775* (Philadelphia: University of Pennsylvania Press, 1996). Ida Altman analyzes Spanish emigration to the New World in *Emigrants and Society: Extremadura and America in the Sixteenth Century* (Berkeley: University of California Press, 1989). For an examination of the disease and mortality involved in European migration to the Caribbean, see Philip D. Curtin, *Death by Migration: Europe's Encounter with the Tropical World in the Nineteenth Century* (Cambridge, England: Cambridge University Press, 1989).

Catherine tekakoüita Iroquoise du Saut
S.t Louis de Montreal en Canada morte
en odeur de Sainteté.

A Female Indian Saint

Kateri Tekakwitha converted to Christianity as a young girl and left her village in the Mohawk Valley to live among other Indians converted by French Jesuits in Kahnawake, a French *reserve* near Montreal. Her mentors considered her a model of female piety, because she refused to take a husband and insisted on living a life of chastity and bodily mortification (see Selection 1). She died at a young age and was quickly venerated by the priests and nuns of New France as "the Lily of the Mohawks." She is currently a candidate for sainthood in the Catholic Church. How is her saintliness conveyed in this image, and how does it compare to the depiction of Indian converts in Illustrations 3.1 and 6.1 (pp. 42 and 106)?

Source: Dechert Collection/Annenberg Rare Book and Manuscript Library/University of Pennsylvania

Constructing Gender
in the Atlantic World

Introduction

Biology divides humans into males and females, but society shapes our notions of gender difference. In other words, nature may determine a person's sex, but gender—the ideas, roles, and behavior associated with being male or female—is constructed by the social world a person inhabits. Each society defines its own standards for masculinity and femininity, for sexual conduct and expression, for a division of labor between men and women; and as with any other social category, gender roles adapt to changing historical circumstances. The Atlantic World offers an interesting theater for studying the historical construction of gender because it brought together peoples with vastly different notions of how the two sexes ought to interact. Each group involved in this collision tried to preserve its own gender roles, but each also found those roles challenged by exposure to new people, environments, and ideas. Like any other system used for ordering human relationships, gender had to be reconstructed in the crucible of the Atlantic World to reflect the new societies that emerged there.

The Europeans who conquered and colonized the Americas brought with them their own gender roles. While values and practices rooted in gender identity varied between European nations, they shared a few bedrock assumptions about ordering relations between the sexes. All European societies were patriarchal in their law and family structure: The male head of the household ruled over his wife, children, and other dependents, controlling the family's resources and representing its members in the marketplace and courthouse. When a couple married, the wife passed from the authority of her father to her husband, and the right to any property she brought to the marriage was likewise typically vested in her husband. This type of social and legal patriarchy associated masculinity with such public activities as trade and politics and femininity with such domestic activities as child-rearing and the household production of food and clothing. Of course, women and men could and did move about in both worlds, but Europeans considered a feminine private sphere and masculine public one essential to a well-ordered society.

The degree to which Europeans transplanted these gender roles to the Americas varied according to local circumstances. In colonial New England, many colonists arrived as members of nuclear families and quickly replicated patterns of marriage, childbearing, and domestic production from the Old World. However, the religious beliefs that motivated many of these colonists also encouraged a female spiritual activism that challenged the male clergy. Ann Hutchinson and Mary Dyer were two such outspoken women whose defiance of traditional church and state authority in religious matters incurred the wrath of male magistrates and led to their banishment from Massachusetts. Elsewhere in the Americas, the demographic disruption caused by high mortality rates and an imbalanced sex ratio among colonists temporarily loosened the bonds of patriarchal authority over European women, enabling them to exert wider marriage choice, more control over property and inheritance, and greater influence in political and religious affairs. This initial flexibility in gender roles gave way to a reassertion of patriarchal power as colonial societies stabilized and developed the institutions necessary to maintain separate male and female spheres.

A good way to examine this process is by looking at the intersection of European colonial populations with Native Americans and Africans. Early European emigration to the Americas tended to be overwhelmingly male, leading many male colonists to pursue economic and sexual partnerships with women who came from societies that constructed gender very differently. In Canada, for example, European fur traders found marriage to Native American women a profitable way of gaining entry to native communities. The Indians of New France came from a society in which kinship was determined matrilineally and much of daily life was matrifocal: Family and clan membership passed through the mother, and clan matrons—the elder women of different lineages—held considerable influence over village politics. Women also were the primary agricultural laborers and managed the planting and harvesting of crops, while men took responsibility for hunting, trade, and diplomacy with outsiders. Missionaries tried to impose a European gender division of labor on their Christian converts, encouraging men to work in the fields and women to learn domestic tasks such as spinning and dairying, but they met with limited success. The extension of the fur trade and preservation of Indian friendship demanded that the French not push the imposition of patriarchy too far, lest marriage alliances fail and converts abandon the faith.

By the eighteenth century, there emerged in Canada a type of European-Indian marriage that fur traders called *marriage à la façon du pays*. In such unions, a male European fur trader took a Native American wife in a ceremony that involved asking the permission of her family and presenting them a gift of trade goods. These women contributed to the labor of the fur trade by continuing such traditional work as stringing snowshoes and making canoes, but they also served as interpreters and negotiators between Indians and Europeans. Missionaries frowned upon such marriages because they followed native rather than Christian custom, were often temporary, and in some cases were even polygamous. Nevertheless, the custom remained an important part of the Canadian fur trade well into the nineteenth century and gave Indian women an influence in the marketplace and diplomatic councils that their European counterparts could not rival.

The intersection of gender, race, and labor in plantation colonies had very different ramifications. In early plantation societies, European men and women often worked side by side in the fields, and female servants were particularly susceptible to the sexual and physical abuse of their masters. As the slave population of a plantation colony increased, masters preferred to put African women to work in the fields alongside their male counterparts, so that white women could cease fieldwork and resume their traditional domestic duties. In this manner, plantation societies associated slavery with a feminized dependence and servility, while creating a standard of female respectability that was limited to whites only. This racial construction of gender is evident in the changing meaning of the word *wench* in colonial Virginia. The English who colonized Virginia initially used *wench* as a derogatory term for women of lower-class status, applying it interchangeably to white servants and black slaves. By the early eighteenth century, when slavery had displaced servitude as the colony's chief form of labor, white colonists used *wench* only in reference to women of African descent.

In Iberian America, the construction of gender roles reflected the distinctive heritage of Spanish and Portuguese colonists as well as their close contact with Native American and African populations. The confluence of Islamic and Christian faiths on the Iberian Peninsula during the medieval era had produced an ideal of femininity that emphasized seclusion and sexual purity. A family's honor depended in a large part upon how well its female members met social standards of piety and modesty, and marriage and female religious orders developed as the appropriate institutions for making sure women met these expectations. In the New World, the offspring of sexual unions between Iberian men and Native American or African women violated Iberian notions of "purity of blood," or the absence of non-Christian ancestry necessary for social and legal legitimacy. Elites placed great value in legal marriage (as recognized by the state and church), because it provided the basis for separating a father's rightful heirs from his illegitimate ones. People of mixed-race ancestry (see Chapter 6, pp. 106–125) lacked such "purity of blood" and often lived in a state of concubinage, or informal marriage, which the clergy frowned upon but society nevertheless tolerated. Thus, a correlation developed between race, social status, and illegitimacy in Iberian colonies: Non-whites, who occupied the lower rungs of the social ladder, were more likely to bear illegitimate children than property-owning whites. Family honor and female chastity became values linked specifically to an elite exhibiting "purity of blood," while the lower orders of society lacked access to the legal recognition and property necessary to achieve such status.

The readings in this chapter come from women who lived or traveled in the Atlantic World between 1600 and 1800. During this time, women generally had lower literacy rates than men, and thus, left far fewer first-person accounts of their lives. Those who did tended to write either spiritual autobiographies or travel narratives. In both cases, women often wrote about topics, such as domestic relations, overlooked by male writers, and they used a distinctive style that reveals the inner dimensions of female experience in a way not available in other sources (this is especially true for spiritual autobiographies). Of course, African and Native American women were even less likely to leave behind the sort of first-person accounts excerpted here (note that one African woman's spiritual autobiography is included on pp. 199–200), but their experiences can be glimpsed in the selections that follow. As you read them, think about how you might use these sources to describe the construction of gender in colonial societies: What role did racial difference play in notions of gender and sexuality? How did religion and labor shape the way men and women interacted in these cross-cultural encounters?

SELECTION 1: A French Nun Remarks on Native American Women

Marie de L'Incarnation was a French nun of the Ursuline order, founded in the sixteenth century to educate girls in the Catholic faith. The Ursulines extended their mission to North America when they established a convent school for Indian girls in Quebec in 1639. L'Incarnation was one of the founders of this convent, and she lived there until her death in 1672. In many ways, she led a remarkable life: A wife at age 18 and a mother and widow by 20, she became a nun and emigrated to America in her late thirties. Her writings provide a detailed record of the Ursuline mission in New France as well as a fascinating portrait of seventeenth-century Quebec society. Her letters are also indispensable to the study of gender relations in New France because she worked closely with native girls and women and because hers is one of the few female voices in a record dominated by male priests. In the following excerpted letters, she describes some of the Indians who came under her tutelage. The praise she heaps upon her converts is indicative of the gendered values and behavior she expected native women to adopt as Christians, but her descriptions of Indians who resisted conversion also tells us about how Christianity upset traditional gender relations within native communities.

There is talk of giving us two girls of this nation [Huron] and two Algon-kins, these in addition to the eighteen that have filled our seminary, not to speak of the day-girls that come here continually. I assure you, Madame, that in France it will be hard to believe the benedictions God continually pours upon our little seminary. I shall give you a few particulars so as to acquaint you with our consolation.

The first Savage seminarian that was given to us, Marie Negabamat by name, was so used to running in the woods that we lost all hope of keeping her in the seminary. The Reverend Father Le Jeune, who had persuaded her father [Noël Negabamat] to give her to us, sent two older Christian girls with her. These remained with her for some time in order to settle her, but to no avail, for she fled into the woods four days later, after tearing a dress we had given her to pieces. Her father, who is an excellent Christian and lives like a saint, or-dered her to return to the seminary, which she did. She had not been here two days when there was a wonderful change. She seemed no longer to be herself, so disposed was she to prayer and the practices of Christian piety, so that today she is an example to the girls of Quebec, although they are all very well brought-up. As soon as she has committed a fault, she comes to ask pardon on her knees and she does the penances she is given with incredible submissiveness and amiability. In a word, it is impossible to look at her without being touched by devotion, so marked is her face by innocence and inner grace.

At the same time we were given a big girl of seventeen years whose name is Marie Amiskouevan. One could not see anything more tractable, more inno-cent, or more candid even than this girl, for we have never surprised her in a lie, which is a great virtue among the Savages. If her companions accuse her, she never excuses herself. She is so ardent in praying to God that it is never necessary to advise her to do so; she even leads the others, and it seems as if she were their mother, so much charity has she towards them. She has great intelligence for retaining what is taught her, especially the mysteries of our holy Faith, which makes us hope she will do great good when she returns to the Savages. She is sought in marriage by a Frenchman, but it is intended to give her to a man of her own nation because of the example it is hoped she will give the other Savages. If God would give someone in France the devout-ness to help her build a little house, this would undoubtedly be a work of very great merit. This girl has helped us greatly in the study of her tongue because she speaks French well. In a word, she wins everyone's heart by her great sweetness and her fine qualities.

Your god-daughter, Marie-Magdeleine Abatenau, was given to us entirely covered with smallpox and still only six years old. She had at that age cared

From *Word from New France: The Selected Letters of Marie de L'Incarnation*, translated and ed-ited by Joyce Marshall (Toronto: Oxford University Press, 1967), 71–75, 104–107.

alone for her father and mother during the malady from which they died and with such skill that she was the wonder of everyone that saw her. No-one more obedient than this child could be seen—she even anticipates obedience, for she is skillful at taking up her position in those places where she foresees we might be able to employ her—and she does everything she is told with such good behaviour and good grace one would take her for a girl of rank. This, then, is your god-daughter, I should gladly say your daughter in Jesus Christ. I shall add for your consolation that she knows her catechism by heart, as well as the Christian prayers, which she recites with a devoutness capable of inspiring like feelings in those that see her.

Marie-Ursule Gamitiens, the god-daughter of Mademoiselle de Luynes, is only five or six years old. Small though she is, we have no trouble getting her to make her Christian devotions, for she is no sooner awake than she prepares herself to pray to God. She says her rosary during Mass and sings hymns in her Savage tongue.

Agnès Chabdikouechich was given to us at the same time. The name Agnès suits her very well, for she is a lamb in gentleness and simplicity. Some time before she entered the seminary she met the Reverend Father de Quen in the woods where she was cutting her provision. She had no sooner seen him than she threw her hatchet aside and said, "Teach me." She did this with such good grace that he was sensibly touched by it and, to satisfy her fervour, brought her and one of her companions to the seminary, where in a short time they were fitted for Holy Baptism. She has made very great progress with us in the knowledge of the mysteries and, as well, in good manners, embroidery, reading, playing the viol, and a thousand other little skills. She is only twelve years old and made her First Communion at Easter with three of her companions.

Nicole Assepanse was given to us the same day at the age of seven. Her parents, who are among the most prominent of the Savages, begged us to receive her for a time because she could not accompany them to the hunt. This girl has a mind so open that she is as capable of instruction as a girl of twenty. She was only five months in the seminary and was able to recount the principal points of our Faith and knew the catechism and Christian practices perfectly. When her mother came to fetch her on her return from the hunt, the innocent had her pray. I admired the simplicity of the mother, who was not yet baptized, in receiving instruction from her daughter with so much ardour and docility.

Overjoyed at hearing her daughter pray and respond to the catechism, she said, "My daughter, you will instruct your father and me. If you wish to remain longer in the seminary where you are so much loved, you will become even better fitted to do it."

The girl nevertheless could not leave her mother whose only child she was, but she said, "Though I wish to go, it is not because I lack for anything. I eat as much as I wish, the virgins give me fine clothes and love me very much, but I cannot leave you."

As she said these words, she was taken away to be brought back to the cabins, where she is admired by all the Savages.

It would take me too long to speak to you separately of them all but I shall tell you in general that these girls love us more than they love their parents, showing no desire to accompany them, which is most extraordinary in the Savages. They model themselves upon us as much as their age and their condition can permit. When we make our spiritual exercises, they keep a continual silence. They dare not even raise their eyes or look at us, thinking that this would interrupt us. But when we are finished, I could not express the caresses they give us, a thing they never do with their natural mothers.

Four of them received communion at Easter. They performed this act with such purity that the slightest shadow of sin frightened them, and with so much ardour and desire for union with Our Lord that, as they waited to receive it, they cried out, "Ah, when will Jesus come to kiss our hearts?"

When the Reverend Father [Claude] Pijart, who had baptized and instructed them for communion, saw them behave with angelic modesty, he could not restrain his tears.

We have had eighteen girls, not to speak of the Savage women and girls, who have permission to enter the place set aside for the instruction of the French and the Savages and come there very frequently.

After instruction and prayers we feast them according to their fashion. Their own hunger is the clock by which they judge when it is time for a meal, so when we prepare food for our seminarians, we must also provide for any others that might unexpectedly arrive. This is the case particularly in winter when the old people cannot accompany the other Savages to the hunt, for if they were not cared for at that time they would die of hunger in the cabins. God granted us the grace to be able to succour them till springtime so that they kept us good company, and it will be a singular consolation to us to be able to continue to do this with the help of charitable persons in France, failing which it will be absolutely impossible, our little seminary not being able to suffice by itself for the great expenditures required for the maintenance of seminarians and assistance to the other Savages as well.

❖   ❖   ❖

In our seminary we have persons great and small, girls and women, that are given to us for a number of reasons as determined in the council of the Savages. We have had two this year, one of whom was removed from a pagan that had taken her as his wife—unknown to her kinsmen, who are Christians, though she was also a pagan. These good converts, who wanted her to be instructed in the Faith so they could give her in marriage to a Christian, could not suffer this injury and gave the man to understand that, if he wished to marry their kinswoman, he must give up another wife he had and also become a Christian. He promised to do so but, as there is no honour among the infidels, he broke his word, which forced the woman's kinsmen to take her from him and give her to us.

The Reverend Father de Quen told us that she would cause us great trouble and that he believed she would break out of the enclosure in a very short time and do her best to return to the pagan, whom she loved. We received her nevertheless with affection. She was sad for two or three days and then suddenly became as gentle as a child. She wished earnestly to be instructed and receive Holy Baptism. Her kinsmen could not believe in so great and sudden a change, for she wished not to see her husband again unless he became a Christian and her kinsmen agreed. Nevertheless, as the Savages are fickle and do not trust each other willingly except after a long proof of fidelity, they took her back to their cabin.

Some time later, when this poor woman was going somewhere, she met her husband. She took flight; he ran after her. She went into the house of a Frenchman; he went in with her. She hid herself for fear of having to speak to him; he declared that he would not leave without speaking to her. At last he did speak to her and did not neglect any sort of flattery that might persuade her to go back to him—but in vain. He grew angry, he shouted, he threatened to kill them all if his wife were not restored to him. But while he was carrying on in this way, she took a little turning without his noticing, made her way to the cabin of her kinsmen and in this way escaped the importunate man. While he was urging her thus, she had been saying in her heart: I wish to believe in earnest. I wish to be baptized. I love obedience.

She said she loved obedience because she had been forbidden to speak to the pagan and not to obey on such occasions is a crime among our new Christians. She recounted everything that had happened but no-one would believe her, and all maintained that she had accompanied the pagan willingly and disobeyed the commandment she had been given. She repeated that she wished to be baptized but, despite her protestations, council was held to decide how her offence should be punished. Some said she should be condemned to death as a perpetual example and that if this offence remained unpunished the women and girls would imitate her disobedience. Others, who were not so ardent, replied that for the first time they should proceed more gently and that it would be sufficient to condemn her to be publicly whipped. So it was decided, and nothing remained but to find someone to execute the sentence.

The most zealous of the company rose, saying, "I shall do it."

Meanwhile the poor innocent woman did not say a word but thought in her heart that this humiliating punishment would be a preparation for baptism. All the women and girls were now greatly ashamed, for by the sentence they had to be present at its execution, which was to take place at the door of the church. The Savages did not wish, however, to execute the sentence without informing Father de Quen, who was then very occupied in the confessional. When he was able to listen, he was told of the evil the woman was believed to have committed and of the resolution to punish her. Without knowing what had happened or how far the matter was to go, he replied that she deserved to be punished and withdrew.

The executioner then led the woman to the door of the church, ordered her to place her hands on the railing of the bridge and uncovered her shoulders. Without complaint and with matchless submissiveness and graciousness, she did everything that was wished of her.

Then the executioner raised his voice, saying, "Harken, harken, Frenchmen. Know that we love obedience. Here is one of our daughters that has disobeyed. So we are going to punish her as you punish your children. And you, women and girls of the Savages-the same will be done to you if you disobey." With these words, he gave her a great lash with the whip. "Count," he said to the woman, "and remember well."

He said this because he was to give her five lashes. When he reached the third, Father de Quen, hearing that it was not coming to an end and that the lashes were being delivered very roughly, came out and called halt to the zealous executioner. The woman dressed herself again with great sweetness and tranquillity and went to see the Father to beg him to baptize her.

But as he did not know of her innocence, he sent her away very roughly, saying, "If you wish me to believe you, go to the Ursulines tomorrow after sunrise and I shall baptize you with your companions if you persevere."

We knew nothing of what had taken place, but the Reverend Father came to see us and gave us the details of the whole story. I must confess, my very dear Mother, that I thought to be angry with him for letting that poor innocent woman be whipped without checking the ill-considered zeal of the Savages, but at last, as the whole thing took place innocently on one side and the other, we had to laugh at the simplicity of the Savages while remaining edified by the patience of the woman.

She anticipated the time and came to see me at daybreak with a group of girls, saying she had come to wait for the Father so she could be baptized. I asked her if she wished earnestly to be numbered among God's children, and she replied that she had come only for that.

"But," I asked her, "what do you say about being whipped? Are you quite content with that?"

"Yes," she said. "I wished to suffer that indignity to prepare myself for baptism and I endured it in peace, since Jesus endured and paid for me."

I confess, my very dear Mother, that I was overjoyed to hear her and to see her so inclined towards grace. I instructed her and sent for the Father. He baptized her, and throughout the ceremony she showed a modesty that gave sufficient evidence that her entreaties had been without pretense. I had her given the name of our first mother, St Angéle, feeling that this was her due since God had converted her in a house of our holy mother's daughter. . .

SELECTION 2: Moravian Women's Spiritual Autobiographies

The Moravians were a Protestant religious sect that originated in Central Europe. In the eighteenth century, many of its German-speaking adherents emigrated to the New World, where they conducted missionary work among Africans and Native Americans in the Caribbean and North America. It was a common practice for Moravians to write or dictate a *lebenslauf*, or personal memoir, which was read and entered into their congregation's records at the time of their death. Women as well as men composed these brief biographies; while they shared a similar narrative structure, they nonetheless allow modern readers to glimpse the individual personalities behind the stories they tell.

The *lebenslauf* provide a unique perspective on female spirituality in the Atlantic World. Many Moravian women acted contrary to traditional gender roles when they embraced their faith, making an independent decision that angered or saddened their relatives. Others preferred to remain physically chaste but used sexual imagery to describe their spiritual union with Christ.

Some Moravians also abandoned the nuclear family for living arrangements in which the sexes lived apart from each other in groups known as choirs and raised their children communally. Three examples of *lebenslauf* from Moravian women are excerpted here; all are examples of how the pursuit of spiritual fulfillment opened new opportunities for women and affected gender roles in the Atlantic World.

Marie Elizabeth Kunz (1732–1769) was born in Pennsylvania and joined the Moravians as a young teenager, after hearing them preach. She left her family to join the Moravian congregation in Bethlehem, Pennsylvania, where she lived in the Single Sisters' Choir until taking a husband. Her lebenslauf *is noteworthy for the sexual imagery with which she describes her spiritual union with Christ.*

Personalia of the late Sister Marie Elisabeth Kunz according to her own, albeit somewhat brief, account.

She was born Minier [i.e., her maiden name] and came into this mortal life in 1732, on January 5, in Cannestoga in the Province of Pennsylvania. When her father moved to Heidelburg, she had the opportunity of hearing Brother Wagner and was strongly awakened during the sermon. After closer acquaintance with Brother and Sister Wagner and other brothers and sisters who came to visit, she had no peace until she received permission to come to the Congregation in Bethlehem. After she had received the same, she arrived there on June 2, 1745, and thus in her fourteenth year. In 1749, on January 6 (the day after her birthday), she was accepted into the Congregation, and on February 2 of the same year, she partook of the flesh and blood of the Bridegroom [Christ] of her soul in the Holy Communion with the Congregation for the first time. When she had been in the Single Sisters' Choir for a while, she noted down the following in her own hand about her heart's intercourse with Him who loves her soul:

In 1754, on November 2, the good Saviour began a special work of grace with my heart. With body and soul I could give myself up just as I was and want nothing else in this world than to depend on Him: for this grace could be felt so strongly in my heart that I thought "there is nothing more for me here"; and it was just as though the tormented body of the Bloody Saviour were hanging there right before my eyes. Now, because it was Communion day, I could hardly wait until I got to enjoy His Body and Blood in the Sacrament, and as I was actually enjoying it I could hardly remember whether I was still here or already in the marriage hall. That was a great day of grace for me, which I shall never forget. And thus the Holy Spirit, the dear Mother, continued His work of Grace, and this was so powerful that sometimes I thought that I cannot remain here any longer. During the Passion Week, in 1755, I

From *Moravian Women's Memoirs: Their Related Lives, 1750–1820*, translated and edited by Katherine M. Faull (Syracuse, N.Y: Syracuse University Press, 1997), 57–59, 77–78, 87–89.

could neither hear nor meditate enough about all that my dearest Friend of souls had suffered for me during these days. My heart swam in tears, and it was amazing to me that the good Saviour had shown so much grace to such a poor maid as I am. For my poverty and my many sins became clear to me in my heart, and it saddened me greatly that I was not yet completely as my true friend wanted in His heart, as befitted my virgin's state, which was very great and important to me, I begged the Saviour with tears to give me the grace to keep my soul and body chaste until I reached His arms and embrace.

In 1762, on November 21, she was joined in Holy Matrimony to Brother David Kunz, the present widower, with the watchword: "Be content again my soul, for the Lord does good to you. Do not forget it, o my heart!" This marriage she conducted contentedly and blessedly until her death. The Saviour also blessed her with three children, namely two sons, David and Jacob, of whom the latter was not seen long in his earthly tabernacle, but the former is in our children's home. She was safely delivered her last child, a daughter, on the 9th of this (year) and remained quite healthy until the 20th. On that day, however, she had a severe headache and thereafter such a high fever that she was conscious of little around her and took notice of nothing. Last Saturday it appeared to be improving somewhat, but in the middle of the night her condition changed so that one could see clearly that her last hour was at hand, as she had been prepared right at the beginning of her illness for her going home. Last Friday she saw her little David one more time and last Saturday she took a heartfelt farewell from her husband. She has now reached the end of all her affliction and now rests in peace after she had lived this mortal life for 37 years, 5 months, 2 weeks, and 2 days.

Magdalene Beulah Brockden (1731–1820) was enslaved in West Africa as a young child and came to Philadelphia as a domestic servant. Although her master was not Moravian, he sent her to Bethlehem to be educated in Christianity and freed her nine years later. She married another African Moravian in 1762. Her lebenslauf, *written in the mid-1750s, is the earliest extant writing by an African woman in North America.*

Our Negro sister Magdalena, who happily departed on January 3rd of this year, left behind the following report.

I was, as is known, a slave or the property of the late Mr. Brockden who bought me from another master, when I was ten years old and from then on I served his family until I was grown. Because my master was much concerned about the salvation of my soul and he saw that it was high time that I was protected from the temptations of the world and brought to a religious society, he suggested to me that I should go to Bethlehem.

Because I had no desire to do so, I asked him rather to sell me to someone else, for at that time I still loved the world and desired to enjoy it fully. However, my master said to me lovingly that I should go to Bethlehem and at least try it. He knew that I would be well treated there. And if it did not suit me there so he would take me back at any time. When I arrived here I was received with such love and friendship by the official workers and all the Brethren that I was much ashamed. (She arrived on November 23, 1743 in Bethlehem.) I soon received permission to remain here. My behaviour in the beginning was so bad; I really tried to be sent away again, which did not happen. The love of the Brethren, however, and in particular the great mercy of the Saviour that I came to feel at this time moved me to stay here. Some time after, my master came here and gave me his permission and blessing, and I became content and happy.

The Saviour showed great mercy to my poor soul, which was so deeply sunk in the slavery of sin that I never thought that I would be freed from these chains and could receive grace. How happy I was for the words, "Also for you did Jesus die on the stem of the cross so that you may be redeemed and eternally blessed." I understood this in faith and received forgiveness for my sins.

◆   ◆   ◆

In 1748 on the 19th May she was baptized in the death of Jesus and on the 26th January 1749 she attained the pleasure of Holy Communion with the congregation. On 21st January 1762 she entered into matrimony with the Negro Brother Andrew, and this marriage was blessed with two sons who have both gone home [i.e., are deceased]. In 1779 on March 30th she became a widow. She enjoyed lasting health until her old age. About fourteen days ago she became seriously ill, and it soon became clear that this illness was to be her end, and this became clear to her also. She fell asleep the above day in the eighty-ninth year of her life.

Anna Barbara Fenstermacher (1709–1790) was born in Germany and emigrated to North America with her husband and children in 1727. Shortly after moving from the countryside to Philadelphia in 1742, she was widowed. In 1744, she joined the Moravians. Her lebenslauf *is noteworthy for the story it tells about women's experiences with childbirth, marriage, and widowhood.*

Our departed sister Anna Barbara Fenstermacher had the following written down about her way through this life.

> I was born on March 28, 1709, in Erstett in the Palatinate, where my father, Martin Rente was a burgher and a blacksmith. My parents raised me as a good Lutheran, and it was also my great pleasure to go to church. In my twelfth year, I went to Holy Communion for the first time and, soon thereafter, I went into service. In my eighteenth year, I took my first husband, Michael Leibert, and bore him ten children, six sons and four daughters. I had my first son while still living in my father's house and, during this birth, I was awakened. As I cried to the Saviour in my soul's troubled state, he forgave my sins, and then I really felt my salvation. When I had recovered, I was crying a great deal, and my mother asked me, "Why are you crying so much? You have a son!" I answered her, "Because I did not die, and I am so blessed, and now I have to go back into the world." And from that time forth I was always concerned as to how I would maintain grace.
>
> In 1727, we moved to this country and, when we had already said our farewells and I was leaving, my mother followed me and said she had something else to say to me, and we sat down, and she began: "When you arrive in the land, don't think

about gaining great wealth, but rather first take care of your children, and see that they come to no harm and don't get bitten by snakes or the like. Second, I have heard for a long time that a congregation of God [the Moravians] is to be founded over the ocean, just as it was in the Apostles' time, and when you hear about it, don't think about the fact that you were brought up in such and such a religion (her husband was Catholic) but rather join with them. They think much of the sufferings of Christ; they move from place to place, but when only three are gathered together, remain with them, for it must be again as it was in the beginning." And so on. That made such an impression on me that I always thought about it.

Once, when I was very ill, I felt my salvation again, and it was always in my heart as though those people would come, about whom my mother had spoken, and when the Brethren came into the land, I believed that they were those people even before I saw them. I heard Count von Zinzendorf [a Moravian leader] himself preaching first of all; but I was also persecuted enough.

Thereupon in March 1742, we moved in to the city where my husband lived for only another six months. There I was, a widow with nine children, until I had four of them with the Congregation. Thereafter, I was married to my late husband, Christian Fenstermacher. In September 1764, we moved to Lititz [Pennsylvania], which was hard for me to do because I had children in Philadelphia, and was still attached to the world.

Thus far her own account.

In 1744, she was received into the Congregation in Philadelphia and admitted to Holy Communion in 1746. In 1768, in Lititz she became a widow for the second time and, in answer to her dearest wish, she received permission to move to Bethlehem and was one of the first inhabitants of the Widows' Choirhouse, where she was quite contented and happy. She often gave witness to the fact that she was now living the most peaceful and contented part of her life and was content with everything. The beautiful services in the congregation were of immeasurable value to her and, for as long as she could, she did not miss a single Opportunity. With thanks she often testified how the dear Saviour had granted her a childlike care and steadfast trust in Him through all her troubles. One of these times had remained with her quite clearly, when she once had had nothing to give her children to eat and had been most worried about this in the night. Early in the morning, a neighbour came as she was in great despair and said "Barbara, during the night I was wondering whether you had anything to eat for yourself and the children." Whereupon she wept and said to him that she had nothing, and if he could lend her a couple of bushels of fruit so she would be very grateful to him. Whereupon he said to her, "I want to give you flour and fruit without expecting payment."

As long as six years ago she had a stroke and, although she recovered straightaway, from that time on we noticed a paralysis on her right side and a weakening of her senses. She often prayed to the Saviour with many tears to help her. Four years ago, she had a heavier stroke and from then on was robbed of most of her senses, could not talk coherently to anyone, and from then on had to be cared for like a small child. Her nurse, Christina Segner, did this with great love and loyalty day and night. For the last year she was in an especially wretched state, that one could hardly look upon or hear her whimpering without heartfelt sympathy. One could understand nothing other than, "Oh, Lord Jesus, oh my Saviour have pity and help me."

Recently, she often got open sores on her body, for which the doctors remained loyal in the attempt to dull her pain, for her bodily suffering was very great. On December 15th, the daily watchword for the congregation was "though I walk in the midst of hostility, thou dost stretch forth thy hand [Psalm 138:7]. I can be comforted with you when my distress is greatest of all Your care for me your child is more than fatherly." One could see that she was nearing her release from all sorrow, and the blessing of the Congregation and her Choir was given to her with the feeling of the nearness of Jesus, with which she passed away on the morning of the 16th quite gently and blessedly in the eighty-second year of her life. Now, in harmony, she will sing above, as we do here, "One thing has brought me through, little lamb, that slaughtered were you!"

SELECTION 3: A Scottish Woman's Impressions of Gender Relations in the British West Indies and North Carolina

Janet Schaw accompanied her brother Alexander on a trip from Edinburgh, Scotland to the Caribbean, North America, and Portugal from 1774 to 1776. The Schaws were middle-aged siblings from a wealthy mercantile family with business connections in the places they visited. They traveled in high style, including female and male servants. Janet's journal reads like the travelogue from what today might be called an "adventure vacation": a trip to an exotic place taken by a wealthy person who likes the idea of roughing it for awhile but never intends to stray too far from the lap of luxury.

In her journal, Schaw recorded her impression of gender relations in the colonial societies she visited. She expressed concern for the ability of European men and women to maintain a proper level of gentility and refinement in the New World, and the evidence she saw of sexual relations between male slave owners and female slaves violated her sense of propriety. In the passages that follow, her descriptions of colonial men, their wives, and their slaves reveal some of the ways in which gender, sexuality, and race intersected in the Atlantic World.

A s I am now about to leave them, you, no doubt, will expect me, to give my opinion as fully on the Inhabitants, as I have done on their Island [Antigua] and manners, but I am afraid you will suspect me of partiality, and were

From *Journal of a Lady of Quality, Being the Narrative of a Journey from Scotland to the West Indies, North Carolina, and Portugal, in the Years 1774 to 1776*, edited by Evangeline Walker Andrews and Charles McLean Andrews (London: Oxford University Press, 1923), 111–15, 153–55.

I to speak of Individuals, perhaps you might have reason, but as to the characters in general I can promise to write without prejudice, and if I only tell truth, they have nothing to fear from my pen. I think the men the most agreeable creatures I ever met with, frank, open, generous, and I dare say brave; even in advanced life they retain the Vivacity and Spirit of Youth; they are in general handsome, and all of them have that sort of air, that will ever attend a man of fashion. Their address is at once soft and manly; they have a kind of gallantry in their manner, which exceeds mere politeness, and in some countries, we know, would be easily mistaken for something more interesting than civility, yet you must not suppose this the politeness of French manners, merely words of course. No, what they say, they really mean; their whole intention is to make you happy, and this they endeavour to do without any other view or motive than what they are prompted to by the natural goodness of their own natures. In short, my friend, the woman that *brings a heart here* will have little sensibility if she carry it away.

I hear you ask me, if there is no alloy to this fine character, no reverse to this beautiful picture. Alas! my friend, tho' children of the Sun, they are mortals, and as such must have their share of failings, the most conspicuous of which is, the indulgence they give themselves in their licentious and even unnatural amours, which appears too plainly from the crowds of Mullatoes, which you meet in the streets, houses and indeed every where; a crime that seems to have gained sanction from custom, tho' attended with the greatest inconveniences not only to Individuals, but to the publick in general. The young black wenches lay themselves out for white lovers, in which they are but too successful. This prevents their marrying with their natural mates, and hence a spurious and degenerate breed, neither so fit for the field, nor indeed any work, as the true bred Negro. Besides these wenches become licentious and insolent past all bearing, and as even a mulattoe child interrupts their pleasures and is troublesome, they have certain herbs and medicines, that free them from such an incumbrance, but which seldom fails to cut short their own lives, as well as that of their offspring. By this many of them perish every year. I would have gladly drawn a veil over this part of a character, which in every thing else is most estimable.

As to the women, they are in general the most amiable creatures in the world, and either I have been remarkably fortunate in my acquaintance, or they are more than commonly sensible, even those who have never been off the Island are amazingly intelligent and able to converse with you on any subject. They make excellent wives, fond attentive mothers and the best house wives I have ever met with. Those of the first fortune and fashion keep their own keys and look after every thing within doors; the domestick Economy is entirely left to them; as the husband finds enough to do abroad. A fine house, an elegant table, handsome carriage, and a crowd of mullatoe servants are what they all seem very fond of. The sun appears to affect the sexes very differently. While the men are gay, luxurious and amorous, the women are modest, genteel, reserved and temperate. This last virtue they have indeed in the extreme; they drink nothing stronger in general than Sherbet, and never eat above one or two things at table, and these the lightest and plainest. The truth is, I can observe no indulgence they allow themselves in, not so much as in scandal [gossip], and if I stay long in this country, I will lose the very idea of that innocent amusement; for since I resided amongst them, I have never heard one woman say a wrong thing of another. This is so unnatural, that I suppose you will (good naturedly) call it cunning; but if it is so, it is the most commendable cunning I ever met with, as nothing can give them a better appearance in the eyes of a stranger.

As we became better acquainted, their reserve wore off, and I now find them most agreeable companions. Jealousy is a passion with which they are entirely unacquainted, and a jealous wife would be here a most ridiculous character indeed. Let me conclude this by assuring you, that I never admired my own sex more than in these amiable creoles. Their Sentiments are just and virtuous; in religion they are serious without ostentation, and perform every duty with pleasure from no other motive but the consciousness of doing right. In their persons they are very genteel, rather too thin till past thirty, after that they grow plump and look much the better for it. Their features are in general high and very regular, they have charming eyes, fine teeth, and the greatest quantity of hair I ever saw, which they dress with taste, and wear a great deal of powder. In short, they want only colour to be termed beautiful, but the sun who bestows such rich taints on every other flower, gives none to his lovely daughters; the tincture of whose skin is as pure as lily, and as pale. Yet this I am convinced is owing to the way in which they live, entirely excluded from proper air and exercise. From childhood they never suffer the sun to have a peep at them, and to prevent him are covered with masks and bonnets, that absolutely make them look as if they were stewed. Fanny who just now is blooming as a new blown rose, was prevailed on to wear a mask, while we were on our Tour, which in a week changed her colour, and if she had persevered I am sure a few months would have made her as pale as any of them. As to your humble Servant, I have always set my face to the weather; wherever I have been. I hope you have no quarrel at brown beauty.

* * *

WILMINGTOWN [NORTH CAROLINA]

I have been in town a few days, and have had an opportunity to make some little observations on the manners of a people so new to me. The ball I mentioned was intended as a civility, therefore I will not criticize it, and tho' I have not the same reason to spare the company, yet I will not fatigue you with a description, which however lively or just, would at best resemble a Dutch picture, where the injudicious choice of the subject destroys the merit of the painting. Let it suffice to say that a ball we had, where were dresses, dancing and ceremonies laughable enough, but there was no object on which my own ridicule fixed equal to myself and the figure I made, dressed out in all my British airs with a high head and a hoop and trudging thro' the unpaved streets in embroidered shoes by the light of a lanthorn [lantern] carried by a black wench half naked. No chair, no carriage—good leather shoes need none. The ridicule was the silk shoes in such a place. I have however gained some most amiable and agreeable acquaintances amongst the Ladies; many of whom would make a figure in any part of the world, and I will not fail to cultivate their esteem, as they appear worthy of mine.

I am sorry to say, however, that I have met with few of the men who are natives of the country [male colonists born in America], who rise much above my former description, and as their natural ferocity is now inflamed by the fury of an ignorant zeal, they are of that sort of figure, that I cannot look at them without connecting the idea of tar and feather. Tho' they have fine women and such as might inspire any man with sentiments that do honour to humanity, yet they know no such nice distinctions, and in this at least are real patriots. As the population of the country is all the view they have in what they call love, and tho' they often honour their black wenches with their attention, I sincerely believe they are excited to that crime by no other desire or motive but that of adding to the number of their slaves.

The difference between the men and the women surprised me, but a sensible man, who has long resided here, in some degrees accounted for it. In the infancy of this province, said he, many families from Britain came over, and of these the wives and daughters were people of education. The mothers took the care of the girls, they were train'd up under them, and not only instructed in the family duties necessary to the sex, but in those accomplishments and genteel manners that are still so visible amongst them, and this descended from Mother to daughter. As the father found the labours of his boys necessary to him, he led them therefore to the woods, and taught the sturdy lad to glory in the stroke he could give with his Ax, in the trees he felled, and the deer he shot; to conjure the wolfe, the bear and the Alligator; and to guard his habition from Indian inroads was most justly his pride, and he had reason to boast of it. But a few generations this way lost every art or science, which their fathers might have brought out, and tho' necessity no longer prescribed these severe occupations, custom has established it as still necessary for the men to spend their time abroad in the fields; and to be a good marksman is the highest ambition of the youth, while to those enervated by age or infirmity drinking grog remained a last consolation.

≈ Discussion Questions ≈

1. According to Marie de L'Incarnation, what kind of transformation did conversion to Christianity cause in the values and behavior of Native American girls and women? Compare her expectations for female converts with those expressed by Isaac Jogues for male converts (Chapter 3, pp. 45–50). How did the new gender roles missionaries expected converts to take cause tensions with nonconverts?

2. How does the language and imagery used in the Moravian memoirs reflect a female perspective on spirituality? In what ways did these women challenge conventional gender expectations when they embraced their faith? What do these three memoirs tell you about the life cycle of Moravian women from their youth to old age?

3. How does Janet Schaw's analysis of the effects of colonization on European men and women reflect notions of gender difference and separate spheres? In her opinion, what are the social costs of interracial sexual unions, and to whom does she assign the blame for such activity? How does her description of white colonial women contrast with her description of female slaves?

4. How did the women who authored these selections participate in the construction of new gender roles and categories for the Atlantic World? How did that construction affect other women, especially those of African or Native American ancestry?

Suggested Readings

The study of gender in the Atlantic World has often been framed in the context of cross-cultural encounters between Africans, Indians, and Europeans. The role of native women and European men in the fur trade is examined in Susan Sleeper-Smith, *Indian Women and French Men: Rethinking Cultural Encounter in the Western Great Lakes* (Amherst Mass.: University of Massachusetts Press, 2001); Sylvia Van Kirk, *Many Tender Ties: Women in Fur-Trade Society, 1670–1870* (Norman, Okla.: University of Oklahoma Press, 1980); and Jennifer S. H. Brown, *Strangers in Blood: Fur Trade Company Families in Indian Country* (Vancouver: University of British Columbia Press, 1980). The conflict between Christianity and traditional Native American gender roles is described in Karen L. Anderson, *Chain Her by One Foot: The Subjugation of Native Women in Seventeenth-Century New France* (New York: Routledge, 1993), and Carol Devens, *Countering Colonization: Native American Women and Great Lakes Missions, 1630–1900* (Berkeley: University of California Press, 1992). For a gendered perspective on the experience of Indian captivity, see June Namias, *White Captives: Gender and Ethnicity on the American Frontier* (Chapel Hill, N.C: University of North Carolina Press, 1993).

Several studies address the intersection of gender, sexuality, and race in New World slavery. For North America, see Kathleen M. Brown, *Good Wives, Nasty Wenches, and Anxious Patriarchs: Gender, Race, and Power in Colonial Virginia* (Chapel Hill, N.C: University of North Carolina Press, 1996), and Deborah Gray White, *Ar'n't I a Woman? Female Slaves in the Plantation South* (New York: W. W. Norton, 1985). For the Caribbean, see *Engendering History: Caribbean Women in Historical Perspective*, edited by Verene Shepherd, Bridget Brereton, and Barbara Bailey (New York: St. Martin's Press, 1995), and Hilary Beckles, *Natural Rebels: A Social History of Enslaved Women in Barbados* (London: Zed Press, 1989). For Latin America, see Susan M. Socolow, *The Women of Colonial Latin America* (Cambridge, England: Cambridge University Press, 2000), and Asuncion Lavrin, *Sexuality and Marriage in Colonial Latin America* (1989; Lincoln, Nebr.: University of Nebraska Press, 1992).

Historians have also studied the construction of gender in early America through the lenses of religion and the law. For studies emphasizing religion, see Laurel Thatcher Ulrich, *Good Wives: Image and Reality in the Lives of Women in Northern New England, 1650–1750* (New York: Alfred A. Knopf, 1982), and Susan Juster, *Disorderly Women: Sexual Politics and Evangelicalism in Revolutionary New England* (Ithaca, N.Y.: Cornell University Press, 1994). For studies emphasizing the law, see Mary Beth Norton, *Founding Mothers and Fathers: Gendered Power and the Forming of American Society* (New York: Alfred A. Knopf, 1996), and Cornelia Hughes Dayton, *Women Before the Bar: Gender, Law, and Society in Connecticut, 1639–1789* (Chapel Hill, N.C.: University of North Carolina Press, 1995).

The Female Combatants (London, 1776)

This British political cartoon lampooned the outbreak of the American Revolution. Britain is depicted as the female figure Britannia, who tells her rebellious subject, "I'll force you to Obedience you Rebellious Slut." The American colonies are represented by the female Indian figure, who responds, "Liberty Liberty for ever Mother while I exist." While the artist clearly intended the image of two women engaged in fisticuffs to be humorous, the cartoon also reflects the Enlightenment's depiction of America as a place younger, less refined, and culturally distinct from Europe (see Selection 1). Colonial revolutionaries embraced the image of the Indian and the name "American" to set themselves apart from the Old World (see Selection 3). What positive attributes do you suppose they associated with Indians? Source: Courtesy of the John Carter Brown Library at Brown University

Enlightenment and Revolution

Introduction

The American War of Independence initiated an era of political upheaval that transformed the Atlantic World between 1775 and
1825. Wars and slave rebellions in the Americas as well as political
revolutions in Europe upset the systems of trade and government that
imperial powers had worked so hard to create since the time of Columbus. Revolutionary ideas followed the currents of trade and travel back
and forth across the Atlantic, spreading the contagion of rebellion and
its unanticipated consequences to new regions. In this era, the Atlantic
World seemed to reach its zenith and its disintegration at the same
time, as the institutions that had allowed it to prosper in the first
place—the slave trade, colonial empires, powerful monarchies—faced
crippling attacks from the discontented and disenfranchised.

The Atlantic revolutions had many causes, each unique to particular circumstances of time and place. The American Revolution
(1775–1783) and the Spanish-American revolutions (1810–1825) are
best described as wars of independence led by colonial elites who resented imperial restrictions on their economic and political autonomy.
By the end of the eighteenth century, there had emerged in North and
South America native-born, or creole, elites descended from the first
waves of European colonizers. These creole elites proudly identified
themselves as "Americans," claiming a cultural and moral superiority
over their African and Indian dependents, while also setting themselves
apart from the European society across the Atlantic. In North and South
America during the late eighteenth century, creole patriots resented the
imperial officials who monopolized high offices of church and state in
their colonies and attacked the arbitrary authority that European
monarchies claimed over them. They fought wars of colonial independence to free themselves from the economic and political restraints imposed upon them by these monarchies, but not necessarily to extend
that same freedom to the dependent peoples over whom they ruled.

In other regions, particularly the Caribbean, slave populations
grew so large relative to the planter class that by the end of the eighteenth century, rebellions became more frequent and costly. The Haitian Revolution (1791–1804) toppled the colonial planter class and

209

raised a banner for the self-emancipation of slaves throughout the Western Hemisphere. The French Revolution (1789–1799) was another species of revolution altogether, a violent convulsion from within French society that destroyed the authority of the monarchy, aristocracy, and church and initiated an age of democratic ferment that reverberated throughout Europe for fifty years.

The common connection between these various revolutionary movements was their ideological foundation in the Enlightenment, an intellectual movement that transformed European science and philosophy between 1680 and 1800. The spirit of the Enlightenment was cosmopolitan. Its adherents, often known by the French term *philosophes* (philosophers), considered themselves "citizens of the world," individuals who recognized their common humanity with others around the globe and who contemplated science, politics, and philosophy in the most universal terms possible. They believed that what was learned or uncovered in one realm of study—cosmology, botany, mathematics—could be applied to the study of another, because all of creation was rationally ordered and worked according to certain immutable natural laws. The *philosophes* most often conveyed this idea through mechanical metaphors, comparing the natural world to a machine whose blueprint could be deciphered through proper observation and experimentation. Just as a craftsman could apply his knowledge of mechanics to building a better clock, so too did the *philosophes* believe that they could apply their grasp of the laws that governed nature to making society more free, prosperous, and harmonious.

The model of a mechanical universe governed by natural laws gave rise to a belief in natural rights, universal liberties held by all people in all societies. The classic statement of natural rights philosophy comes from John Locke's *Second Treatise on Government*, written in the 1680s to justify parliamentary resistance to the Stuart monarchy in England. Locke challenged the absolutist authority of monarchs by arguing that human beings possess natural rights to life, liberty, and property. According to Locke, all governments were contractual and therefore limited in power. When a government ceased to protect the natural rights of its citizens, the people had a right to replace it.

During the Age of Revolutions, Locke's natural rights philosophy was adopted and popularized by a host of radical thinkers and revolutionaries on both sides of the Atlantic. An obvious source of the appeal of Locke's argument was its universality. While Locke wrote in a distinctly English tradition about rights and liberties, subsequent theorists applied his ideas across national and cultural boundaries. Colonial elites, political radicals, and enslaved Africans adopted natural rights rhetoric to make their own case for rebellion, and in doing so, made Lockean principles about self-government and human rights part of the common intellectual fabric of the Atlantic World. The foundational documents of the American and French Revolutions, the Declaration of Independence and the Declaration of Rights of Man and

Citizen, respectively, are examples of Locke's profound influence on the Atlantic revolutions and our own modern notions of democracy.

Despite the many variations in their causes and consequences, the Atlantic revolutions shared a general commitment to replacing forms of absolutist political power with representative government. *Philosophes* challenged the divine right of kings, a political doctrine that argued that monarchs derived their power from God and therefore rebellion against them violated God's will. Political revolutionaries in Europe and the Americas extended this attack to all forms of hereditary power, including the social and economic privileges that aristocrats enjoyed by virtue of their birth. The equality of all citizens before the law became an important component of the revolutionary agenda, and the republics of ancient Greece and Rome replaced absolutist monarchies as the model for national government in the Americas. Of course, few of the Atlantic revolutions succeeded in creating stable republics, and many reverted to some form of de facto absolutist power in the form of dictators or military strongmen. Nevertheless, the Enlightenment dealt a fatal blow to the institution of hereditary kingship and made possible the emergence of modern nation-states out of the colonial empires that had previously governed the Atlantic World.

The readings in this chapter examine the intersection of the Enlightenment and the Atlantic revolutions of 1775 to 1825. In the first selection, a French expatriate living in British North America uses Enlightenment ideas about human nature and the environment to explain how European colonists have turned into "Americans." In the second, a transatlantic revolutionary uses natural rights philosophy to attack the hereditary powers of monarchs and aristocrats. In the third selection, a Spanish-American revolutionary expresses a creole nationalism grounded in Enlightenment notions about self-government. As you read these selections, try to pick out the themes and ideas that unite them. How do they make use of natural rights theory to attack the traditional forms of government that have ruled the Atlantic World? What types of government do they expect to replace those older models?

SELECTION 1: **A French Expatriate Describes Colonial Society in British North America**

Hector St. John de Crèvecoeur's life was buffeted and changed several times by the revolutionary struggles of the Atlantic World. He came to North America as a French military officer in 1755. After France surrendered Canada to Britain in 1763, he became a naturalized British subject, traveled throughout eastern North America, and settled in New York. His loyalism during the American Revolution forced him to return to Europe, where he published *Letters from an American Farmer* in 1782. The book's glowing descriptions of American society made him a literary celebrity, and the French Crown appointed him an ambassador to the new United States. He returned from this diplomatic service during the French Revolution, but this time avoided his political enemies by retreating to the French countryside, where he died in 1813.

Crèvecoeur's career illustrated the transatlantic kinship between the American and French revolutions. Although not a revolutionary himself, he embraced Enlightenment notions about human progress, the order of nature, and the irrepressible expansion of liberty. In "What is an American?"—the most famous essay from *Letters from an American Farmer*—he described North America as a place where the environment transformed European immigrants into a society that was more equal, prosperous, and just than that they had left behind.

I wish I could be acquainted with the feelings and thoughts which must agitate the heart and present themselves to the mind of an enlightened Englishman when he first lands on this continent [North America]. He must greatly rejoice that he lived at a time to see this fair country discovered and settled; he must necessarily feel a share of national pride when he views the chain of settlements which embellish these extended shores. When he says to himself, "This is the work of my countrymen, who, when convulsed by factions, afflicted by a variety of miseries and wants, restless and impatient, took refuge here. They brought along with them their national genius, to which they principally owe what liberty they enjoy and what substance they possess." Here he sees the industry of his native country displayed in a new manner and traces in their works the embryos of all the arts, sciences, and ingenuity which flourish in Europe. Here he beholds fair cities, substantial villages, extensive fields, an immense country filled with decent houses, good roads, orchards, meadows, and bridges where an hundred years ago all was wild, woody, and uncultivated! What a train of pleasing ideas this fair spectacle must suggest; it is a prospect which must inspire a good citizen with the most heart-felt pleasure. The difficulty consists in the manner of viewing so extensive a scene. He is arrived on a new continent; a modern society offers itself to his contemplation, different from what he had hitherto seen. It is not composed, as in Europe, of great lords who possess everything and of a herd of people who have nothing. Here are no aristocratical families, no courts, no kings, no bishops, no ecclesiastical dominion, no invisible power giving to a few a very visible one, no great manufactures employing thousands, no great refinements of luxury. The rich and the poor are not so far removed from each other as they are in Europe. Some few towns excepted, we are all tillers of the earth, from Nova Scotia to West Florida. We are a people of cultivators scattered over an immense territory, communicating with each other by means of good roads and navigable rivers, united by the silken bands of mild government, all respecting the

---

From J. Hector St. John de Crèvecoeur, "What is an American?" in *Letters from an American Farmer* (1782; New York: E. P. Dutton, 1926), 39–44, 55–58.

laws without dreading their power, because they are equitable. We are all animated with the spirit of an industry which is unfettered and unrestrained, because each person works for himself. If he travels through our rural districts,
he views not the hostile castle and the haughty mansion, contrasted with the
clay-built hut and miserable cabin, where cattle and men help to keep each
other warm and dwell in meanness, smoke, and indigence. A pleasing unifor-
mity of decent competence appears throughout our habitations. The meanest
of our log-houses is a dry and comfortable habitation. Lawyer or merchant
are the fairest titles our towns afford; that of a farmer is the only appellation
of the rural inhabitants of our country. It must take some time ere he can reconcile himself to our dictionary, which is but short in words of dignity and
names of honour. There, on a Sunday, he sees a congregation of respectable
farmers and their wives, all clad in neat homespun, well mounted, or riding in
their own humble waggons. There is not among them an esquire, saving the
unlettered magistrate. There he sees a parson as simple as his flock, a farmer
who does not riot on the labour of others. We have no princes for whom we
toil, starve, and bleed; we are the most perfect society now existing in the
world. Here man is free as he ought to be, nor is this pleasing equality so tran-
sitory as many others are. Many ages will not see the shores of our great lakes
replenished with inland nations, nor the unknown bounds of North America
entirely peopled. Who can tell how far it extends? Who can tell the millions of
men whom it will feed and contain? For no European foot has as yet travelled
half the extent of this mighty continent!

   The next wish of this traveller will be to know whence came all these people. They are a mixture of English, Scotch, Irish, French, Dutch, Germans, and
Swedes. From this promiscuous breed, that race now called Americans have
arisen. The eastern provinces must indeed be excepted as being the unmixed
descendants of Englishmen. I have heard many wish that they had been more
intermixed also; for my part, I am no wisher and think it much better as it has
happened. They exhibit a most conspicuous figure in this great and variegated
picture; they too enter for a great share in the pleasing perspective displayed in
these thirteen provinces. I know it is fashionable to reflect on them, but I respect them for what they have done; for the accuracy and wisdom with which
they have settled their territory; for the decency of their manners; for their
early love of letters; their ancient college, the first in this hemisphere; for their
industry, which to me who am but a farmer is the criterion of everything.
There never was a people, situated as they are, who with so ungrateful a soil
have done more in so short a time. Do you think that the monarchical ingredi-
ents which are more prevalent in other governments have purged them from
all foul stains? Their histories assert the contrary.

   In this great American asylum, the poor of Europe have by some means met
together, and in consequence of various causes; to what purpose should they
ask one another what countrymen they are? Alas, two thirds of them had no
country. Can a wretch who wanders about, who works and starves, whose life
is a continual scene of sore affliction or pinching penury—can that man call
England or any other kingdom his country? A country that had no bread for
him, whose fields procured him no harvest, who met with nothing but the
frowns of the rich, the severity of the laws, with jails and punishments, who

owned not a single foot of the extensive surface of this planet? No! Urged by a variety of motives, here they came. Everything has tended to regenerate them: new laws, a new mode of living, a new social system; here they are become men: in Europe they were as so many useless plants, wanting vegetative mould and refreshing showers; they withered, and were mowed down by want, hunger, and war; but now, by the power of transplantation, like all other plants they have taken root and flourished! Formerly they were not numbered in any civil lists of their country, except in those of the poor; here they rank as citizens. By what invisible power hath this surprising metamorphosis been performed? By that of the laws and that of their industry. The laws, the indulgent laws, protect them as they arrive, stamping on them the symbol of adoption; they receive ample rewards for their labours; these accumulated rewards procure them lands; those lands confer on them the title of freemen, and to that title every benefit is affixed which men can possibly require. This is the great operation daily performed by our laws. Whence proceed these laws? From our government. Whence that government? It is derived from the original genius and strong desire of the people ratified and confirmed by the crown. This is the great chain which links us all, this is the picture which every province exhibits, Nova Scotia excepted. There the crown has done all; either there were no people who had genius or it was not much attended to; the consequence is that the province is very thinly inhabited indeed; the power of the crown in conjunction with the musketos has prevented men from settling there. Yet some parts of it flourished once, and it contained a mild, harmless set of people. But for the fault of a few leaders, the whole was banished. The greatest political error the crown ever committed in America was to cut off men from a country which wanted nothing but men!

What attachment can a poor European emigrant have for a country where he had nothing? The knowledge of the language, the love of a few kindred as poor as himself, were the only cords that tied him; his country is now that which gives him his land, bread, protection, and consequence; *Ubi panis ibi patria* [where my bread is, there is my country] is the motto of all emigrants. What, then, is the American, this new man? He is either an European or the descendant of an European; hence that strange mixture of blood, which you will find in no other country. I could point out to you a family whose grandfather was an Englishman, whose wife was Dutch, whose son married a French woman, and whose present four sons have now four wives of different nations. *He* is an American, who, leaving behind him all his ancient prejudices and manners, receives new ones from the new mode of life he has embraced, the new government he obeys, and the new rank he holds. He becomes an American by being received in the broad lap of our great Alma Mater. Here individuals of all nations are melted into a new race of men, whose labours and posterity will one day cause great changes in the world. Americans are the western pilgrims who are carrying along with them that great mass of arts, sciences, vigour, and industry which began long since in the East; they will finish the great circle. The Americans were once scattered all over Europe; here they are incorporated into one of the finest systems of population which has ever appeared, and which will hereafter become distinct by the power of the different climates they inhabit. The American ought therefore to love this country much better than that wherein either he or his forefathers were born. Here the rewards of his industry follow with equal steps the progress of his labour; his labour is founded on the basis of nature, self-interest; can it want a stronger allurement? Wives and children, who before in vain demanded of him a morsel of bread, now, fat and frolicsome, gladly help their father to clear those fields whence exuberant crops are to arise to feed and to clothe them all, without any part being claimed, either by a despotic prince, a rich abbot, or a mighty lord. Here religion demands but little of him: a small voluntary salary to the minister and gratitude to God; can he refuse these? The American is a new man, who acts upon new principles; he must therefore entertain new ideas and form new opinions. From involuntary idleness, servile dependence, penury, and useless labour, he has passed to toils of a very different nature, rewarded by ample subsistence. This is an American.

❖ ❖ ❖

Europe contains hardly any other distinctions but lords and tenants; this fair country alone is settled by freeholders, the possessors of the soil they cultivate, members of the government they obey, and the framers of their own laws, by means of their representatives. This is a thought which you have taught me to cherish; our distance from Europe, far from diminishing, rather adds to our usefulness and consequence as men and subjects. Had our forefathers remained there, they would only have crowded it and perhaps prolonged those convulsions which had shaken it so long. Every industrious European who transports himself here may be compared to a sprout growing at the foot of a great tree; it enjoys and draws but a little portion of sap; wrench it from the parent roots, transplant it, and it will become a tree bearing fruit also. Colonists are therefore entitled to the consideration due to the most useful subjects; a hundred families barely existing in some parts of Scotland will here in six years cause an annual exportation of 10,000 bushels of wheat, 100 bushels being but a common quantity for an industrious family to sell if they cultivate good land. It is here, then, that the idle may be employed, the useless become useful, and the poor become rich; but by riches I do not mean gold and silver—we have but little of those metals; I mean a better sort of wealth—cleared lands, cattle, good houses, good clothes, and an increase of people to enjoy them.

There is no wonder that this country has so many charms and presents to Europeans so many temptations to remain in it. A traveller in Europe becomes a stranger as soon as he quits his own kingdom; but it is otherwise here. We know, properly speaking, no strangers; his is every person's country; the variety of our soils, situations, climates, governments, and produce hath something which must please everybody. No sooner does an European arrive, no matter of what condition, than his eyes are opened upon the fair prospect: he hears his language spoke; he retraces many of his own country manners; he perpetually hears the names of families and towns with which he is acquainted; he sees happiness and prosperity in all places disseminated; he meets with hospitality, kindness, and plenty everywhere; he beholds hardly any poor; he seldom hears of punishments and executions; and he wonders at the elegance of our towns, those miracles of industry and freedom. He cannot admire enough our rural districts, our convenient roads, good taverns, and our many accommodations; he involuntarily loves a country where everything is so lovely. When in England, he was a mere Englishman; here he stands on a larger portion of the globe, not less than its fourth part, and may see the productions of the north, in iron and naval stores; the provisions of Ireland; the grain of Egypt; the indigo, the rice of China. He does not find, as in Europe, a crowded society where every place is overstocked; he does not feel that perpetual collision of parties, that difficulty of beginning, that contention which oversets so many. There is room for everybody in America; has he any particular talent or industry? He exerts it in order to procure a livelihood, and it succeeds. Is he a merchant? The avenues of trade are infinite. Is he eminent in any respect? He will be employed and respected. Does he love a country life? Pleasant farms present themselves; he may purchase what he wants and thereby become an American farmer. Is he a labourer, sober and industrious? He need not go many miles nor receive many informations before he will be hired, well fed at the table of his employer, and paid four or five times more than he can get in Europe. Does he want uncultivated lands? Thousands of acres present themselves, which he may purchase cheap. Whatever be his talents or inclinations, if they are moderate, he may satisfy them. I do not mean that every one who comes will grow rich in a little time; no, but he may procure an easy, decent maintenance by his industry. Instead of starving, he will be fed; instead of being idle, he will have employment: and these are riches enough for such men as come over here. The rich stay in Europe; it is only the middling and poor that emigrate. Would you wish to travel in independent idleness, from north to south, you will find easy access, and the most cheerful reception at every house; society without ostentation; good cheer without pride; and every decent diversion which the country affords, with little expense. It is no wonder that the European who has lived here a few years is desirous to remain; Europe with all its pomp is not to be compared to this continent for men of middle stations or labourers.

An European, when he first arrives, seems limited in his intentions, as well as in his views; but he very suddenly alters his scale; two hundred miles formerly appeared a very great distance, it is now but a trifle; he no sooner breathes our air than he forms schemes and embarks in designs he never would have thought of in his own country. There the plenitude of society confines many useful ideas and often extinguishes the most laudable schemes, which here ripen into maturity. Thus Europeans become Americans. . . .

SELECTION 2: A Transatlantic Revolutionary's Attack on Monarchy and Aristocracy

The international revolutionary cause in the eighteenth-century Atlantic World had no voice more eloquent than Thomas Paine's. A native of England, he emigrated to Pennsylvania on the eve of the American Revolution, where he achieved fame as the author of the pro-independence pamphlet *Common*

Sense in 1776. After the American Revolution, his radicalism drew him to France, where he worked as a member of the revolutionary National Assembly. Shifting political fortunes landed him in prison, where he wrote *The Age of Reason* (1794), an attack on Christianity and a defense of the Enlightenment notion of natural religion, or deism. In 1802 he returned to North America, but his reputation for atheism had soured his name, and he died in obscurity in 1809.

The most common theme in Paine's political writings was the inconsistency of hereditary privilege with natural law. Paine railed against monarchy and aristocracy as unjust systems of social and political power, designed only to perpetuate the lordship of a chosen few over the disenfranchised many. He gave fullest expression to this argument in *The Rights of Man*, his defense of the democratic principles of the French Revolution against their chief critic, the British statesman Edmund Burke. In the passage excerpted here, Paine lays out the choice he sees ahead, between a past bound by tradition and ignorance to false privilege or a future transformed by representative government and the recognition of the natural rights of all.

R eason and ignorance, the opposites of each other, influence the great bulk of mankind. If either of these can be rendered sufficiently extensive in a country, the machinery of government goes easily on. Reason shows itself, and ignorance submits to whatever is dictated to it.

The two modes of government which prevail in the world, are, 1st, government by election and representation; 2d, government by hereditary succession. The former is generally known by the name of republic; the latter by that of monarchy and aristocracy.

Those two distinct and opposite forms, erect themselves on the two distinct and opposite bases of reason and ignorance. As the exercise of government requires talents and abilities, and as talents and abilities cannot have hereditary descent, it is evident that hereditary succession requires a belief from man, to which his reason cannot subscribe, and which can only be established upon his ignorance; and the more ignorant any country is, the better it is fitted for this species of government.

On the contrary, government in a well constituted republic, requires no belief from man beyond what his reason authorizes. He sees the *rationale* of the whole system, its origin, and its operation; and as it is best supported when best understood, the human faculties act with boldness, and acquire, under this form of government, a gigantic manliness.

As, therefore, each of those forms acts on a different basis, the one moving freely by the aid of reason, the other by ignorance; we have next to consider, what it is that gives motion to that species of government which is called

From Thomas Paine, *The Rights of Man, Part First* (1791), in *The Political Works of Thomas Paine*, (New York: Calvin Blanchard, 1860), 95–102.

mixed government, or, as it is sometimes ludicrously styled, a government of *this, that, and t'other.*

The moving power in this species of government is, of necessity, corruption. However imperfect election and representation may be in mixed governments, they still give exertion to a greater portion of reason than is convenient to the hereditary part; and therefore it becomes necessary to buy the reason up. A mixed government is an imperfect every-thing, cementing and soldering the discordant parts together, by corruption, to act as a whole. Mr. Burke appears highly disgusted, that France, since she had resolved on a revolution, did not adopt what he calls "a British constitution"; and the regret which he expresses on this occasion, implies a suspicion, that the British constitution needed something to keep its defects in countenance.

In mixed governments, there is no responsibility; the parts cover each other till responsibility is lost; and the corruption which moves the machine, contrives at the same time its own escape. When it is laid down as a maxim, that a *king can do no wrong*, it places him in a state of similar security with that of idiots and persons insane, and responsibility is out of the question, with respect to himself. It then descends upon the [prime] minister, who shelters himself under a majority in parliament, which by places, pensions, and corruption, he can always command; and that majority justifies itself by the same authority with which it protects the minister. In this rotatory motion, responsibility is thrown off from the parts, and from the whole.

When there is a part in a government which can do no wrong, it implies that it does nothing; and is only the machine of another power, by whose advice and direction it acts. What is supposed to be the king, in mixed governments, is the cabinet; and as the cabinet is always a part of the parliament, and the members justifying in one character what they act in another, a mixed government becomes a continual enigma; entailing upon a country, by the quantity of corruption necessary to solder the parts, the expense of supporting all the forms of government at once, and finally resolving itself into a government by committee; in which the advisers, the actors, the approves, the justifiers, the persons responsible, and the persons not responsible, are the same person.

By this pantomimical contrivance, and change of scene and character, the parts help each other out in matters, which, neither of them singly, would presume to act. When money is to be obtained, the mass of variety apparently dissolves, and a profusion of parliamentary praises passes between the parts. Each admires, with astonishment, the wisdom, the liberality and disinterestedness of the other; and all of them breathe a pitying sigh at the burdens of the nation.

But in a well-conditioned republic, nothing of this soldering, praising and pitying, can take place; the representation being equal throughout the country, and complete in itself, however it may be arranged into legislative and executive, they have all one and the same natural source. The parts are not foreigners to each other, like democracy, aristocracy, and monarchy. As there are no discordant distinctions, there is nothing to corrupt by compromise, nor confound by contrivance. Public measures appeal of themselves to the understanding of the nation, and, resting on their own merits, disown any flattering application to vanity. The continual whine of lamenting the burden of taxes, however successfully it may be practised in mixed governments, is inconsistent with the sense and spirit of a republic. If taxes are necessary, they are of course advantageous; and if they require an apology, the apology itself implies an impeachment. Why then is man thus imposed upon, or why does he impose upon himself.

When men are spoken of as kings and subjects, or when government is mentioned under distinct or combined heads of monarchy, aristocracy, and democracy, what is it that *reasoning* man is to understand by the terms? If there really existed in the world two more distinct and separate *elements* of human power, we should then see the several origins to which those terms would descriptively apply; but as there is but one species of man, there can be but one element of human power, and that element is man himself. Monarchy, aristocracy, and democracy are but creatures of imagination; and a thousand such may be contrived as well as three.

◆　◆　◆

From the revolutions of America and France, and the symptoms that have appeared in other countries, it is evident that the opinion of the world is changing with respect to systems of government, and that revolutions are not within the compass of political calculations. The progress of time and circumstances, which men assign to the accomplishment of great changes, is too mechanical to measure the force of the mind, and the rapidity of reflection, by which revolutions are generated; all the old governments have received a shock from those that already appear, and which were once more improbable, and are a greater subject of wonder, than a general revolution in Europe would be now.

When we survey the wretched condition of man, under the monarchical and hereditary systems of government, dragged from his home by one power, or driven by another, and impoverished by taxes more than by enemies, it becomes evident that those systems are bad, and that a general revolution in the principle and construction of governments is necessary.

What is government more than the management of the affairs of a nation? It is not, and from its nature cannot be, the property of any particular man or family, but of the whole community at whose expense it is supported; and though by force or contrivance it has been usurped into an inheritance, the usurpation cannot alter the right of things. Sovereignty, as a matter of right, appertains to the nation only, and not to any individual; and a nation has at all times an inherent, indefeasible right to abolish any form of government it finds inconvenient, and establish such as accords with its interest, disposition, and happiness. The romantic and barbarous distinctions of men into kings and subjects, though it may suit the condition of courtiers cannot that of citizens; and is exploded by the principle upon which governments are now founded. Every citizen is a member of the sovereignty, and as such can acknowledge no personal subjection; and his obedience can be only to the laws.

When men think of what government is, they must necessarily suppose it to possess a knowledge of all the objects and matters upon which its authority is to be exercised. In this view of government, the republican system, as established by America and France, operates to embrace the whole of a nation: and the knowledge necessary to the interest of all the parts, is to be found in the centre, which the parts by representation form; but the old governments are on a construction that excludes knowledge as well as happiness; government by monks, who know nothing of the world beyond the walls of a convent, is as consistent as government by kings.

What were formerly called revolutions, were little more than a change of persons, or an alteration of local circumstances. They rose and fell like things of course, and had nothing in their existence or their fate that could influence beyond the spot that produced them. But what we now see in the world, from the revolutions of America and France, are a renovation of the natural order of things, a system of principles as universal as truth and the existence of man, and combining moral with political happiness and national prosperity.

I. Men are born, and always continue, free and equal, in respect to their rights. Civil distinctions, therefore, can be founded only on public utility.

II. The end of all political associations is the preservation of the natural and imprescriptible rights of man, and these rights are liberty, property, security, and resistance of oppression.

III. The nation is essentially the source of all sovereignty; nor can any individual, or any body of men, be entitled to any authority which is not expressly derived from it.

In these principles there is nothing to throw a nation into confusion, by inflaming ambition. They are calculated to call forth wisdom and abilities, and to exercise them for the public good, and not for the emolument or aggrandizement of particular descriptions of men or families. Monarchical sovereignty, the enemy of mankind and the source of misery, is abolished; and sovereignty itself is restored to its natural and original place, the nation.—Were this the case throughout Europe, the cause of wars would be taken away.

It is attributed to Henry IV. of France, a man of an enlarged and benevolent heart, that he proposed, about the year 1620, a plan for abolishing war in Europe. The plan consisted in constituting an European congress, or, as the French authors style it, a pacific republic; by appointing delegates from the several nations, who were to act, as a court of arbitration, in any disputes that might arise between nation and nation.

Had such a plan been adopted at the time it was proposed, the taxes of England and France, as two of the parties, would have been at least ten millions sterling annually, to each nation, less than they were at the commencement of the French revolution.

To conceive a cause why such a plan has not been adopted, (and that instead of a congress for the purpose of preventing war, it has been called only to *terminate* a war, after a fruitless expense of several years,) it will be necessary to consider the interest of governments as a distinct interest to that of nations.

Whatever is the cause of taxes to a nation, becomes also the means of revenue to a government. Every war terminates with an addition of taxes, and consequently with an addition of revenue; and in any event of war, in the manner they are now commenced and concluded, the power and interest of governments are increased. War, therefore, from its productiveness, as it easily furnishes the pretence of necessity for taxes and appointments to places and office, becomes the principal part of the system of old governments; and to establish any mode to abolish war, however advantageous it might be to nations, would be to take from such government the most lucrative of its branches. The frivolous matters upon which war is made, show the disposition and avidity of governments to uphold the system of war, and betray the motives upon which they act.

Why are not republics plunged into war, but because the nature of their government does not admit of an interest distinct from that of the nation? Even Holland, though an ill-constructed republic, and with a commerce extending over the world, existed nearly a century without war: and the instant the form of government was changed in France, the republican principles of peace, and domestic prosperity and economy, arose with the new government; and the same consequences would follow the same causes in other nations,

As war is the system of government on the old construction, the animosity which nations reciprocally entertain, is nothing more than what the policy of their governments excite, to keep up the spirit of the system. Each government accuses the other of perfidy, intrigue and ambition, as a means of heating the imagination of their respective nations, and incensing them to hostilities. Man is not the enemy of man, but through the medium of a false system of government. Instead, therefore, of exclaiming against the ambition of kings, the exclamation should be directed against the principle of such governments; and instead of seeking to reform the individual, the wisdom of a nation should apply itself to reform the system.

Whether the forms and maxims of governments which are still in practice, were adapted to the condition of the world at the period they were established, is not in this case the question. The older they are the less correspondence can they have with the present state of things. Time, and change of circumstances and opinions have the same progressive effect in rendering modes of government obsolete, as they have upon customs and manners. Agriculture, commerce, manufactures, and the tranquil arts, by which the prosperity of nations is best promoted, require a different system of government and a different species of knowledge to direct its operations, to what might have been the former condition of the world.

As it is not difficult to perceive, from the enlightened state of mankind, that the hereditary governments are verging to their decline, and that revolutions on the broad basis of national sovereignty, and government by representation, are making their way in Europe, it would be an act of wisdom to anticipate their approach, and produce revolutions by reason and accommodation, rather than commit them to the issue of convulsions.

From what we now see, nothing of reform in the political world ought to be held improbable. It is an age of revolutions, in which every thing may be looked for. The intrigue of courts, by which the system of war is kept up, may provoke a confederation of nations to abolish it: and an European congress to patronize the progress of free government, and promote the civilization of nations with each other is an event nearer in probability, than once were the revolutions and alliances of France and America.

SELECTION 3: **A Creole Revolutionary's Vision for the Future of Spanish America**

Known as *El Libertador* in his native Venezuela, Simón Bolívar was the most famous of Latin America's creole revolutionaries. As a general and a statesman, he helped forge the independent nations of Venezuela, Colombia, Ecuador, Peru, and Bolivia, and he was an early and eloquent advocate of Latin American nationalism.

Bolívar's social background and intellectual influences resemble closely those of George Washington, Thomas Jefferson, and other revolutionary leaders in North America. His parents were members of Venezuela's planter aristocracy, and his private tutor educated him in the classic works of the Enlightenment. As a young man, he traveled in Europe and was drawn to the political radicalism of many of Latin American expatriates. Between 1810 and 1825, he led the struggle for independence in Andean South America, a conflict that Bolívar himself called a "War to the Death." After independence, he worked to forge a confederation of Andean states, but he died in 1830 after political rivals had forced him from office.

One of Bolívar's most famous works was "The Jamaica Letter," which he wrote during an interlude of Caribbean exile in 1815, in hopes of attracting British support to his cause. In this essay, Bolívar described the causes and course of the Spanish-American revolutions and his vision of a post-revolutionary South America founded on Enlightenment principles of government. The Jamaica Letter complements Crèvecoeur's "What is an American?" and Paine's *Rights of Man* by illustrating the universal appeal of Enlightenment thinking to colonial peoples who asserted their own national identities during the Age of Revolutions in the Atlantic World.

Success will crown our efforts, because the destiny of America has been irrevocably decided; the tie that bound her to Spain has been severed. Only a concept maintained that tie and kept the parts of that immense monarchy together. That which formerly bound them now divides them. The hatred that the [Iberian] Peninsula has inspired in us is greater than the ocean between us. It would be easier to have the two continents meet than to reconcile the spirits of the two countries. The habit of obedience; a community of interest, of understanding, of religion; mutual goodwill; a tender regard for the birthplace and good name of our forefathers; in short, all that gave rise to our hopes, came to us from Spain. As a result there was born a principle of affinity that seemed eternal, notwithstanding the misbehavior of our rulers which weak-

From *Selected Writings of Bolivar*, compiled by Vicente Lecuna, edited by Harold A. Bierck, Jr., and translated by Lewis Bertrand, two volumes, second edition (New York: The Colonial Press, 1951), 1:104–105, 109–112, 115–117, 121–122.

ened that sympathy, or, rather, that bond enforced by the domination of their rule. At present the contrary attitude persists: we are threatened with the fear of death, dishonor, and every harm; there is nothing we have not suffered at the hands of that unnatural step-mother—Spain. The veil has been torn asunder. We have already seen the light, and it is not our desire to be thrust back into darkness. The chains have been broken; we have been freed, and now our enemies seek to enslave us anew. For this reason America fights desperately, and seldom has desperation failed to achieve victory.

Because successes have been partial and spasmodic, we must not lose faith. In some regions the Independents triumph, while in others the tyrants have the advantage. What is the end result? Is not the entire New World in motion, armed for defense? We have but to look around us on this hemisphere to witness a simultaneous struggle at every point.

❖   ❖   ❖

It is even more difficult to foresee the future fate of the New World, to set down its political principles, or to prophesy what manner of government it will adopt. Every conjecture relative to America's future is, I feel, pure speculation. When mankind was in its infancy, steeped in uncertainty, ignorance, and error, was it possible to foresee what system it would adopt for its preservation? Who could venture to say that a certain nation would be a republic or a monarchy; this nation great, that nation small? To my way of thinking, such is our own situation. We are a young people. We inhabit a world apart, separated by broad seas. We are young in the ways of almost all the arts and sciences, although, in a certain manner, we are old in the ways of civilized society. I look upon the present state of America as similar to that of Rome after its fall. Each part of Rome adopted a political system conforming to its interest and situation or was led by the individual ambitions of certain chiefs, dynasties, or associations. But this important difference exists: those dispersed parts later reestablished their ancient nations, subject to the changes imposed by circumstances or events. But we scarcely retain a vestige of what once was; we are, moreover, neither Indian nor European, but a species midway between the legitimate proprietors of this country and the Spanish usurpers. In short, though Americans by birth we derive our rights from Europe, and we have to assert these rights against the rights of the natives, and at the same time we must defend ourselves against the invaders. This places us in a most extraordinary and involved situation. Notwithstanding that it is a type of divination to predict the result of the political course which America is pursuing, I shall venture some conjectures which, of course, are colored by my enthusiasm and dictated by rational desires rather than by reasoned calculations.

The rôle of the inhabitants of the American hemisphere has for centuries been purely passive. Politically they were non-existent. We are still in a position lower than slavery, and therefore it is more difficult for us to rise to the enjoyment of freedom. Permit me these transgressions in order to establish the issue. States are slaves because of either the nature or the misuse of their constitutions; a people is therefore enslaved when the government, by its nature or its vices, infringes on and usurps the rights of the citizen or subject. Applying these principles, we find that America was denied not only its freedom but even an active and effective tyranny. Let me explain. Under absolutism there are no recognized limits to the exercise of governmental powers. The will of the great sultan, khan, bey, and other despotic rulers is the supreme law, carried out more or less arbitrarily by the lesser pashas, khans, and satraps of Turkey and Persia, who have an organized system of oppression in which inferiors participate according to the authority vested in them. To them is entrusted the administration of civil, military, political, religious, and tax matters. But, after all is said and done, the rulers of Ispahan are Persians; the viziers of the Grand Turk are Turks; and the sultans of Tartary are Tartars. China does not bring its military leaders and scholars from the land of Genghis Khan, her conqueror, notwithstanding that the Chinese of today are the lineal descendants of those who were reduced to subjection by the ancestors of the present-day Tartars.

How different is our situation! We have been harassed by a conduct which has not only deprived us of our rights but has kept us in a sort of permanent infancy with regard to public affairs. If we could at least have managed our domestic affairs and our internal administration, we could have acquainted ourselves with the processes and mechanics of public affairs. We should also have enjoyed a personal consideration, thereby commanding a certain unconscious respect from the people, which is so necessary to preserve amidst revolutions. That is why I say we have even been deprived of an active tyranny, since we have not been permitted to exercise its functions.

Americans today, and perhaps to a greater extent than ever before, who live within the Spanish system occupy a position in society no better than that of serfs destined for labor, or at best they have no more status than that of mere consumers. Yet even this status is surrounded with galling restrictions, such as being forbidden to grow European crops, or to store products which are royal monopolies, or to establish factories of a type the Peninsula itself does not possess. To this add the exclusive trading privileges, even in articles of prime necessity, and the barriers between American provinces, designed to prevent all exchange of trade, traffic, and understanding. In short, do you wish to know what our future held?—simply the cultivation of the fields of indigo, grain, coffee, sugar cane, cacao, and cotton; cattle raising on the broad plains; hunting wild game in the jungles; digging in the earth to mine its gold—but even these limitations could never satisfy the greed of Spain.

So negative was our existence that I can find nothing comparable in any other civilized society, examine as I may the entire history of time and the politics of all nations. Is it not an outrage and a violation of human rights to expect a land so splendidly endowed, so vast, rich, and populous, to remain merely passive?

As I have just explained, we were cut off and, as it were, removed from the world in relation to the science of government and administration of the state. We were never viceroys or governors, save in the rarest of instances; seldom archbishops and bishops; diplomats never; as military men, only subordinates; as nobles, without royal privileges. In brief, we were neither magistrates nor financiers and seldom merchants—all in flagrant contradiction to our institutions.

Emperor Charles V made a pact with the discoverers, conquerors, and settlers of America, and this, as Guerra puts it, is our social contract. The monarchs of Spain made a solemn agreement with them, to be carried out on their own account and at their own risk, expressly prohibiting them from drawing on the royal treasury. In return, they were made the lords of the land, entitled to organize the public administration and act as the court of last appeal, together with many other exemptions and privileges that are too numerous to mention. The King committed himself never to alienate the American provinces, inasmuch as he had no jurisdiction but that of sovereign domain. Thus, for themselves and their descendants, the *conquistadores* possessed what were tantamount to feudal holdings. Yet there are explicit laws respecting employment in civil, ecclesiastical, and tax-raising establishments. These laws favor, almost exclusively, the natives of the country who are of Spanish extraction. Thus, by an outright violation of the laws and the existing agreements, those born in America have been despoiled of their constitutional rights as embodied in the code.

❖   ❖   ❖

More than anyone, I desire to see America fashioned into the greatest nation in the world, greatest not so much by virtue of her area and wealth as by her freedom and glory. Although I seek perfection for the government of my country, I cannot persuade myself that the New World can, at the moment, be organized as a great republic. Since it is impossible, I dare not desire it; yet much less do I desire to have all America a monarchy because this plan is not only impracticable but also impossible. Wrongs now existing could not be righted, and our emancipation would be fruitless. The American states need the care of paternal governments to heal the sores and wounds of despotism and war. The parent country, for example, might be Mexico, the only country fitted for the position by her intrinsic strength, and without such power there can be no parent country. Let us assume it were to be the Isthumus of Panamá, the most central point of this vast continent. Would not all parts continue in their lethargy and even in their present disorder? For a single government to infuse life into the New World; to put into use all the resources for public prosperity; to improve, educate, and perfect the New World, that government would have to possess the authority of a god, much less the knowledge and virtues of mankind.

The party spirit that today keeps our states in constant agitation would assume still greater proportions were a central power established, for that power—the only force capable of checking this agitation—would be elsewhere. Furthermore, the chief figures of the capitals would not tolerate the preponderance of leaders at the metropolis, for they would regard these leaders as so many tyrants. Their resentments would attain such heights that they would compare the latter to the hated Spaniards. Any such monarchy would be a misshapen colossus that would collapse of its own weight at the slightest disturbance.

Mr. de Pradt [a French writer] has wisely divided America into fifteen or seventeen mutually independent states, governed by as many monarchs. I am in agreement on the first suggestion, as America can well tolerate seventeen nations; as to the second, though it could easily be achieved, it would serve no purpose. Consequently, I do not favor American monarchies. My reasons are these: The well-understood interest of a republic is limited to the matter of its preservation, prosperity, and glory. Republicans, because they do not desire powers which represent a directly contrary viewpoint, have no reason for expanding the boundaries of their nation to the detriment of their own resources, solely for the purpose of having their neighbors share a liberal constitution. They would not acquire rights or secure any advantage by conquering their neighbors, unless they were to make them colonies, conquered territory, or allies, after the example of Rome. But such thought and action are directly contrary to the principles of justice which characterize republican systems; and, what is more, they are in direct opposition to the interests of their citizens, because a state, too large of itself or together with its dependencies, ultimately falls into decay. Its free government becomes a tyranny. The principles that should preserve the government are disregarded, and finally it degenerates into despotism. The distinctive feature of small republics is permanence: that of large republics varies, but always with a tendency toward empire. Almost all small republics have had long lives. Among the larger republics, only Rome lasted for several centuries, for its capital was a republic. The rest of her dominions were governed by divers laws and institutions.

The policy of a king is very different. His constant desire is to increase his possessions, wealth, and authority; and with justification, for his power grows with every acquisition, both with respect to his neighbors and his own vassals, who fear him because his power is as formidable as his empire, which he maintains by war and conquest. For these reasons I think that the Americans, being anxious for peace, science, art, commerce, and agriculture, would prefer republics to kingdoms. And, further, it seems to me that these desires conform with the aims of Europe.

❖   ❖   ❖

I shall tell you with what we must provide ourselves in order to expel the Spaniards and to found a free government. It is *union*, obviously; but such union will come about through sensible planning and well-directed actions rather than by divine magic. America stands together because it is abandoned by all other nations. It is isolated in the center of the world. It has no diplomatic relations, nor does it receive any military assistance; instead, America is attacked by Spain, which has more military supplies than any we can possibly acquire through furtive means.

When success is not assured, when the state is weak, and when results are distantly seen, all men hesitate; opinion is divided, passions rage, and the enemy fans these passions in order to win an easy victory because of them. As soon as we are strong and under the guidance of a liberal nation which will lend us her protection, we will achieve accord in cultivating the virtues and talents that lead to glory. Then will we march majestically toward that great prosperity for which South America is destined. Then will those sciences and arts which, born in the East, have enlightened Europe, wing their way to a free Colombia, which will cordially bid them welcome. . . .

⤳ Discussion Questions ⤳

1. Where do you see evidence of the Enlightenment's celebration of nature, natural law, and human progress in Crèvecoeur's writing? According to him, what distinctive social factors in colonial society accounted for the transformation of Europeans into Americans?

2. How does Paine link the American and French revolutions in his attack on monarchy and aristocracy? Why does he consider hereditary power a violation of natural law? Why does he believe republican forms of government are more consistent with natural law?

3. According to Bolívar, why is Spain an "unnatural step-mother" for its colonies? Bolívar lived a generation after Crèvecoeur and Paine: Where do you see evidence of those two earlier writers in "The Jamaica Letter"? Consider especially Bolívar's definition of "Americans" and his prescription for the future government of Latin America.

4. All three authors in this chapter were well traveled and spent considerable time on both sides of the Atlantic. How do you think that experience affected their political ideas and agendas? Where do you think they would have agreed or disagreed in their predictions for the future of the Atlantic World?

Suggested Readings

Classic studies of the Age of Revolutions include E. J. Hobsbawm, *The Age of Revolution: Europe, 1789–1848* (London: Weidenfeld and Nicholson, 1962), and R. R. Palmer, *The Age of Democratic Revolution: A Political History of Europe and America, 1760–1800*, 2 volumes (Princeton, N.J.: Princeton University Press, 1959). Both of these works provide an introduction to the Enlightenment ideology that inspired the Age of Revolutions, but neither addresses the Latin American wars of independence in any detail. In *The Many-Headed Hydra: Sailors, Slaves, Commoners, and the Hidden History of the Revolutionary Atlantic* (Boston: Beacon Press, 2000), Peter Linebaugh and Marcus Rediker take a different approach, emphasizing the role that an international working class of sailors, servants, and slaves played in fomenting political upheaval and anti-slavery sentiment in the northern Atlantic World. Lester D. Langley provides a comparative history of the American, Haitian, and Latin American revolutions in *The Americas in the Age of Revolution, 1750–1850* (New Haven, Conn.: Yale University Press, 1996). Also useful for its treatment of North America, the Caribbean, and South America is Max Savelle, *Empires to Nations: Expansion in America, 1713–1824* (Minneapolis, Minn.: University of Minnesota Press, 1974). A more recent study of the impact of the American Revolution on the British West Indies is Andrew Jackson O'Shaughnessy, *An Empire Divided: The American Revolution and the British Caribbean* (Philadelphia: University of Pennsylvania Press, 2000).

The ideological links between the American and French Revolutions are explored in Susan Dunn, *Sister Revolutions: French Lightning, American Light* (New York: Faber and Faber, Inc., 1999); Patrice L. R. Higonnet, *Sister Republics: The Origins of French and American Republicanism* (Cambridge, Mass.: Harvard University Press, 1988); and Lloyd S. Kramer, *Lafayette in Two Worlds: Public Cultures and Personal Identities in an Age of Revolutions* (Chapel Hill, N.C.: University of North Carolina Press, 1996). The transatlantic connections between the Enlightenment and the Age of Revolutions are also examined in Henry Steele Commager, *The Empire of Reason: How Europe Imagined and America Realized the Enlightenment* (Garden City, N.Y.: Anchor Press/Doubleday, 1977). A good overview of the causes and consequences of the Latin American wars of independence is Richard Graham, *Independence in Latin America: A Comparative Approach*, second edition (New York: McGraw-Hill, Inc., 1994). Also see John Lynch, *The Spanish American Revolutions, 1808–1826*, second edition (New York: W. W. Norton, 1986).

Europe Supported by Africa and America

John Stedman commissioned this artwork for his narrative of his adventures in Surinam (see Chapter 5, Selection 2, pp. 95–104), depicting the three populations he encountered there—Europeans, Africans, and Indians—as three female figures with arms entwined. How does the figure of Europe differ from that of Africa and America? What is the significance of the figures' nakedness? Do you suppose Stedman meant this image to be a criticism or endorsement of the historical forces that created and sustained the Atlantic World?

Source: "Europe Supported by Africa & America," engraving by William Blake, 1792, from *John Gabriel Stedman's Narrative of a Five Years Expedition Against the Revolted Negroes of Surinam*, edited by Richard Price and Sally Price (Baltimore: John Hopkins University Press, 1988). Photo courtesy of Richard and Salle Price

Out of the Atlantic Crucible

Introduction

No singular event heralded the end of the Atlantic World System in the way that Columbus's first voyage marked its beginning. The Atlantic World had a long demise, as illustrated by the protracted battle to end slavery in the Americas. The economic and political ties that bound together Africa, Europe, and the Americas changed gradually but significantly over the course of the nineteenth century, bringing an end to the empires that had ruled and profited from the Atlantic World. Nevertheless, the Atlantic World left important legacies for the modern era, and one does not have to look far to find evidence of its continuing impact on our own world.

In 1823, United States President James Monroe warned the nations of Europe not to interfere with the newly independent nations of Latin America. In return, Monroe promised, the United States would not meddle in the affairs of Europe. The Monroe Doctrine, as this policy became known, had no real teeth: The United States lacked the military and naval power to enforce it. More significantly, however, it gave formal expression to a reality that had been reshaping the Atlantic World since 1775. Politically, the two hemispheres were growing apart; former colonies were gaining their independence and expressing new nationalist identities that emphasized their distance and autonomy from the Old World. While some European powers retained their sugar island colonies in the Caribbean well into the twentieth century, the independent nation state had become the norm of political organization in the Americas by 1825.

While Europe's political domination of the Western Hemisphere went into eclipse, its economic power there remained strong. In nineteenth-century Latin America, British and German merchants and investors rushed to fill the gap left by the destruction of Spanish imperial rule. This reliance on European capital and industry perpetuated the economic dependence of the old colonial system in Latin America well after political independence had been achieved. In the southern United States, the plantation complex continued to thrive after independence, as planters sold their new cash crop, cotton, to textile manufacturers in Britain and the northern United States. Indeed, the explosive growth of industrial production in Britain, the northern United States, France, and Germany in the nineteenth century created a new web of international trade in which those nations with industrial capacity continued to exploit other regions of the world for their raw materials, only now on a global scale.

European imperialism, in other words, did not end with the Atlantic World. Quite to the contrary, it became even more powerful as it shifted into Africa and Asia. Powered by Industrial Age improvements in transportation (railroads, steamships, canals) and military technology (ironclad warships, machine guns), Britain, Germany, and France competed intensely for overseas empire in Africa, Asia, and the Pacific. The plantation complex traveled with them, and colonizers applied it to extracting rubber, tea, sugar, gold, diamonds, and other raw materials from these regions. Indigenous peoples in these regions faced the same onslaught from epidemic diseases, coerced labor, and religious missions that Native Americans had encountered in the Atlantic World.

The transoceanic migrations that shaped the Atlantic World also continued well after the decline of the Atlantic empires. Emigration from Europe to the Americas grew at an even greater pace after 1800. Latin American independence ended the restrictive immigration policy that the Spanish had imposed on their colonies, allowing British, German, and Italian emigrants to settle in South America. In North America, European immigration prior to 1850 was dominated by Irish, German, and Scandinavian peoples; after 1880, Italians, Poles, and Russian Jews made the Atlantic crossing in large numbers. The end of slavery in the New World also revived the immigration of indentured servants for the plantation economies of the Caribbean, bringing East Indians in large numbers to the British West Indies after 1833. As the nineteenth century progressed, the Pacific Ocean became another highway of migration, traveled by Chinese indentured servants to North and South America. In short, so long as the demand for labor remained high in the Americas, immigration there continued apace.

In some respects, the Atlantic World never came to an end. Rather, it morphed into something else, on a much grander scale. We live in an age of global travel and communication, of world markets and multinational corporations, of multiethnic communities with populations from every corner of the globe. All of these characteristics of our modern world have roots in the Atlantic World, although modern technology may make the wooden ships and muskets of the Atlantic World appear quaint by comparison. We should not let that glaring technological gap fool us. On the human scale, there is still much that bears comparison between the Atlantic World and our modern one whenever we talk about contact, exchange, and conflict between human populations around the globe.

The readings in this chapter suggest one such inquiry: What type of legacy have notions of race that were forged in the Atlantic World left for modern society? The colonization of the Americas brought together for the first time African, Native American, and European peoples, and out of this collision there emerged racial categories and social orders peculiar to the New World. As colonial empires gave way to nation states, the issue of race confronted all who contemplated the future of the Americas. In the selections in this chapter, three observers offer their differing impressions of race relations in the Atlantic World during the early nineteenth century. As you read these selections, think of the historical factors that might account for the different experiences and opinions of these writers. How did their views anticipate the continuing significance of race in the modern world's social, economic, and political systems?

SELECTION 1: A German Traveler Describes the Race-Based Social Order of Mexico

Alexander von Humboldt, a native of Germany, crossed the Atlantic in 1799 and spent five years in the Americas. His travels focused on the Andes and Mexico, but on his way home, he also visited Philadelphia and Washington, D.C.—a stop that informed his comparisons of the United States and Latin America. Humboldt's primary interests were scientific: He gathered information about flora, fauna, geology, and other aspects of the natural world. He was also a keen student of history and politics, and much of what he wrote about Latin America reflected Enlightenment-era criticism of Spain's conquest and government of its New World dominions. Upon returning to Europe, Humboldt gained celebrity for his American travels, and he spent the rest of his life working as a scientist and diplomat.

In 1811 he published his most famous work, the four-volume *Political Essay on the Kingdom of New Spain*. Most of the *Political Essay* deals with Mexico's natural resources, particularly its mineral wealth, but the picture Humboldt painted of a mature colonial society on the verge of political independence is what still attracts historians to this source today. With the voice of a detached, scientific observer, he took measure of Mexico's population and dissected its race-based social order. In the passage that follows, he comments on African and Indian slavery and the nature of the color prejudice that determined rank in this society.

The kingdom of New Spain is, of all the European colonies under the torrid zone, that in which there are the fewest Negroes. We may almost say that there are no slaves. We may go through the whole city of Mexico without seeing a black countenance. The service of no house is carried on with slaves.

From Alexander von Humboldt, *Political Essay on the Kingdom of New Spain*, edited by Mary Maples Dunn (New York: Alfred A. Knopf, 1972), 84–90.

Figure 12.1   Independent States in the Americas, c. 1825
National boundaries in Western Hemisphere.
Source: Adapted from Max Savelle, *Empires to Nations: Expansion in America, 1713–1824*
(Minneapolis: University of Minnesota Press, 1974), 265.

From this point of view Mexico presents a singular contrast to Havana. Lima and Caracas. From information in the enumeration [census] of 1793 it appears that in all New Spain there are not six thousand Negroes and not more than nine or ten thousand slaves, of whom the greatest number belong to the ports of Acapulco and Vera Cruz or the warm regions of the coasts. The slaves are four times more numerous in Caracas which does not contain a sixth of the population of Mexico. The Negroes of Jamaica are to those of New Spain in the proportion of 250 to 1 ! In the West India islands, Peru and even Caracas, the progress of agriculture and industry in general depends on the augmentation of Negroes. In the island of Cuba, for example, where the annual exportation of sugar has risen in twelve years from 400,000 to 1,000,000 quintals [88 million to 220 million lbs.], between 1792 and 1803 nearly 55,000 slaves have been introduced. But in Mexico the increase of colonial prosperity is nowise occasioned by a more active slave trade, and the progress of sugar cultivation which has taken place in New Spain has not perceptibly increased the number of slaves. Of the 74,000 Negroes annually furnished by Africa to America and Asia, not above 100 land on the coast of Mexico.

By the laws there can be no Indian slaves in the Spanish colonies, and yet by a singular abuse wars give rise to a state very much like that of the African slave. In Mexico the prisoners taken in the petty warfare which is carried on almost without interruption on the frontiers of the provincias internas [northern provinces of Mexico] experience an unhappy fate. They are generally of the nation of the Apaches, and they are dragged to Mexico where they languish in the dungeons of a correction house. Their ferocity is increased by solitude and despair. Transported to Vera Cruz and Cuba, they soon perish, like every savage Indian removed from the high table land into the lower and hotter regions. These prisoners sometimes break from their dungeons and commit the most atrocious cruelties in the surrounding countries. It is high time that the government interested itself in these unfortunate persons whose number is small and their situation so much the easier to be ameliorated.

However, the slaves in Mexico, as in all the other Spanish possessions, are somewhat more under the protection of the laws than the Negroes of the other European colonies. These laws are always interpreted in favor of liberty. The government wishes to see the number of freedom increased. A slave who by his industry has procured a little money may compel his master to give him his liberty on paying the moderate sum of 1,500 or 2,000 livres [£62 or £83]. Liberty cannot be refused to a Negro on the pretext that he cost the triple of the sum, or that he possesses a particular talent for some lucrative employment. A slave who has been cruelly used acquires on that account his freedom by the law, if the judge do justice to the cause of the oppressed, but it may be easily conceived that this beneficent law must be frequently eluded. I saw, however, in Mexico in the month of July, 1803, an example of two Negroes to whom the magistrate gave their liberty because their mistress, a lady from the islands, had wounded them all over the body with scissors, pins and knives. In the course of this shocking process the lady was accused of having knocked out the teeth of the slaves with a key when they complained of a fluxion [bleeding] in the gums which prevented them from working.

To complete the table of the elements of which the Mexican population is composed, it remains for us to point out rapidly the differences of caste which spring from the mixture of the pure races with one another. These castes constitute a mass almost as considerable as the Mexican Indians. We may estimate the total of the individuals of mixed blood at nearly 2,400,000. From a refinement of vanity, the inhabitants of the colonies have enriched their language with terms for the finest shades of the colors which result from the degeneration of the primitive color. It may be useful to explain these denominations because they have been confounded by many travelers. and because this confusion frequently causes no small embarrassment to those who read Spanish works on the American possessions.

The son of a white (creole or European) and a native of copper color is called mestizo. His color is almost a pure white, and his skin is of a particular transparency. The small beard and small hands and feet, and a certain obliquity of the eyes, are more frequent indications of the mixture of Indian blood than the nature of the hair. If a mestiza marry a white man, the second generation differs hardly in anything from the European race. As very few Negroes have been introduced into New Spain, the mestizos probably compose 7/8 of the whole castes. They are generally accounted of a much more mild character than the mulattos, descended from whites and Negresses, who are distinguished for the violence of their passions and a singular volubility of tongue. The descendants of Negroes and Indian women bear the strange name of *Chino*, Chinese. On the coast of Caracas and, as appears from the laws, even in New Spain, they are called zambos. This last denomination is now principally limited to the descendants of a Negro and a female mulatto, or a Negro and a Chinese female. From these common zambos they distinguish the zambos prietos who descend from a Negro and a female zamba. From the mixture of a white man with a mulatto comes the cast of *cuarterón*. When a female cuarteron marries a European or creole, her son bears the name of *quinterón*. A new alliance with a white banishes to such a degree the remains of color that the children of a white and a quinterón are white also.

In a country governed by whites, the families reputed to have the least mixture of Negro or mulatto blood are also naturally the most honored. In Spain it is almost a title of nobility to descend neither from Jews nor Moors. In America the greater or less degree of whiteness of skin decides the rank which man occupies in society. A white who rides barefooted on horseback thinks he belongs to the nobility of the country. Color establishes even a certain equality among men who, as is universally the case where civilization is either little advanced or in a retrograde state, take a particular pleasure in dwelling on the prerogatives of race and origin. When a common man disputes with one of the titled lords of the country, he is frequently heard to say, "Do you think me not so white as yourself?" This may serve to characterize the state and source of the actual aristocracy. It becomes, consequently, a very interesting business for the public vanity to estimate accurately the fractions of European blood which belong to the different castes.

It often happens that families suspected of being of mixed blood demand from the high court of justice a declaration that they belong to the whites.

These declarations are not always corroborated by the judgment of the senses. We see very swarthy mulattoes who have had the address to get themselves "whitened" (this is the vulgar expression). When the color of the skin is too repugnant to the judgment demanded, the petitioner is contented with an expression somewhat problematical—"that such or such individuals may consider themselves as whites."

The reader will no doubt desire to have a discussion of what is the influence of this mixture of races on the general well-being of society? And what is the degree of enjoyment and individual happiness which a man of cultivated mind can procure amidst such a collision of interests, prejudices and feelings?

When a European transports himself into these distant regions of the new continent, he feels oppressed at every step with the influence which the colonial government has for centuries exercised over the minds of the inhabitants. A well-informed man, who merely interests himself in the intellectual development of the species, suffers less perhaps than the man who is endowed with great sensibility. The former institutes a comparison with the mother country; from maritime communication he procures books and in-struments; he sees with ecstasy the progress which the exact sciences have made in the great cities of Spanish America; and the contemplation of nature in all her grandeur and the astonishing variety of her productions, indemnifies his mind for the privations to which his position condemns him. But the man of sensibility must seek in the Spanish colonies for everything agreeable in life within himself alone. It is in this way that isolation and solitude have their attractions for him if he wishes to enjoy peaceably the advantages afforded by the excellence of the climate, the aspect of a never-fading verdure; and the political calm of the new world. While I freely give these ideas to the world, I am not censuring the moral character of the inhabitants of Mexico or Peru; nor do I say that the people of Lima are worse than those of Cadiz. I am rather inclined to believe what many other travelers have observed before me, that the Americans are endowed by nature with a gentleness of manners rather approaching to effeminacy, as the energy of several European nations easily degenerates into harshness. The want of sociability so universal in the Spanish colonies and the hatreds which divide the castes of greatest affinity, the effects of which shed a bitterness over the life of the colonists, are solely due to the political principles by which these regions have been governed since the sixteenth century. A government, aware of the true interests of humanity, will be able to diffuse information and instruction, and by extinguishing gradually the monstrous inequality of rights and fortunes, will succeed in augmenting the physical prosperity of the colonists; but it will find immense difficulties to overcome before rendering the inhabitants sociable, and teaching them to consider themselves mutually in the light of fellow citizens.

Let us not forget than in the United States society is formed in a very different manner from what it is in Mexico and the other continental regions of the Spanish colonies. Penetrating into the Alleghany mountains, the Europeans found immense forests in which a few tribes of hunters wandered up and down, attached by no tie to an uncultivated soil. At the approach of the new colonists, the natives gradually retired towards the western savannas in the neighborhood of the Mississippi and the Missouri. In this manner free men of the same race and the same origin became the first elements of a new people.

In New Spain and Peru, if we except the missions, the colonists nowhere returned to the state of nature. Fixing themselves in the midst of agricultural nations, who themselves lived under governments equally complicated and despotic, the Europeans took advantage of the preponderancy of their civilization, their cunning, and the authority they derived from the conquest. This particular situation, and the mixture of races of which the interests are diametrically opposite, became an inexhaustible source of hatred and disunion. In proportion as the descendants of the Europeans became more numerous than those sent over directly by the mother country, the white race divided into two parties, of which the ties of blood cannot heal the resentments. The colonial government from a mistaken policy wished to take advantage of these dissensions. The greater the colony, the greater the suspicion of the administration. According to the ideas which unfortunately have been adopted for ages, these distant regions are considered as tributary to Europe. Authority is there distributed not in the manner which the public interest requires, but according as the dread of seeing a too rapid increase in the prosperity of the inhabitants seems to dictate. Seeking security in civil dissensions, in the balance of power, and in a complication of all the springs of the great political machine, the mother country foments incessantly the spirit of party and hatred among the castes and constituted authorities. From this state of things arises a rancor which disturbs the enjoyments of social life.

SELECTION 2: A French Traveler Considers the Future of Race Relations in the United States of America

Alexis de Tocqueville was a young French nobleman who toured the United States of America from 1831 to 1832. Although the nominal purpose of his trip was to investigate reforms in the American penal system, he quickly shifted his focus to a much larger topic: how the rise of political democracy in the United States was transforming social relations. He published his observations in *Democracy in America*, the first part of which appeared in 1835 and the second in 1840. Like Humboldt before him, Tocqueville brought a spirit of a scientific observation to his work, evaluating American society as if he were encountering a new kind plant or animal species. He found in the United States a laboratory for the social transformations unleashed by the Enlightenment and Age of Revolutions, and he believed those changes would eventually sweep the Old World.

The excerpt below comes from an essay in *Democracy in America* titled "The Present and Probable Future Condition of the Three Races that Inhabit the Territory of the United States." Like the selection from Humboldt, it concerns the coming together of African, Native American, and European peoples, but describes very different results from that collision. While much of his language will strike modern readers as racist, Tocqueville nevertheless takes an unflinching look at the costs that white democracy in the United States imposed on the other racial groups living there.

The territory now occupied or claimed by the American Union spreads from the shores of the Atlantic to those of the Pacific ocean. On the east and west its limits are those of the continent itself. On the south it advances nearly to the tropic, and it extends upward to the icy regions of the north.

The human beings who are scattered over this space do not form, as in Europe, so many branches of the same stock. Three races naturally distinct, and I might almost say hostile to each other, are discoverable among them at the first glance. Almost insurmountable barriers had been raised between them by education and by law, as well as by their origin and outward characteristics; but fortune has brought them together on the same soil, where, although they are mixed, they do not amalgamate, and each race fulfils its destiny apart.

❖   ❖   ❖

The Europeans introduced among the savages of North America firearms, ardent spirits, and iron: they taught them to exchange for manufactured stuffs the rough garments which had previously satisfied their untutored simplicity. Having acquired new tastes, without the arts by which they could be gratified, the Indians were obliged to have recourse to the workmanship of the whites; but in return for their productions the savage had nothing to offer except the rich furs which still abounded in his woods. Hence the chase [hunting] became necessary, not merely to provide for his subsistence, but in order to procure the only objects of barter which he could furnish to Europe. While the wants of the natives were thus increasing, their resources continued to diminish.

From the moment when a European settlement is formed in the neighbourhood of the territory occupied by the Indians, the beasts of chase takes the alarm. Thousands of savages, wandering in the forest and destitute of any fixed dwelling, did not distrub them; but as soon as the continuous sounds of European labour are heard in the neighbourhood, they begin to flee away, and retire to the west, where their instinct teaches them that they will find deserts of immeasurable extent. "The buffalo is constantly receding," say Messrs. Clarke and Cass in their Report of the year 1829; "a few years since they approached the base of the Allegany; and a few years hence they may even be rare upon the immense plains which extend to the base of the Rocky mountains." I have been assured that this effect of the approach of the whites is often felt at two hundred leagues' distance from the frontier. Their influence is thus exerted over tribes whose name is unknown to them, and who suffer the evils of usurpation long before they are acquainted with the authors of their distress.

———————

From Alexis de Tocqueville, *Democracy in America,* 2 volumes (1835; New York: J. & H. G. Langley, 1841), 1:362, 367–370, 386, 389–391, 404–407, 412.

Bold adventures soon penetrate into the country the Indians have deserted, and when they have advanced about fifteen or twenty leagues from the extreme frontiers of the whites, they begin to build habitations for civilized beings in the midst of the wilderness. This is done without difficulty, as the territory of a hunting-nation is ill defined; it is the common property of the tribe, and belongs to no one in particular, so that individual interests are not concerned in the protection of any part of it.

A few European families, settled in different situations at a considerable distance from each other, soon drive away the wild animals which remain between their places of abode. The Indians, who had previously lived in a sort of abundance, then find it difficult to subsist, and still more difficult to procure the articles of barter which they stand in need of.

To drive away their game is to deprive them of the means of existence, as effectually as if the fields of our agriculturists were stricken with barrenness; and they are reduced, like famished wolves, to prowl through the forsaken woods in quest of prey. Their instinctive love of their country attaches them to the soil which gave them birth, even after it has ceased to yield anything but misery and death. At length they are compelled to acquiesce, and to depart: they follow the traces of the elk, the buffalo, and the beaver, and are guided by those wild animals in the choice of their future country. Properly speaking, therefore, it is not the Europeans who drive away the native inhabitants of America; it is famine which compels them to recede; a happy distinction which had escaped the casuists of former times, and for which we are indebted to modern discovery.

It is impossible to conceive the extent of the sufferings which attend these forced emigrations. They are undertaken by a people already exhausted and reduced; and the countries to which the new-comers betake themselves are inhabited by other tribes which receive them with jealous hostility. Hunger is in the rear, war awaits them, and misery besets them on all sides. In the hope of escaping from such a host of enemies, they separate, and each individual endeavours to procure the means of supporting his existence in solitude and secresy, living in the immensity of the desert like an outcast in civilized society. The social tie, which distress had long since weakened, is then dissolved; they have lost their country, and their people soon deserts them; their very families are obliterated; the names they bore in common are forgotten, their language perishes, and all the traces of their origin disappear. Their nation has ceased to exist, except in the recollection of the antiquaries of America and a few of the learned of Europe.

◆   ◆   ◆

The Indians will perish in the same isolated condition in which they have lived; but the destiny of the negroes is in some measure interwoven with that of the Europeans. These two races are attached to each other without intermingling; and they are alike unable entirely to separate or to combine. The most formidable of all the ills which threaten the future existence of the United States, arises from the presence of a black population upon its territory; and in contemplating the causes of the present embarrassments or of the future dangers of the United States, the observer is invariably led to consider this as a primary fact.

◆   ◆   ◆

I see that in a certain portion of the territory of the United States at the present day, the legal barrier which separated the two races is tending to fall away, but not that which exists in the manners of the country; slavery recedes, but the prejudice to which it has given birth remains stationary. Whosoever has inhabited the United States, must have perceived, that in those parts of the Union in which the negroes are no longer slaves, they have in nowise drawn nearer to the whites. On the contrary, the prejudice of the race appears to be stronger in the states which have abolished slavery, than in those where it still exists; and nowhere is it so intolerant as in those states where servitude has never been known.

It is true, that in the north of the Union, marriages may be legally contracted between negroes and whites, but public opinion would stigmatize a man who should connect himself with a negress as infamous, and it would be difficult to meet with a single instance of such a union. The electoral franchise has been conferred upon the negroes in almost all the states in which slavery has been abolished; but if they come forward to vote, their lives are in danger. If oppressed, they may bring an action at law, but they will find none but whites among their judges; and although they may legally serve as jurors, prejudice repulses them from that office. The same schools do not receive the child of the black and of the European. In the theatres, gold cannot procure a seat for the servile race beside their former masters; in the hospitals they lie apart; and although they are allowed to invoke the same Divinity as the whites, it must be at a different altar, and in their own churches with their own clergy. The gates of heaven are not closed against these unhappy beings; but their inferiority is continued to the very confines of the other world. When the negro is defunct, his bones are cast aside, and the distinction of condition prevails even in the equality of death. The negro is free, but he can share neither the rights, nor the pleasures, nor the labour, nor the afflictions, nor the tomb of him whose equal he has been declared to be; and he cannot meet him upon fair terms in life or in death.

In the south, where slavery still exists, the negroes are less carefully kept apart; they sometimes share the labour and the recreations of the whites; the whites consent to intermix with them to a certain extent, and although the legislation treats them more harshly, the habits of the people are more tolerant and compassionate. In the south the master is not afraid to raise his slave to his own standing, because he knows that he can in a moment reduce him to the dust at pleasure. In the north, the white no longer distinctly perceives the barrier which separates him from the degraded race, and he shuns the negro with the more pertinacity, because he fears lest they should some day be confounded together.

Among the Americans of the south, nature sometimes reasserts her rights, and restores a transient equality between the blacks and the whites; but in the north, pride restrains the most imperious of human passions. The American of the northern states would perhaps allow the negress to share his licentious pleasures, if the laws of his country did not declare that she may aspire to be the legitimate partner of his bed; but he recoils with horror from her who might become his wife.

Thus it is, in the United States, that the prejudice which repels the negroes seems to increase in proportion as they are emancipated, and inequality is sanctioned by the manners while it is effaced from the laws of the country. But if the relative position of the two races which inhabit the United States, is such as I have described, it may be asked why the Americans have abolished slavery in the north of the Union, why they maintain it in the south, and why they aggravate its hardships there? The answer is easily given. It is not for the good of the negroes, but for that of the whites, that measures are taken to abolish slavery in the United States.

❖   ❖   ❖

As soon as it is admitted that the whites and the emancipated blacks are placed upon the same territory in the situation of two alien communities, it will readily be understood that there are but two alternatives for the future; the negroes and the whites must either wholly part or wholly mingle. I have already expressed the conviction which I entertain as to the latter event. I do not imagine that the white and the black races will ever live in any country upon an equal footing. But I believe the difficulty to be still greater in the United States than elsewhere. An isolated individual may surmount the prejudices of religion, of his country, or of his race, and if this individual is a king he may effect surprising changes in society; but a whole people cannot rise, as it were, above itself. A despot who should subject the Americans and their former slaves to the same yoke, might perhaps succeed in commingling their races; but as long as the American democracy remains at the head of affairs, no one will undertake so difficult a task; and it may be foreseen that the freer the white population of the United States becomes, the more isolated will it remain.

I have previously observed that the mixed race is the true bond of union between the Europeans and the Indians; just so the mulattoes are the true means of transition between the white and the negro; so that wherever mulattoes abound, the intermixture of the two races is not impossible. In some parts of America, the European and the negro races are so crossed by one another, that it is rare to meet with a man who is entirely black or entirely white: when they are arrived at this point, the two races may really be said to be combined; or rather to have been absorbed in a third race, which is connected with both, without being identical with either.

Of all the Europeans the English are those who have mixed least with the negroes. More mulattoes are to be seen in the south of the Union than in the north, but still they are infinitely more scarce than in any other European colony: Mulattoes are by no means numerous in the United States; they have no force peculiar to themselves, and when quarrels originating in differences of colour take place, they generally side with the whites, just as the lacqueys of the great in Europe assume the contemptuous airs of nobility to the lower orders.

The pride of origin, which is natural to the English, is singularly augmented by the personal pride which democratic liberty fosters among the Americans:

the white citizen of the United States is proud of his race, and proud of himself. But if the whites and the negroes do not intermingle in the north of the Union, how should they mix in the south? Can it be supposed for an instant, that an American of the southern states, placed, as he must for ever be, between the white man with all his physical and moral superiority, and the negro, will ever think of preferring the latter? The Americans of the southern states have two powerful passions which will always keep them aloof; the first is the fear of being assimilated to the negroes, their former slaves; and the second, the dread of sinking below the whites, their neighbours.

If I were called upon to predict what will probably occur at some future time, I should say, that the abolition of slavery in the south, will, in the common course of things, increase the repugnance of the white population for the men of colour. I found this opinion upon the analogous observation which I already had occasion to make in the north. I there remarked, that the white inhabitants of the north avoid the negroes with increasing care, in proportion as the legal barriers of separation are removed by the legislature; and why should not the same result take place in the south? In the north, the whites are deterred from intermingling with the blacks by the fear of an imaginary danger; in the south, where the danger would be real, I cannot imagine that the fear would be less general.

If, on the one hand, it be admitted (and the fact is unquestionable), that the coloured population perpetually accumulates in the extreme south, and that it increases more rapidly than that of the whites; and if, on the other hand, it be allowed that it is impossible to foresee a time at which the whites and the blacks will be so intermingled as to derive the same benefits from society; must it not be inferred, that the blacks and the whites will, sooner or later, come to open strife in the southern states of the Union? But if it be asked what the issue of the struggle is likely to be, it will readily be understood, that we are here left to form a very vague surmise of the truth. The human mind may succeed in tracing a wide circle, as it were, which includes the course of future events; but within that circle a thousand various chances and circumstances may direct it in as many different ways; and in every picture of the future there is a dim spot, which the eye of the understanding cannot penetrate. It appears, however, to be extremely probable, that in the West India islands the white race is destined to be subdued, and the black population to share the same fate upon the continent.

In the West India islands the white planters are surrounded by an immense black population; on the continent, the blacks are placed between the ocean and an innumerable people, which already extends over them in a dense mass from the icy confines of Canada to the frontiers of Virginia, and from the banks of the Missouri to the shores of the Atlantic. If the white citizens of North America remain united, it cannot be supposed that the negroes will escape the destruction with which they are menaced; they must be subdued by want or by the sword. But the black population which is accumulated along the coast of the gulf of Mexico, has a chance of success, if the American Union is dissolved when the struggle between the two races begins. If the federal tie were broken, the citizens of the south would be wrong to rely upon any lasting succour from their northern countrymen. The latter are well aware that the danger can never reach them; and unless they are constrained to march to the assistance of the south by a positive obligation, it may be foreseen that the sympathy of colour will be insufficient to stimulate their exertions.

Yet, at whatever period the strife may break out, the whites of the south, even if they are abandoned to their own resources, will enter the lists with an immense superiority of knowledge and of the means of warfare; but the blacks will have numerical strength and the energy of despair upon their side; and these are powerful resources to men who have taken up arms. The fate of the white population of the southern states will, perhaps, be similar to that of the Moors in Spain. After having occupied the land for centuries, it will perhaps be forced to retire to the country whence its ancestors came, and to abandon to the negroes the possession of a territory, which Providence seems to have more peculiarly destined for them, since they can subsist and labour in it more easily than the whites.

❖   ❖   ❖

If it be impossible to anticipate a period at which the Americans of the south will mingle their blood with that of the negroes, can they allow their slaves to become free without compromising their own security? And if they are obliged to keep that race in bondage, in order to save their own families, may they not be excused for availing themselves of the means best adapted to that end? The events which are taking place in the southern states of the Union, appear to be at once the most horrible and the most natural results of slavery. When I see the order of nature overthrown, and when I hear the cry of humanity in its vain struggle against the laws, my indignation does not light upon the men of our own time who are the instruments of these outrages; but I reserve my execration for those who, after a thousand years of freedom, brought back slavery into the world once more.

Whatever may be the efforts of the Americans of the south to maintain slavery, they will not always succeed. Slavery, which is now confined to a single tract of the civilized earth, which is attacked by Christianity as unjust, and by political economy as prejudicial, and which is now contrasted with democratic liberties and the information of our age, cannot survive. By the choice of the master or the will of the slave, it will cease; and in either case great calamities may be expected to ensue. If liberty be refused to the negroes of the south, they will in the end seize it for themselves by force; if it be given, they will abuse it ere long.

SELECTION 3: A Free Black's Incendiary Call for the Destruction of Slavery

David Walker was a shopkeeper and leader of Boston's free black community when he published *An Appeal to the Coloured Citizens of the World* in 1829. A child of a free mother and enslaved father, he had grown up in Wilmington, North Carolina and traveled in the South before settling in Boston in 1825. Like many African Americans of his era, he practiced Methodism, one of the first

Protestant denominations to seek converts among free and enslaved blacks in the Americas. His Christian faith and learning influenced his attack on slavery, which relied extensively on scriptural authority and appeals to divine justice.

Walker's *Appeal* raised a militant voice for the anti-slavery cause in the Atlantic World. The book's language and imagery were incendiary, encouraging active resistance to the institution of slavery. Walker disseminated his message by distributing copies to black sailors and missionaries, who carried them into the cities and plantations of the American South and Caribbean. Slaveholders typically seized and destroyed copies of the book whenever possible and tightened anti-literacy slave laws in its wake. Most important, Walker framed his argument, as the title suggests, as a universal call to blacks, free or slave. Referring to his audience as "true-hearted sons of Africa," he gave voice to an emerging African-American consciousness in the Atlantic World that was animated and united by the anti-slavery cause.

Ignorance, my brethren, is a mist, low down into the very dark and almost impenetrable abyss of which, our fathers for many centuries have been plunged. The christians, and enlightened of Europe, and some of Asia, seeing the ignorance and consequent degradation of our fathers, instead of trying to enlighten them, by teaching them that religion and light with which God had blessed them, they have plunged them into wretchedness ten thousand times more intolerable, than if they had left them entirely to the Lord, and to add to their miseries, deep down into which they have plunged them, tell them, that they are an *inferior* and *distinct race* of beings, which they will be glad enough to recall and swallow by and by. Fortune and misfortune, two inseparable companions, lay rolled up in the wheel of events, which have from the creation of the world, and will continue to take place among men until God shall dash worlds together.

When we take a retrospective view of the arts and sciences—the wise legislators—The Pyramids, and other magnificent buildings—the turning of the channel of the river Nile, by the sons of Africa or of Ham [Noah's son, cursed by his father to serve others], among whom learning originated, and was carried thence into Greece, where it was improved upon and refined. Thence among the Romans, and all over the then enlightened parts of the world, and it has been enlightening the dark and benighted minds of men from then, down to this day. I say, when I view retrospectively, the renown of that once mighty people, the children of our great progenitor, I am indeed cheered. Yea further, when I view that mighty son of Africa, Hannibal, one of the greatest generals of antiquity, who defeated and cut off so many thousands of the

From David Walker, *Appeal to the Coloured Citizens of the World* (1829) in *Walker's Appeal, with a Brief Sketch of His Life,* by Henry Highland Garnet (New York: J. H. Tobitt, 1848), 29–31, 40–43, 53–56, 80–81.

white Romans or murderers, and who carried his victorious arms, to the very gate of Rome, and I give it as my candid opinion, that had Carthage been well united and had given him good support, he would have carried that cruel and barbarous city by storm. But they were disunited, as the colored people are now, in the United States of America, the reason our natural enemies are enabled to keep their feet on our throats.

Beloved brethren—here let me tell you, and believe it, that the Lord our God, as true as he sits on his throne in heaven, and as true as our Saviour died to redeem the world, will give you a Hannibal, and when the Lord shall have raised him up, and given him to you for your possession, O my suffering brethren! remember the divisions and consequent sufferings of *Carthage* and of *Hayti*. Read the history particularly of Hayti, and see how they were butchered by the whites, and do you take warning. The person whom God shall give you, give him your support and let him go his length, and behold in him the salvation of your God. God will indeed, deliver you through him from your deplorable and wretched condition under the christians of America. I charge you this day before my God to lay no obstacle in his way, but let him go.

The whites want slaves, and want us for their slaves, but some of them will curse the day they ever saw us. As true as the sun ever shone in its meridian splendor, my colour will root some of them out of the very face of the earth. They shall have enough of making slaves of, and butchering, and murdering us in the manner which they have. No doubt some may say that I write with a bad spirit, and that I being a black, wish these things to occur. Whether I write with a bad or a good spirit, I say if these things do not occur in their proper time, it is because the world in which we live does not exist, and we are deceived with regard to its existence. It is immaterial however to me, who believe, or who refuse—though I should like to see the whites repent peradventure God may have mercy on them, some however, have gone so far that their cup must be filled.

But what need have I to refer to antiquity, when Hayti, the glory of the blacks and terror of tyrants, is enough to convince the most avaricious and stupid of wretches—which is at this time, and I am sorry to say it, plagued with that scourge of nations, the Catholic religion; but I hope and pray God that she may yet rid herself of it, and adopt in its stead the Protestant faith; also, I hope that she may keep peace within her borders and be united, keeping a strict look out for tyrants, for if they get the least chance to injure her, they will avail themselves of it, as true as the Lord lives in heaven. But one thing which gives me joy is, that they are men who would be cut off to a man, before they would yield to the combined forces of the whole world—in fact, if the whole world was combined against them, it could not do any thing with them, unless the Lord delivers them up.

❖   ❖   ❖

Men of colour, who are also of sense, for you particularly is my appeal designed. Our more ignorant brethren are not able to penetrate its value. I call upon you therefore to cast your eyes upon the wretchedness of your brethren and to do your utmost to enlighten them—*go to work and enlighten your brethren !*—let the Lord see you doing what you can to rescue them and yourselves from degradation. Do any of you say that you and your family are free and happy and what have you to do with wretched slaves and other people? So can I say, for I enjoy as much freedom as any of you, if I am not quite as well off as the best of you. Look into our freedom and happiness and see of what kind they are composed!! They are of the very lowest kind—they are the very *dregs!*—they are the most servile and abject kind, that ever a people was in possession of! If any of you wish to know how free you are, let one of you start and go thro' the southern and western States of this country, and unless you travel as a slave to a white man (a servant is a *slave* to the man whom he serves,) or have your free papers (which if you are not careful they will get from you) if they do not take you up and put you in jail, and if you cannot give evidence of your freedom, sell you into eternal slavery, I am not a living man; or any man of color, immaterial who he is or where he came from, if he is not the 4th from the "*Negro race*," (as we are called,) the white christians of America will serve him the same, they will sink him into wretchedness & degradation forever while he lives. And yet some of you have the hardihood to say that you are free & happy! May God have mercy on your freedom and happiness! I met a colored man in the street a short time since, with a string of boots on his shoulder; we fell into conversation, and in course of which I said to him, what a miserable set of people we are! He asked why?—Said I, we are so subjected under the whites, that we cannot obtain the comforts of life, but by cleaning their boots and shoes, old clothes, waiting on them, shaving them, etc. Said he, (with the boots on his shoulders,) "I am completely happy!!! I never want to live any better or happier than when I can get a plenty of boots and shoes to clean!!!" Oh! how can those who are actuated by avarice only, but think that our creator made us to be an inheritance to them forever, when they see that our greatest glory is centered in such mean and low objects? Understand me, brethren, I do not mean to speak against the occupations by which we acquire enough and sometimes scarcely that, to render ourselves and families comfortable through life. I am subjected to the same inconvenience, as you all. My objections are, to our *glorying* and being *happy* in such low employments; for if we are men, we ought to be thankful to the Lord for the past, and for the future. Be looking forward with thankful hearts to higher attainments than *wielding the razor* and *cleaning boots and shoes.* The man whose aspirations are not *above,* and even *below* these, is indeed, ignorant and wretched enough. I advance it therefore to you, not as a *problematical,* but as an unshaken and forever immoveable *fact,* that your full glory and happiness, as well as all other colored people under heaven, shall never be fully consummated, but with the *entire emancipation of your enslaved brethren all over the world.* You may therefore, go to work and do what you can to rescue, or join in with tyrants to oppress them and yourselves, until the Lord shall come upon you all like a thief in the night. For I believe it is the will of the Lord that our greatest happiness shall consist in working for the salvation of our whole body. When this is accomplished a burst of glory will shine upon you, which will indeed astonish you and the world. Do any of you say this will never be done? I assure you that God will accomplish it—if nothing else will answer, he will hurl tyrants and devils into *atoms* and make way for his people. But O my brethren! I say unto you again, you must go to work and *prepare the way* of the Lord.

There is a great work for you to do, as trifling as some of you may think of it. You have to prove to the Americans and the world, that we are MEN, and not *brutes* as we have been represented, and by millions treated. Remember, to let the aim of your labours among your brethren, and particularly the youths, be the dissemination of education and religion. It is lamentable, that many of our children go to school, from four until they are eight or ten, and sometimes fifteen years of age, and leave school knowing but a little more about the grammar of their language than a horse does about handling a musket—and not a few of them are really so ignorant, that they are unable to answer a person correctly, general questions in geography, and to hear them read would only be to disgust a man who has a taste for reading; which, to do well, as trifling as it may appear to some, (to the ignorant in particular) is a great part of learning. Some few of them, may make out to scribble tolerably well, over a half sheet of paper, which I believe has hitherto been a powerful obstacle in our way, to keep us from accquiring knowledge. An ignorant father, who knows no more than what nature has taught him, together with what little he acquires by the senses of hearing and seeing, finding his son able to write a neat hand, sets it down for granted that he has as good learning as any body; the young, ignorant gump, hearing his father or mother, who perhaps may be ten times more ignorant, in point of literature, than himself, extolling his learning, struts about in the full assurance, that his attainments in literature are sufficient to take him through the world, when, in fact, he has scarcely any learning at all!!!!

◆   ◆   ◆

How can the preachers and people of America believe the Bible? Does it teach them any distinction on account of a man's color? Hearken, Americans! to the injunctions of our Lord and Master, to his humble followers.

"And Jesus came and spake unto them saying, all power is given unto me in heaven and in earth.

Go ye, therefore, and teach all nations, baptizing them in the name of the Father, and of the Son, and of the Holy Ghost, Teaching them to observe all things whatsoever I have commanded you; and lo, I am with you alway, even unto the end of the world. Amen."

I declare, that the very face of these injunctions appears to be of God and not of man. They do not show the slightest degree of distinction. "Go ye, therefore," (says my divine Master) "and teach all nations," (or in other words, all people) "baptizing them in the name of the Father, and of the Son, and of the Holy Ghost." Do you understand the above, Americans? We are a people, notwithstanding many of you doubt it. You have the Bible in your hands, with this very injunction. Have you been to Africa, teaching the inhabitants thereof the words of the Lord Jesus? "Baptizing them in the name of the Father, and of the Son, and of the Holy Ghost." Have you not, on the contrary, entered among us, and learnt us the art of throat-cutting, by setting us to fight, one against another, to take each other as prisoners of war, and sell to you for small bits of calicoes, old swords, knives, etc. to make slaves for you and your children? This being done, have you not brought us among you, in chains and handcuffs, like brutes, and treated us with all the cruelties and rigour your ingenuity could invent, consistent with the laws of your country, which (for the blacks) are tyrannical enough? Can the American preachers appeal unto God, the Maker and Searcher of hearts, and tell him, with the Bible in their hands, that they make no distinction on account of men's colour? Can they say, O God! thou knowest all things—thou knowest that we make no distinction between thy creatures to whom we have to preach thy Word? Let them answer the Lord; and if they cannot do it in the affirmative, have they not departed from the Lord Jesus Christ, their master? But some may say, that they never had or were in possession of a religion, which makes no distinction, and of course they could not have departed from it. I ask you then, in the name of the Lord, of what kind can your religion be? Can it be that which was preached by our Lord Jesus Christ from Heaven? I believe you cannot be so wicked as to tell him that his Gospel was that of *distinction*. What can the American preachers and people take God to be?—Do they believe his words? If they do, do they believe that he will be mocked? Or do they believe because they are whites and we blacks, that God will have respect to them? Did not God make us as it seemed best to himself? What right, then, has one of us, to despise another and to treat him cruel, on account of his colour, which none but the God who made it can alter? Can there be a greater absurdity in nature, and particularly in a free republican country? But the Americans, having introduced slavery among them, their hearts have become almost seared, as with an hot iron, and God has nearly given them up to believe a lie in preference to the truth ! ! ! and I am awfully afraid that pride, prejudice, avarice and blood, will, before long, prove the final ruin of this happy republic, or land of liberty ! ! ! Can any thing be a greater mockery of religion than the way in which it is conducted by the Americans? It appears as though they are bent only on daring God Almighty to do his best—they chain and handcuff us and our children and drive us around the country like brutes, and go into the house of the God of justice to return Him thanks for having aided him in their infernal cruelties inflicted upon us. Will the Lord suffer this people to go on much longer, taking his holy name in vain? Will he not stop them, PREACHERS and all? O Americans! Americans !!I call God—I call angels—I call men, to witness, that your DESTRUCTION *is at hand*, and will be speedily consummated unless you REPENT.

◆   ◆   ◆

Remember Americans, that we must and shall be free, and enlightened as you are, will you wait until we shall, under God, obtain our liberty by the crushing arm of power? Will it not be dreadful for you? I speak Americans for your good. We must and shall be free I say, in spite of you. You may do your best to keep us in wretchedness and misery, to enrich you and your children but God will deliver us from under you. And Wo, Wo, will be to you if we have to obtain our freedom by fighting. Throw away your fears and prejudices then, and enlighten us and treat us like men, and we will like you more than we do now hate you, and tell us now no more about colonization [resettling free blacks in Africa] for America is as much our country, as it is yours—Treat us like men, and there is no danger but we will all live in peace and happiness together. For we are not like you, hard hearted, unmerciful, and unforgiving.

What a happy country this will be, if the whites will listen. What nation under heaven, will be able to do any thing with us, unless God gives us up into his hand? But Americans, I declare to you, while you keep us and our children in bondage, and treat us like brutes, to make us support you and your families, we cannot be your friends. You do not look for it; do you? Treat us then like men, and we will be your friends. And there is not a doubt in my mind, but that the whole of the past will be sunk into oblivion, and we yet, under God, will become a united and happy people. The whites may say it is impossible, but remember that nothing is impossible with God.

The Americans may say or do as they please, but they have to raise us from the condition of brutes to that of respectable men, and to make a national acknowledgement to us for the wrongs they have inflicted on us. As unexpected, strange, and wild as these propositions may to some appear, it is no less a fact, that unless they are complied with, the Americans of the United States, though they may for a little while escape, God will yet weigh them in a balance, and if they are not superior to other men, as they have represented themselves to be, he will give them wretchedness to their very heart's content.

⁓ Discussion Questions ⁓

1. What does Humboldt find peculiar about the racial caste system in Mexico? According to him, what historical circumstances have given rise to it? What are its long-term effects on Mexican society?

2. Summarize Tocqueville's conclusions about the fate of Indians and Africans in the United States. According to him, why have their experiences in dealing with whites followed opposite paths?

3. How did David Walker make use of the Haitian Revolution, the Enlightenment, and Christianity in his call for an end to slavery? What evidence does his argument present of a distinctly African-American identity in the Atlantic World?

4. Tocqueville describes the Spanish-American model of racial intermarriage as the only alternative to race war in the United States. Humboldt sees in the United States the opposite of the "hatred and disunion" of the racial caste system in Mexico. Walker predicts divine retribution if slaves are not fully enfranchised in American society. Why were these authors so pessimistic about the future of race relations in the societies they observed? How does modern society continue to struggle with the issues of racial difference identified by these authors?

Suggested Readings

An excellent overview of European imperialism that explores the links between the Atlantic empires and those established in Africa and Asia in the nineteenth century is D. K. Fieldhouse, *The Colonial Empires from the Eigh-*

teenth Century (New York: Delacorte Press, 1966). Philip D. Curtin has written several books that deal with nineteenth-century imperialism in a context useful for students of the Atlantic World. See especially *The World and the West: The European Challenge and the Overseas Response in the Age of Empire* (New York: Cambridge University Press, 2000); *Disease and Empire: The Health of European Troops in the Conquest of Africa* (New York: Cambridge University Press, 1998); and *Death by Migration: Europe's Encounter with the Tropical World in the Nineteenth Century* (New York: Cambridge University Press, 1989).

A comparative perspective on the transition from colonial to national identities in the Atlantic World is provided in *Colonial Identity in the Atlantic World, 1500–1800*, edited by Nicholas P. Canny and Anthony Pagden (Princeton, N.J.: Princeton University Press, 1987). Also useful in this regard for Latin America is D. A. Brading, *The First America: The Spanish Monarchy, Creole Patriots, and the Liberal State, 1492–1867* (New York: Cambridge University Press, 1991). For more on Mexico in the era of Alexander von Humboldt, see *Mexico in the Age of Democratic Revolutions, 1750–1850*, edited by Jaime E. Rodríguez O. (Boulder, Colo.: Lynne Rienner, 1994). For more on race relations in the United States in the era of Alexis de Tocqueville and David Walker, see Reginald Horsman, *Race and Manifest Destiny: The Origins of American Racial Anglo-Saxonism* (Cambridge, Mass.: Harvard University Press, 1981).